INNER VOICES

Abbey Simon

with Garnet Ungar

Cover photo © by Christian Steiner

Design and copyediting by Oxford Editing

Printed in the United States of America

First Printing, 2017

ISBN-13: 978-0692922408

ISBN-10: 0692922407

CONTENTS

PREFACE

Between 1880 and 1920, millions of Eastern European Jews left their homes in search of a better life in the United States. Hundreds of thousands settled in New York City, which became the capital of Jewish America. Four key people from the Russian Empire were part of this wave of immigrants. Elli Sheldin (1857-1935) and his wife Augusta Sheldin (1859-1935), came from Minsk. Gottlieb Simon (c. 1864-?), and his wife, Dvorah Stollowitz Simon (1865-?), arrived in 1902. The Sheldins brought their daughter, Vera (1891-c. 1935), and the Simons brought their son, Solomon (1891-c. 1960). Vera and Solomon were married in 1915 and their only child, born on January 8, 1920, was called Abbey Henry Simon.

Sixty years later, in the early 1980s, I was a teenaged piano student in Calgary, Canada, and learned about the famous Abbey Simon from pianists who lived there. He was sometimes referred to as "Crabby Abbey" and was known as a tough, ruthless teacher with a temper. I also knew him from my repeatedly-played cassette of his Chopin scherzos and Mendelssohn Variations sérieuses. After doing a Bachelor of Music degree at the University of Toronto, I had returned to the University of Calgary for my master's, and it was there, on November 4, 1990, that I met Abbey Simon for the first time. He was giving a masterclass and playing the Schumann Quintet with the Manhattan String Quartet. I was scheduled to play first in his masterclass and showed up a bit early to the concert hall. He was alone, standing in the middle of the stage, holding a cup of coffee the size of his head and looking...

crabby. I said, "Hello," and he said, "Hello." There was no nonsense. I liked him instantly. In the class, I played about half of the Chopin Third Ballade before he stopped me and said, "Well, that's very good, but it all sounds the same." His saying "That's very good" was all it took for me to relax and feel worthy of his presence. For the next half hour, he gave me a series of suggestions for phrasing, pedaling, technique, and articulation, and every one was insightful, immediately applicable, and absolutely right. One of them was "You have to give the audience your interpretation on a silver platter." Each suggestion was offered only once. You had to understand it the first time, there was no repetitive drilling. The rest of the masterclass, where my fellow students played, was the same.

I was his page turner for the performance of the quintet and came to the first rehearsal expecting a certain kind of playing based on his recording of the Chopin scherzos—muscular, driving, and with a brilliant tone that, as I later learned, owed a lot to the bright Baldwin piano. When I sat beside him, he was a different pianist. His fingers floated over the keyboard, each one subtly caressing the key with a different depth and color. The playing was incredibly sensitive and perfectly controlled, and not as aggressive as I expected. He sat still, his gaze penetrating into the keyboard, and he groaned, loudly, along with the music. On the first run-through of the quintet he played one wrong note. The second time was perfect. The horrendously difficult octave passages in the scherzo were dashed off with musical spontaneity and freedom despite difficulties most pianists pray merely to survive. All the thorny passages in the first movement with the hands playing in octaves flowed like liquid. The difficulties were something to be toyed with and enjoyed.

He required me to keep my hand on the music rack at all

times. He hardly glanced at the score—he had it memorized—but every once in awhile, he would look at me while playing and mutter, "Where am I?" and I had to point to that place in the music. He did this perhaps twenty times in the course of the piece.

Before the concert, the stagehand asked him if he was ready. His response was, "I've never been ready in my life." Despite the perfection of the rehearsals, Mr. Simon did not play well in the concert. His nerves got the better of him, and he sounded like a different person. Over subsequent years, I heard him perform many solo recitals and concertos, and these performances were all flawless except one, when he played the Beethoven "Emperor" Concerto at the University of Evansville, where I currently teach. Again, after essentially perfect rehearsals, the performance was oddly jumbled. When he says, "I played extremely well," you can believe it's the truth. When he says, "It was a disaster," you can believe that too. There's not much in between. During the course of preparing this book, I had the opportunity to listen to several more live recordings, and they tended to fall into the perfect category.

As I approached the end of my master's degree, I was looking for somewhere to do a doctorate, and I knew I wanted to study with Abbey Simon. I had a serious girlfriend who was heading to the University of Texas at Austin, and I wanted to be near her. At the time, there was a big blue book which had an index of every music teacher in the country and where they taught. I looked up Abbey Simon and his name was linked to two schools—Juilliard and the University of Houston. I did the geography—Houston was an easy drive to Austin. I wrote to Mr. Simon asking if he would accept me as a student in Houston. I was elated that he did.

At the beginning of our first lesson, he gave me a stern

warning: "Everybody knows I'm the loudest piano teacher in the world. I yell constantly, so don't take it personally." Other students sometimes got offended. One stopped studying with him for a year because of the yelling. Another student muttered, "Asshole" after playing for him in a masterclass.

The first thing I played for him at UH was Debussy's "Reflets dans l'eau." I played a page or so before he interrupted me:

"Well, it's fine but it's much too slow. Life is a short affair, you have to get to the end!"

"I've been listening to this Claudio Arrau recording and…"

"Oh, well, Claudio Arrau, he's dead. As a matter of fact, that may have been the case when he recorded it."

"One of his posthumous recordings?"

"Exactly."

I felt that Mr. Simon's reputation as a cruel teacher was undeserved. He was direct, but the fact that his comments were phrased as jokes suggested that he was comfortable being human around me, letting his guard down, and somehow being on the same side of the difficulties along with me. I enjoyed playing for him and that continued for all the years I studied with him. There was always a good-naturedness and generosity about him that made it easy to accept all the criticism. During many lessons, I sat there as he hurled insults at me, but because they were so cleverly phrased, I was too busy laughing to feel hurt. The fact that he felt free to be so blunt and not tiptoe around my feelings made the whole matter of playing the piano seem less a matter of life or death. Also, the comments were always directed at the playing rather than at me personally.

Most of my lessons consisted of about forty-five minutes of concentrated suggestions, all insightful, but with little repetition or opportunity to apply them. Mr. Simon was not there to practice with you—that was your affair. The rest of the lesson consisted of stories from his career, the sheer breadth and quantity of which inspired this book. I would often prompt him by bringing up a famous name or situation, and almost invariably he had a related personal story. A typical example was one occasion when I mentioned a CD I had just acquired of Josef Hofmann's 1937 Fiftieth Jubilee concert. The cover features a photograph of Hofmann silhouetted against an enormous audience at the old Metropolitan Opera House in New York. I asked Simon if he was in that audience. His typically casual response was, "Oh, I rehearsed the solo piano part with the orchestra for that concert." His stories often sounded almost like fairy tales, too far-fetched, too entertaining, too strange to be true. But in the course of researching this book, I had access to a wealth of printed material that bears them out in every detail. Every name, concert, orchestra, city and town, is confirmed in black and white.

When experiencing Simon's skill as a raconteur, one is reminded of films of Artur Rubinstein—he is the charismatic center of attention. He becomes rather bored and distant when others begin to speak. There is a cadence to his speech, a quasi-rhyme paced to maximize poetry and suspense. Along with Simon's sensitivity to musical sound comes an affinity for different accents. Simon has an ear for languages and years of living in Geneva have perfected his French.

Our senses of humor seem to gel, and he will often finish my jokes in mid-sentence. Recently, I was confirming when I would arrive at his apartment:

"Is it ok if I arrive at 3:30?"

"I'll be here. I can't promise I'll be alive, but I'll be here."

"Well, if I smell somethi…"

"That's it, exactly."

He is critical of himself, sometimes referring to himself as a ridiculous egomaniac or a retarded child or as "The Great Abbey Simon." He remarks, "I thought being senile would be fun." But sometimes, he does not appreciate being the brunt of jokes. Once he was practicing in his studio while a group of us students stood outside. He burst out of his room, saying, "I've never played so badly in my life." I recycled an old Jack Benny line: "Oh cheer up, sure you have!" He glowered at me.

In many later encounters, he repeatedly opened up about his own experiences, struggles, fears, and brought me into his personal life with real generosity of spirit that gave me courage as a musician. He talks to me as his musical peer, although I am nothing close to it. His generosity with time, supportiveness when it came to important performances, and dozens of extravagant meals at expensive restaurants meant I always felt encouraged. For some reason, I always played my best for him, and having him around before a performance gave me confidence. Backstage before my doctoral solo recital, he said, "Let yourself go. Don't go out there and practice." This is probably the best pre-concert suggestion I've ever had.

Nowadays, Simon continues to drive his car around Houston, fly regularly across the Atlantic, concertize, practice, and teach at the University of Houston. He talks about making another CD, of preparing the next recital program. His life is his work—it is what matters to him above all. For many years, he has been under the management of Gurtman and Murtha. When his wife, Dina, died in May 2014, they were preparing for their seventy-third anniversary. He has two adult grandchildren. His back gives him constant pain, making it difficult to walk. But walk he does. He says he is clinically depressed but he doesn't sound like it. He speaks pessimistically, but there is a twinkle in his eye, a love of ideas and music, dry wit, and observation. He gets around at ninety-seven like a much younger man.

Simon has had health issues—ongoing asthma, frequent colds, shingles, broken fingers, and several other painful, if not life-threatening, illnesses. But he rarely cancels concerts. As a teacher, he always shows up to lessons and teaches energetically, no matter how badly he is feeling that day. Simon talks about being depressed but still seems to have so much vitality, joie de vivre, and sense of humor. His mind hasn't lost anything. He jokes that he never had any to lose.

The bulk of the autobiographical material of this book, contained in the first seven chapters, is taken from a series of interviews I conducted with Mr. Simon from 2015 to 2017 in Houston and Geneva. During the months of interviews for this book, Simon fought off a pickpocket outside his apartment building in Geneva. The young man pulled Simon's wallet from his back pocket and Simon grabbed his wrist and shouted at him until he released the wallet. In February of 2016, Simon wrapped his car around a light post and broke his arm, wrist, and several fingers. After months of intensive physical therapy, Simon returned to the stage in early 2017 to give his annual recital at the University of Houston.

As I write this, I am listening to a live recording of his Chopin E-Major Scherzo, played at the University of Evansville when he was eighty-one. I am trying to focus on the writing but I can't. In all the difficult passages, he not only overcomes the difficulty, but toys with it, finds inner voices, balances it beautifully, clearly, and inventively, all with a hundred dynamic shades. His interpretation has minuscule silences in the middle of the texture, gauged perfectly for clarity, focus, and communication—all on a silver platter.

-Garnet Ungar

ACKNOWLEDGEMENTS

The editor wishes to thank many people who have helped in the writing of this book. First, many of Abbey Simon's former students have contributed their experiences and insights and are quoted in the text:

Andrew Cooperstock, Professor, University of Colorado Boulder

Charles Foreman, Professor Emeritus, University of Calgary

Daniel Glover, Concert Pianist

Christopher Johnson, Concert Pianist and Teacher

David Korevaar, Professor, University of Colorado Boulder

Joseph Matthews, Professor Emeritus, Chapman University

Alice Rybak, Former Professor, University of Denver

Karen Shaw, Professor, Indiana University

John Spradling, Concert Pianist and Teacher

Philip Thomson, Associate Professor, University of Akron

Jerico Vasquez, Associate Professor, Shorter University

Roger Wright, Concert Pianist and Teacher

Two other former students, both concert pianists, deserve special note. The first, Hsia-Jung Chang, has created a compelling series of video interviews with Simon, available on YouTube under Mandala Studios Interviews. These videos give a taste of Simon's style as a raconteur that cannot be fully conveyed in print. The second, Frederic Chiu, devoted many hours to proofreading, de facto editing, encouragement, and genealogical sleuthing.

Donald Manildi, Curator of the International Piano Archives at the University of Maryland, has supplied obscure documents and recordings as well as agreeing to host a new collection of Abbey Simon's complete materials at IPAM.

Two prominent published scholars, Howard Pollack, Professor at the University of Houston, and Sandra Mangsen, Professor Emerita at the University of Western Ontario, have contributed their invaluable guidance.

Mr. Simon's son, Jonathan, and his wife, Suzanne, have helped with information, documentation, corrections, ideas, hospitality, and enthusiasm.

Emma Dederick, Electronic Music Resources Librarian at Indiana University, devoted hours to locating dates and recordings for all of Mr. Simon's recitals at that institution.

Joe Salerno, recording engineer, furnished audio recordings of several International Piano Festival luncheons at the University of Houston.

Marc Aubort, multiple Grammy-winning recording engineer, shared his valuable recollections of many recording sessions with Mr. Simon.

My employer, the University of Evansville, generously granted a year's sabbatical in which to research this book.

Undoubtedly the most significant contributor, without whom this would have been a much shorter book, was Mr. Simon's late wife, Dina. Although I met Dina only once, twenty-five years ago, her posthumous presence was continuously felt as I perused the thousands of documents she lovingly saved over the decades.

Chapter One
BEGINNINGS: 1920-1930

My parents came to the US as children. We had a very good family life in a lovely part of New York, up in the northern part of the Bronx, at 870 East 175th Street. Nearby there was a big street, going for miles and miles, called the Grand Concourse. It was the Bronx's answer to Park Avenue. With doormen, uniformed elevator operators, and canopies everywhere, it was very elegant. There was a wonderful hotel, still there, called the Concourse Plaza, which was two blocks away from Yankee Stadium, and the Biograph Film Studios had their building on our Street. I remember once seeing a famous actor, Milton Sills, running down the street in his underwear while filming a scene from a movie. It was a different world.

I come from an enormous family of doctors, and if you're sick between Boston and Florida, you will undoubtedly be treated by a relative of mine. My father was a sort of peacemaker in the family. He used to coach students and relatives who were taking their Regents Exams, which is a standardized test in New York State. He used to get phone calls saying, "Uncle Sol, I passed!" He was a dentist who also wrote songs, plays, and stories. He taught me how to read when I was four, and by the time I was six, I could read everything ever written.

It was a Jewish household, but not religious. If my parents had any sign of religion, it was from their parents. From the womb, I was automatically and totally furious at the idea of religion. I loved my mother's parents, but I never could warm up to the Simon grandparents—they were very Orthodox and demanding. I refused to participate in the ceremonies, and there were scenes all the time. I remember once, for the Jewish High Holidays, my grandfather was in synagogue and everybody had to wear a hat. As soon as I could, I got out and threw it away. I was not Bar Mitzvahed—I refused to go through the rigors of learning Hebrew. I disliked the sound of it, along with Arabic and Yiddish. I'm embarrassed about the fact that Yiddish was my first language, a byproduct of my grandparents living with us when I was very young.

My parents loved music and were concert and opera goers but not musicians. I had two favorite uncles, both from my mother's side of the family. Neither of them was a professional musician either. One was another dentist who put himself through dental school playing piano in jazz bands. As a child, I used to play four-hand jazz with him at the piano. The other was a businessman who had two young children to support. He was the Jascha Heifetz of the mandolin—he would play everything, including Paganini studies, in the most extraordinary way. The extended family would all meet at our house, and there was always music being played. Also, we almost invariably listened to the Sunday afternoon live concerts of the New York Philharmonic on the radio, and many musicians from the Philharmonic lived in our apartment house or in that part of New York City.

When I was maybe three years old, I was playing on the floor and the three-note NBC theme came on the radio: G-E-C. I went from the other end of the room to the piano and somehow played those exact notes. That was the first time they thought I had any musical talent. From then on, I never considered any occupation but music. In that way, I'm a very lucky man—how many people know what they want to be by the time they're three? My parents were very supportive of my musical interests. They would have been supportive if I had wanted to be a plumber. But they would have preferred I be a doctor, because I was the black sheep of the family.

My first piano teacher was a Russian gentleman called Boris Zhivov. He taught me to read music, and he did one of the most important things, which I resisted, from the Russian tradition. Like Czerny, who made Liszt sight-read on certain days when they did nothing else, Zhivov would make me sit down and sight-read Mozart overtures. I remember playing the overture to *The Marriage of Figaro* for four hands when I could barely read the notes. I hated sight-reading because I knew everything by ear. Zhivov was a wonderful teacher. I was with him from about age five to seven.

One time Zhivov took me to play for Ernest Hutcheson at the Juilliard School. I started my piece in the wrong key, in D Major, and Hutcheson was very angry and rude. He thought it was some sort of put on. He said, "Play it in D-flat." I said to him, "I'm sorry I made this mistake," and I played it in D-flat. I could play anything I heard in any key. He was duly impressed.

Fig. 1. *Abbey Simon with his mother, c. 1930. Photograph courtesy of Jonathan Simon.*

There was a famous restaurant chain called Horn and Hardart, and their gimmick was that you placed the money in a slot and took the food out of a compartment. These restaurants were called automats. They had a radio program on Sunday mornings on CBS: *The Horn and Hardart Children's Hour.* One week it was in New York, the next week it was in Philadelphia. I would write a piece every other week and perform it on the radio. They were the nonsense pieces of a seven- or eight-year-old. When Charles Lindbergh flew across the Atlantic in 1927, I composed a piece with the left hand rumbling to imitate the airplane's engine. It finished with a combination of the *Marseillaise* and *The Star-Spangled Banner*. Another piece was inspired by a picture on our wall of Hiawatha in a canoe. It was in the traditional ABA form, with a middle theme that was my idea of American Indian music. I must have played on the radio program for several months. I was never nervous because I was playing only my own compositions, and I never knew from one moment to the next what notes I'd be playing. I also played on WNYC radio when I was nine years old, and in September of 1929, I won honorable mention in The Brooklyn Free Music Society Contest.

A month later, the Great Depression hit. Everybody was desperate, and you'd see people on the street with big bags of apples trying to sell you one. The first wristwatch I ever got was an Ingersoll from somebody who couldn't pay my father's dentist bill. My mother's family all moved in together. One day, I went down to the bank with my father to cash a check and suddenly, there was a gate across the entrance. The bank had closed its doors. When we walked back up the hill to our apartment, in all probability, all the money we had was in my father's pockets.

I was rather poor in athletics and was always the last one to be chosen for a team. I hated it. One day, when I was maybe eight years old, I was having a difficult moment with my father, whom I adored. I had gotten a bad grade in PT and I said, "Let's face it, I can't climb a rope up to the third floor. I'm no good at basketball, I'm no good at stickball, and I just don't enjoy it." I was however mad about tennis, and I was quite good at it. William Tilden, the No. 1 ranked tennis player in the world, was giving tennis lessons a few blocks away, but it was Depression time and we certainly couldn't afford him. I was complaining about my lack of athletic prowess to my father when he said, "The trouble with you is that you're a snob." It struck me like a revelation, "Dad, you're absolutely right, I am a snob! The others can do nothing that I can do. I'm in a class by myself." The other kids were perfectly nice neighborhood kids, we got along very well, but I put myself way above them. Also, I was reading things that you can't imagine, that I probably didn't understand.

In those days, Leopold Godowsky lived on Seventy-Third Street at a hotel, which is still in existence, called the Ansonia. If the Waldorf Astoria was the place for money, the Ansonia was the place for intelligentsia. The Ansonia lodged Capablanca, one of the greatest chess players of all time. The famous dancer, Albertina Rasch, lived there with her husband, the movie composer Dimitri Tiomkin, who won several Academy Awards. Later, I also had many friends who lived there. David Saperton, the head of the piano department at The Curtis Institute of Music, lived diagonally across the street on Seventy-First Street. He had a gorgeous sound, fabulous fingers, and wonderful musical instincts. When other people were giving single debut recitals, he gave a week of debut recitals in New York, before I was born, in Aeolian Hall. He played a different program every night. By the third night, they were calling him the marathon pianist. He was also married to Godowsky's daughter, Vanita. Godowsky's other daughter, Dagmar, was a star of silent films. Godowsky's son, Leopold Jr., was married to George Gershwin's younger sister, Frances.

The intimates of Godowsky referred to him as "Popsy." Godowsky would sit down at the piano and there would be Josef Hofmann, Rachmaninoff, and Josef Lhévinne going "Mein Gott, unbelievable!" However, when those three went out on the stage at Carnegie Hall, there was pandemonium, but as somebody once wrote, when Godowsky went onstage, it was a wet

cigar. There is a famous story about Busoni walking into Steinway's in Berlin, and somebody was playing the piano, and he
said, "Is that a player piano or Godowsky?"

They were all such ridiculous, phony intellectuals. The names
Hofmann gave his pieces, like *Kaleidoskop* and *Chromaticon*, were a
symbol of the pretentious times. All sorts of things were in vogue
then health-wise, for example, phrenology, that make today look
like a very calm place. Hofmann felt my forehead where I had,
like many young children, two big bumps and he said, "Like
Beethoven." Really, though, it was just a time of boobs. Albert
Einstein was also part of the group. They would let him play
chamber music with them, and apparently one of them once
yelled out to him, "For God's sake, can't you count?"

We had a very dear family friend, Dr. Wanderman, who was
a friend of many musicians. He was the doctor for Leopold
Godowsky and Josef Hofmann, who was the head of Curtis. He
was also a close friend of David Saperton. When I was about
eight, Dr. Wanderman brought me to play for Saperton, who
wanted me to be brought back to Godowsky's birthday party
that night. Hofmann would be there, along with all the most
famous musicians in the world. I didn't know all their names, but
one name I did know: George Gershwin. I had no real pieces to
play, just my own compositions and improvisations. Finally, the
time came for me to do my parlor tricks. Godowsky gave me a
little theme and said, "Improvise in the Russian style," so I improvised in the Russian style, very Tchaikovsky-ish. He went into
a rage and said, "If you are so unsophisticated and have never
really taken any lessons, how do you know what is the Russian
style?" Apparently, I answered, "Well, anybody who knows anything about music would know that's the Russian style." I never
cottoned to Godowsky. I have the feeling that he was irked that I
was unimpressed with him, but I was sitting on pins and needles

for my chance to meet George Gershwin. Hofmann, however, took a liking to me because I could do the same things he could do as a kid—play anything in any key and improvise forever. I stayed there until about ten o'clock at night, when my father had to take me home. I never got to meet Gershwin, he must have arrived after I left.

Right after I played for Josef Hofmann, I was taken to a concert of the Curtis Orchestra, which I had never heard. This sixteen-year-old giant walked out on stage in Carnegie Hall, and he was playing something called the Tchaikovsky Piano Concerto. That fellow was Jorge Bolet. He had entered Curtis at thirteen playing the "Appassionata" Sonata. I had never heard any of this repertoire, although I think I knew by ear the Grieg Concerto. With all this excitement, my career began.

Chapter Two
CURTIS: 1931-1939

The Curtis Institute of Music opened in 1924. It was a special school for the gifted created by Mary Louise Curtis Bok, with guidance from Leopold Stokowski and Josef Hofmann. Josef Hofmann became director of the Curtis Institute in 1927 and urged Mrs. Bok to make the school tuition-free because he felt the quality of the students was not worthy of the world-class faculty. That policy took effect in 1928.

I became a student at Curtis in 1931. When I was at Curtis, the youngest student at the time was a little Cuban girl, Margaret Ross, and I was next to youngest. Third youngest was Rafael Druian, who was three years older than I. He became the concertmaster of the Cleveland Symphony. I was admitted, so far as I can remember, to two departments—piano and composition. But I wasn't really composing anymore when I got to Curtis, and I never dedicated myself to it. All my compositions sounded like Rachmaninoff and Ravel, which would have been alright if they hadn't written them already! Although it was Hofmann who admitted me to Curtis, by the time I arrived there, Hofmann was teaching less and less, and by 1933, he had resumed his annual foreign tours and was at Curtis only sporadically. Even when he was there, he was not a very communicative teacher or person. He would sit down and say, "Well, I do this, why don't you try this?" He expected me to do it as an eleven-year-old. When I played in the Curtis recitals, sometimes he would be there but he never said anything. The only true student of Hofmann was Shura Cherkassky. Hofmann even used to take him on tour with him.

I had horrible health, and my family was against my going to Curtis. My uncles and aunts all said, "He'll never live through the winter in Philadelphia." I used to miss ten days out of every month due to illness in grade school in New York, but I never missed a single day at Curtis. I used to dread going back to New York in the summertime because I'd have to be a regular boy again. In the first year, my mother came with me to Philadelphia and we took a little apartment. It was a brutal change. The New York State Board of Education said I still had school work, so I had a private tutor in math. I also had to be an auditor to a lot of chamber music to fulfill the law about how many hours I would spend in school a week. The first chamber music concert I grudgingly went to was a recital of Elisabeth Schumann, the famous German singer. I was knocked out.

It was part of my nature to read the classics—English, French, German, and I liked to read while the radio was on. Radio was marvelous because it was not just looking at the flat screen and seeing everything. When you listened to a detective story, you became the characters, and everybody took on the face that you gave them.

When I came into Curtis, I was just beginning to doubt the idea that babies came with the stork. By the end of my first week, I knew every conceivable perversion. When I was twelve or thirteen at summer camp, I wrote the hit song of the show, called *I Want a Sweater with Bumps.*

Children of the Rockefellers were not spoiled the way we were at Curtis. There were only seven or eight practice rooms there—the rest were all teaching studios—so we were given our own grand pianos. Even back home in the summertime in New York, someone at the door asked for Mr. Simon, and that was me in short pants. They brought in a Steinway that Curtis had arranged for me.

I was the low man on the totem pole and really didn't know anything. I could barely play the Beethoven G Major Sonata from opus 49. People would talk about opus 53 and I'd wonder, "What's opus 53?" Many of them had musical parents and had been in musical atmospheres all their lives, whereas my parents were not professional musicians. One of my new friends, who was a couple of years older but much further advanced, was playing something called the Schumann Piano Concerto. I came home in hysterics and said, "I'll never be able to do anything like that!" But within two years, I was no longer impressed by him. It was a very small school, just two hundred students or so. I learned more, especially when I first came to Curtis, from the students than I did from the teachers. Your teacher you saw once a week, your colleagues you saw every day.

Horn and Hardart still wanted me to be on their *Children's Hour*, this time in Philadelphia, so I went down automatically on a Sunday morning. Soon after I was hauled into the office at Curtis and reprimanded because we weren't allowed to perform without permission. Maybe it was just my paranoia, as a child of the Depression, but I lived in fear of seeing my name on the bulletin board at Curtis because that would mean I was kicked out of the school. Being accepted there didn't mean you would last very long.

When I first got to Curtis, I had to learn the French system of *solfège*, and was also given a composition class with this very old man, Rosario Scalero, who was the teacher of Samuel Barber, Gian Carlo Menotti, and Vincent Persichetti. I came into my first lesson with him wearing short pants, looking like a four-year-old. He said, "You write-a dis-a cantus firmus," and I said, "What's a cantus firmus?" He said, "Oh my, leave me!" and that was the end of the composition lessons.

Curtis had its own box at the Academy of Music, and we could go hear the Philadelphia Orchestra whenever we wanted.

In those days, Stokowski was conducting, and you've never heard anything like it. I remember the first time I heard pieces like *Daphnis et Chloé*, *La Mer*, and *Petrushka*, the music overwhelmed me so that I was drunk with the sound. I had difficulty walking to the streetcar afterwards.

When I was about twelve, I moved into Sokoloff's boarding house on Spruce Street, where all the rooms were filled with Curtis students. There were two other pianists, two oboists, one violinist, and one bassoonist all living in the same building. They all became principal players in the major orchestras. I had my own furnished room. Curtis paid thirty-one dollars a month for my room and bath, plus breakfast and one other meal a day. That was what things cost during the Depression. The Sokoloff's oldest son was Vladimir (Billy), who became a very distinguished pianist and chamber music player. He and the pianist Ralph Berkowitz played most of the chamber music at Curtis. Billy married Eleanor Blum, who was a student of David Saperton. She still teaches at Curtis.

Every year at Curtis, we'd have a Christmas party that was one of the great social events of Philadelphia. It was held in the old Casimir Hall, which is a marvelous auditorium of about 250 to 300 seats, which were removed. There was a different theme every year. One year it was the circus, so we were all sent down to a costumer's to get circus costumes. Another year, it was horse racing. It was insane.

At Curtis I formed a lifelong trio of friends with Jorge Bolet and Sidney Foster. Bolet was the oldest, born in 1914, and then Foster in 1917. All three of us auditioned for Curtis and were accepted as boys—Foster at ten, Bolet at thirteen. We all studied with David Saperton, although Foster had also studied with Isabelle Vengerova from age ten to twelve. All three of us went on to have long performing careers. Bolet had already graduated and was off into the real world for the second half of my time at Curtis, but Sidney and I, who had much in common from the beginning, were thick as thieves. Like me, Sidney had perfect pitch, played easily by ear, and improvised in various styles for much of his childhood, only beginning formal lessons and note reading at age nine. We also shared a sense of humor. For example, when Curtis held its auditions, and we were very young and very short, we would go into a studio next to the audition room and split the Chopin étude in thirds between us at tremendous tempo, as loud as possible. When it was over, only one of us would walk out.

For the first twenty years of my life or so, I wanted to be Jorge Bolet. One day I was shaving at the mirror and I said, "You're never going to play octaves 1-4, 2-5, the way the other people play sixths. You're not going to be six feet four inches tall and weigh 240 pounds, and you have to face up to the fact that you're going to be the smallest pianist." Bolet was a very easygoing person and a sweet guy, and he was a lazy fellow. He knew he could learn anything by the time I finished talking about it. He was a wonderful reader, but he really played a relatively small repertoire. When I was maybe eleven years old, I heard him play the twelve *Transcendental Études* at a student recital at Curtis.

My mother tragically died when I was about fifteen—I think she was forty-three. My father and I moved to a smaller apartment on the Grand Concourse in the Bronx because he thought we should be closer to his sister in case I needed any help. Sidney came to spend one summer with us. I was killing myself learning the Godowsky *Fledermaus* transcription, and Sidney asked me, "Why are you wasting all your time learning that garbage?" When school opened up in August, I went back to Philadelphia and went downstairs in the basement like John Wayne, looking for Jorge Bolet to play the *Fledermaus* for him. I never did play it for him, except when he heard me play it in a recital at Curtis.

We had a student pianist at Curtis who was considerably older—he had already been to Europe—and his name was Richard Goodman. He was an extraordinary man. He was from Baltimore, and my future wife knew him from there. He started his Curtis graduation recital with the Schumann Toccata, and that was the first time in my life I heard it performed, although I had studied it and brought it to lessons. I've still never heard a better performance of the piece. It was he who introduced me to the early preludes of Shostakovich. He knew them all. Another time he said, "Listen to this, this is the greatest piece ever," and played Ravel's *Valses nobles et sentimentales* for me—I had never heard any Ravel music before that, except "Ondine." The first time I heard the Prokofiev Third Sonata was when Richard played it.

Hofmann, Berceuse, op. 20, no. 5, mm. 1-5

mm. 33-34

During one of my early years at Curtis, I was called upon to play the bass drum in the school orchestra with Fritz Reiner conducting. We were rehearsing Tchaikovsky's Symphony No. 4. The opening of the last movement requires the bass drum to come in precisely at the end of a long line of very fast sixteenth notes. When I had difficulty coming in, I yelled out to Reiner, "I don't understand your beat!" He was so offended that he moved me and the bass drum up to the front of the stage, and when it was time for me to come in, gave me the most enormous beat imaginable.

From 1933 to 1941, Curtis had regular weekly afternoon radio broadcasts, called *The Curtis Institute Musicale,* on the Columbia Network. They always used a small piano piece, the Berceuse by Josef Hofmann, as the theme song. Every week a different student pianist would play it live on the radio. Of course, we only played the first few bars. One afternoon in around 1935, they asked me to play it. I said, "With pleasure," since I knew the first eight bars from memory. They knew very well I was a poor sight-reader and had arranged it so that the *On the Air* light stayed on long after the broadcast had ended. Suddenly, I had to read my way through this entire piece while the red light stayed on, and the piece becomes tricky to sight-read. They were sitting in the lobby, roaring with laughter. I think Hofmann might have been there, too.

At Curtis, most of the students played jazz. I even made some records for fun with two friends, Mary Norris and Albert Tipton. Mary studied with David Saperton, and Albert was a great flutist and conductor. I also had a cousin, Sylvia Milstein, who was a nightclub singer. She would go around to audition at various music publishing houses and when I was about fourteen or fifteen, I would accompany her. I wrote somewhere from six to twelve audition tunes for her—the words too. They all offered me jobs as a composer, but I said, "No, I'm above that."

One summer back in New York, Sidney had a job in a restaurant, accompanying a singer. When he left for a bigger place, I took over his job. It was in a very old, beautiful building on

Fifty-Eighth Street, maybe twenty stories high, and in the back of the lobby, there was a big curtain, behind which was a very discreet restaurant called the Round Room. The food was exquisite, and I doubt if anybody walked away with a check for less than 200 dollars. In would come some wealthy businessman after work, and before long, some gorgeous call girl would come down from one of the apartments to join him, and after a while, they would go back upstairs. I played popular tunes on the piano and accompanied a singer. There was the usual little glass tip jar on top of the piano, and I was earning at least fifty or sixty dollars a night, which was a lot of money back then. After that I played in an even more expensive place, a very famous Italian restaurant in New York City.

In Philadelphia, we practically lived in this drugstore. In those days, drugstores had everything—food, soda fountain, etc. Sidney, Jorge Bolet, one or two other people, and I always ate lunch there—it cost fifteen cents. You could pay a dime or so for a little cardboard punchboard, with rows and rows of places to put a little metal puncher, and if you were lucky, you got a prize. One day, Sidney spent a dime and, lo and behold, he won a pipe. I said, "That's a beautiful pipe," and he said, "You can have it. However, you have to smoke it." Sidney was a heavy cigarette smoker by the time he was six years old or something like that. So I bought a package of pipe tobacco, which was named *Revelation,* and from the first puff I took, I was hooked for life. During his time at Curtis, David Saperton lived in New York, and commuted to Philadelphia three days a week to teach. He stayed at a hotel in Philadelphia. There was one scary year when, because of the Depression, many of the departments at Curtis closed. They said I would be better off taking lessons with Saperton at his apartment in New York. For that year, even though I was a Curtis student, I lived in New York.

Oscar Shumsky was the star of Curtis. He was an incredible violinist. The age gap between us was too great for us to be terribly close, but I worshiped him. There were also masses of talented cellists at Curtis in those days: Sammy Mayes and I were kids together; he was older than I was. He was remarkable. There was Leonard Rose, who was absolutely extraordinary. There was Frank Miller, and Victor Gottlieb. Angelica Morales was one of the most brilliant of the Hofmann students. When I met her, I had to be eight years old; she was eighteen or nineteen, and she was gorgeous. I went to her concert in Carnegie Hall, and I remember a line in her review: "She looked like an angel and played like an angel." When she left Curtis she went to study with Emil von Sauer, who was a pupil of Liszt. She married him, although Sauer was probably forty or fifty years older than she was. She later taught at the University of Kansas. Shura Cherkassky was at least ten years older than I. He was living in Baltimore, then came to Curtis, was the No. 1 protégé of Josef Hofmann, and was marvelous, an absolutely beautiful pianist. I met Samuel Barber when I was ten years old and he was in his twenties, so there was a big difference in age, and I was always in awe of him. Barber was a marvelous composer, and he was an excellent pianist and an excellent singer. Gary Graffman and I never got very close. I knew him, but there was a few years' difference in our age, when those years made a lot of difference.

We studied languages with Martha Türk, who taught us German, and René Daudon, who taught us French. I had much more talent for languages than any of the other people in the class. I remember one year, I did my exam so quickly that I ended up doing the others for the entire class. Another time, we were doing an oral translation from German to English, and I used the Yiddish word *Bissel* instead of *Bisschen*. The whole class, which was predominantly Jewish, started to laugh, and I vowed from then on I would never speak a word of Yiddish. Then Germany became the enemy, and I vowed I would never speak a word of German. I was that simple a person.

The most important teacher at Curtis was Renée Longy-Miquelle. She later taught at Juilliard and I knew her there. Her father, Georges Longy, was the founder of the Longy School in Boston. Her husband, Georges Miquelle, was the principal cellist of the Detroit Symphony. I was in Madame Miquelle's big sight-reading class, and we had to transpose Bach chorales at sight. So long as I heard somebody play the chorale before me, I could make any transposition they wanted, but one day, the ax fell—I was called first and my terrible sight-reading was uncovered. Of course, the class was again howling with laughter because they all knew about my tricks. Madame Miquelle looked at me and said, "You have been deceiving me all these years. You will never do this again. From now on, whenever you see me, you will go to the nearest piano and sight-read."

After several years at Curtis, I was finally re-admitted to the composition department and took Scalero's class again. All my exercises for him were wrong, and I was so desperate and terrified of being thrown out that I said to my friend, Sol Kaplan, who was one of his favorite students, "What is it I'm doing wrong?" Sol said, "I'll give you my old exercises. They're all perfect, just copy them." I copied and submitted them expecting a pat on the head, and they were still all wrong.

Josef Hofmann performed yearly recitals at Curtis from 1935 until his last Curtis recital in 1938. I heard him play, among other repertoire:

Bach-Liszt, Prelude and Fugue in A Minor, BWV 543
Beethoven, Sonata in C Major, op. 53 ("Waldstein"); Sonata in A-flat Major, op. 110

Brahms, Quintet for Piano and Strings, op. 34
Chopin, Fantasy in F Minor, op. 49; Ballade in F Minor, op.
52; Préludes, op. 28; Sonata in B Minor, op. 58; many
smaller works
Liszt, *Mephisto Waltz*
Schumann, *Carnaval*, op. 9; Sonata in F Minor, op. 14;
Kreisleriana, op. 16
Scriabin, Sonata No. 4 in F-sharp Major, op. 30

Hofmann was the real bridge to the nineteenth century. When
I was a child, I had never heard a piano sound that good. He was
famous for supposedly having very small hands, but I can't think
of anything he had any difficulty with. He had a special piano
with a smaller keyboard and slightly narrower keys.

Sometimes, having a good ear is not the best thing in the
world. It helps you get away with murder, and Hofmann was
famous as being the world's worst sight-reader. When he was
occasionally forced to play chamber music, he would play one of
the quintets with the Curtis Quartet. He had the music in front
of him, but he never looked at it. It was like he was playing a
piano concerto. He plowed his way through, paying no attention
to the other four guys on stage.

We students also played chamber music reluctantly, and it
wasn't well-taught. For my early lessons, I was playing the Bach
Brandenburg Concerto No. 1 and the Beethoven E-flat-Major
Woodwind Quintet. Our teacher was Louis Bailly, the violist of
the famous Flonzaley Quartet, and he was completely insane.
He always sat to the right of the pianist. If you were a girl, he
would keep pinching your leg, and if you were a boy, he would
pound out every beat on it. Afterwards, you were lucky if you
could walk again. When he was conducting the Curtis String
Orchestra, they would have secret rehearsals without him.

Isabelle Vengerova and Abram Chasins, who were also on faculty, performed several times while I was there. Vengerova's playing was very beautiful. My piano teacher, David Saperton, recorded the Chopin Études and the Godowsky transcriptions of the Études on 78 rpm records when I was still at Curtis. He could play everything. Saperton also performed three recitals during my earlier years at Curtis, from 1932 to 1935. The first two were almost exclusively Godowsky, including the *Passacaglia on the Opening Theme of Schubert's 'Unfinished Symphony,'* and the third was a program of Beethoven, Chopin, Rachmaninoff, Moszkowski, and Liszt. The Godowsky concerts were dreadful—Godowsky lived for complications—and Saperton invariably got lost in that *Passacaglia* around the 200th variation. I hated that piece!

Saperton married Vanita Godowsky, who was an enormous woman. He thought that would help his career, but it didn't turn out that way. Saperton was another gigantic eater and became a very fat man. I never liked him. He was a difficult person, and there was never a sign of affection. I never thought he taught us anything. You would come into a lesson and you knew he was there because you saw this huge cloud of cigar smoke around his desk. You'd be playing something, and then this voice came out of the fog saying, "You're playing three minutes and already I'm bored," or "That fingering you're doing is ridiculous." You didn't even realize he could see what you were doing.

Saperton was very strong about not letting you indulge in "pretty for pretty's sake," which was a strong point of mine when I was fifteen or sixteen. He would say, "All your tempi are beautiful. Pick one!" He got me to look at the bigger picture and not turn everything into forty pieces.

Whereas Vengerova always had a weekly performance class for her students, Saperton had no studio class where we could play. Instead, the night before you were playing in a student recital, you'd be playing in the hall all alone and suddenly at ten o'clock, he'd walk in and say things like, "You can't be serious. You can't play like that. I think we'd better postpone this concert."

I once ran away from Curtis. I had played Chopin's F-Minor Ballade for my lesson, and when it was over, I went down to one of the practice rooms to try and absorb what little I had learned. In came another Saperton student, Jeanette Weinstein, who was two or three years older than I was and a phenomenal pianist. She said to me, very superior, "Why aren't you observing those rests? They are a very important part of the theme." I looked at her as if she was crazy. Saperton had not mentioned those rests, which are a crucial part of the piece. I was so angry that I walked out of the practice room, went down to the bus terminal on Market Street, and got on a bus to New York. My father had an office in the Paramount Building in those days. I walked in and he said, "What are you doing here?" I said, "I'm leaving the Curtis Institute of Music," and he said, "You're not leaving the Curtis Institute of Music. Get on the next bus and go back."

Saperton's original name was Sapirstein. We used to say things like, "Well, I have to see old Sappy," or "I have a lesson with Sappy today." One day we got a typewritten notice saying he had changed his name, and it was pronounced "*Say*perton." It didn't change things much. Now we could say, "We're gonna go see *Say*py." Musicians changed their names all the time. Leopold Stokowski's original name was Stokes—he was about as Polish as I am. It was Arthur Judson of Columbia Artists who said, "With a name like Stokes, you're never going to get anywhere. Now you're Stokowski." When Sidney Finkelstein won the Leventritt Competition, it was apparently also Judson who said, "Now you're Sidney Foster."

We didn't have many visiting artists at Curtis, although Artur Rubinstein came in 1938. At that time, he was not a household name in the United States. I even remember going to a lesson and saying, "Mr. Saperton, I've just listened to a marvelous record by someone named Artur Rubinstein!"

I did hear many pianists outside of Curtis, including Artur Schnabel playing the thirty-two Beethoven sonatas in New York. Today, all you have to do is drop your hat and somebody's playing the thirty-two sonatas, but in those days, he was the only person who did it. Schnabel was also about the only one who played the Schubert sonatas, although Clifford Curzon played them sometimes, but later. I played for many people. I played for Schnabel, but it was wasted on me and wasted on him. I was very unimpressed with him even though I was maybe thirteen. I was so childish; when I was fifteen, I was going on five.

In 1936, I heard Rosalyn Tureck play the Brahms B-flat-Major Concerto with the Philadelphia Orchestra. I didn't play the Brahms B-flat, I think it might have been the very first time I heard it, although I was with such musically sophisticated people that I could never admit it. I thought her performance was excellent. It was around this time that I learned the Brahms D-Minor Concerto. I was being a big man: "Oh I'm learning the Brahms D-Minor."

I had a dear cousin, Lillian Friedlander, who was quite a good pianist herself. One day, she said she had a pair of tickets to hear Josef Lhévinne in Carnegie Hall. I was very impressed with his concert. I remember thinking, "Maybe I don't know enough, but if he's as good as I think he is, he'd be teaching at Curtis and not at Juilliard." At that point in my life, there was one thing in the world, and that was the Curtis Institute of Music. At that concert, Lhévinne played a whole stack of Chopin études. After the étude in thirds, the public went mad. So he decided to play it again, and it fell apart! One of the big pianists asked him afterwards, "Josef, what happened?" He said, "I started too fast!" So you see, it can happen to the best of us.

In 1937, Josef Hofmann gave his Golden Jubilee Concert at the old Metropolitan Opera House, commemorating his American debut in the same venue fifty years earlier. Part of the program was Anton Rubinstein's Concerto No. 4 with the Curtis Symphony Orchestra. It was one of the three or four concerti I knew, and I had one rehearsal with the orchestra. It was the first time I had played with orchestra, but I don't think I rehearsed the whole concerto. There were many students who rehearsed it, and by the time Hofmann came, we had all learned the Rubinstein Concerto, including Jeanette Weinstein. She came from Bismarck, North Dakota and had phenomenal fingers, and her playing had an emotional range from minus two thousand to minus two thousand and one. I think Bolet played it also. I still have never performed it. Later, I wanted to make a record of it, but I realized that there were four other Rubinstein concertos that maybe I should also play, and no one was interested in recording them.

In 1937, I opened a concert of Saperton students with the Bach-Liszt Fantasy and Fugue in G minor. Later in the program, I played the Kreisler-Rachmaninoff *Liebesleid* and the Ravel "Alborada del gracioso." I was very full of myself; I thought I had played very well at that recital. The next night, I played a recital for the Curtis Concert Bureau, which got us little engagements when they decided we were ready, and I got fifty dollars for this. It was in a place called Sleighton Farms, which was the girls' state reform school. I remember coming there and being given dinner, which was an enormous steak. I was a nervous wreck and there was a huge dog in the room, so I looked around and then just gave my steak to the dog.

We didn't have any piano literature classes. You said to the teacher, "I've learned this," or "What do you think I should learn?" We did have a record library at Curtis, but they were cumbersome 78s. It was a big job to hear them, but I listened to a lot of records anyway. There really weren't many records of pianists—only Horowitz, Rubinstein, and Casadesus.

Godowsky's original music is pretty awful, but we all had to learn some of it. I learned some of the *Triakontameron* in the summertime when I was home in New York, in 1936 or 1937. They were a set of graded piano pieces for students, like the *Mikrokosmos* of Bartók, but not in the same class. Also, I learned two pieces of the *Java Suite*: "The Gardens of Buitenzorg" and "The Chattering Monkeys," because they were amusing and nice. The *Java Suite*—complicated salon music—was probably the only decent thing Godowsky wrote. I played three of the Études. I played *Symphonic Metamorphosis on Themes from Die Fledermaus* a great deal. The *Artist's Life* Waltzes I learned but never performed. Earl Wild and I were once talking about *Artist's Life*, which are even more

Fig. 2. *Josef Hofmann's Golden Jubilee Concert. College Park, National Archives.*

Fig. 3. *Abbey Simon at 17. Photograph courtesy of Jonathan Simon.*

difficult than the *Fledermaus,* and more complicated. He played it, and so did Bolet, but the consensus was if you played it Monday and didn't practice it Tuesday, you were lost Wednesday. It was just too much work. I think it's the same with everybody—there's a period when you're very young, when you want to learn some of these pieces because they're so difficult, because you have to beat them, and it's wonderful. The first time I learned the Liszt *Don Juan Fantasy,* I learned it for one reason—because everybody said it was impossible. I learned

Fig. 4. *Abbey Simon, c. 1940. Photograph courtesy of Jonathan Simon.*

all the Liszt *Transcendental Études,* too. Years ago, there would be a run on a piece. Everyone would be playing the *Mephisto Waltz* to close their programs, and then people got tired of it, and everybody started playing *Islamey,* including me.

Most of what we played at Curtis was from the nineteenth century—not much original Bach, Mozart, or Schubert, and no contemporary music. About six Bach transcriptions were

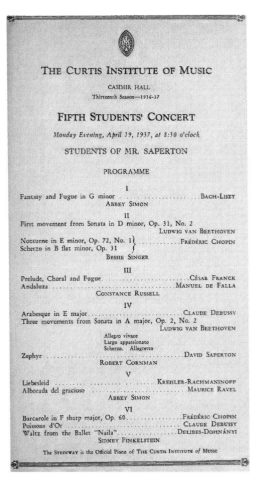

The Curtis Institute of Music
CASIMIR HALL
Thirteenth Season—1936-37

FIFTH STUDENTS' CONCERT

Monday Evening, April 19, 1937, at 8:30 o'clock

STUDENTS OF MR. SAPERTON

PROGRAMME

I
Fantasy and Fugue in G minor .... BACH-LISZT
ABBEY SIMON

II
First movement from Sonata in D minor, Op. 31, No. 2
LUDWIG VAN BEETHOVEN
Nocturne in E minor, Op. 72, No. 1 \
Scherzo in B flat minor, Op. 31 / .... FRÉDÉRIC CHOPIN
BESSIE SINGER

III
Prelude, Choral and Fugue .... CÉSAR FRANCK
Andaluza .... MANUEL DE FALLA
CONSTANCE RUSSELL

IV
Arabesque in E major .... CLAUDE DEBUSSY
Three movements from Sonata in A major, Op. 2, No. 2
LUDWIG VAN BEETHOVEN
Allegro vivace
Largo appassionato
Scherzo. Allegretto
Zephyr .... DAVID SAPERTON
ROBERT CORNMAN

V
Liebesleid .... KREISLER-RACHMANINOFF
Alborada del gracioso .... MAURICE RAVEL
ABBEY SIMON

VI
Barcarole in F sharp major, Op. 60 .... FRÉDÉRIC CHOPIN
Poissons d'Or .... CLAUDE DEBUSSY
Waltz from the Ballet "Naila" .... DELIBES-DOHNÁNYI
SIDNEY FINKELSTEIN

The STEINWAY is the Official Piano of THE CURTIS INSTITUTE of MUSIC

Fig. 5. *Curtis Institute of Music Fifth Students' Recital programme, 19 April 1937, Curtis Institute of Music Archives.*

played. The Bach-Liszt Prelude and Fugue in A Minor was played to death. So was the Bach-D'Albert transcription of that D-Major organ Prelude and Fugue. All of Vengerova's students I heard mostly played the Bach-Liszt A-Minor, and some of them played the Bach-Busoni C-Major Toccata, Adagio, and Fugue. People rarely played original Bach works such as the *Well-Tempered Clavier.* Somebody played the Bach A-Minor English Suite, but I don't remember hearing the Partitas or French Suites. Then taste changed and everybody went to the originals, so that later, when I played a transcription, I got nasty remarks. Now transcriptions have come back, but that's only recently. I played a number of pieces on the Curtis radio program, including Saperton's *Zephyr,* a piece we all played, two pages of nonsense.

In 1938, Josef Hofmann decided to retire, I don't know what the reason was. Saperton left not long after, when Rudolf Serkin came in. Saperton couldn't possibly get along with Serkin—they played a completely opposite kind of repertoire. I was scheduled to graduate that year anyway, so it didn't make any difference to me. I might have been tempted to stay on and take some lessons with Serkin, except I couldn't stand him or his playing. I think it was also that I couldn't stand anything—still can't—German.

I graduated with a diploma from Curtis on May 9, 1939, one of only twenty-four students. In those days, there wasn't much of a curriculum, set length of study, or set graduation age. We just studied until they said, "You're graduating." After I graduated, Curtis started giving a Bachelor of Arts degree in conjunction with the University of Pennsylvania, but it wasn't a degree in Piano Performance, just a Bachelor's degree.

When I left Curtis, I knew four concertos: the Rubinstein 4th, the Brahms D-Minor, the Chopin F-Minor, and the Beethoven 3rd. There was still a world of repertoire I didn't know. My graduation recital took place on March 14, 1940. My program was:

Bach-Busoni, Toccata, Adagio and Fugue in C Major, BWV 564
Schumann, *"Abegg" Variations*, op. 1
Beethoven, Sonata in E Major, op. 109
Chopin, Nocturne in F-sharp Minor, op. 48, no. 2; four Études in D-flat Major, op. 25, no. 8; F Major, op. 25, no. 3; F Minor (Posthumous); C-sharp Minor, op. 10, no. 4
Rachmaninoff, Prelude in E-flat Major, op. 23, no. 6
Ravel, "Alborada del gracioso"
Godowsky, *Music Box*
Balakirev, *Islamey*

Around this time, I was playing with some Curtis students at a summer resort in Pennsylvania. A young woman came in to

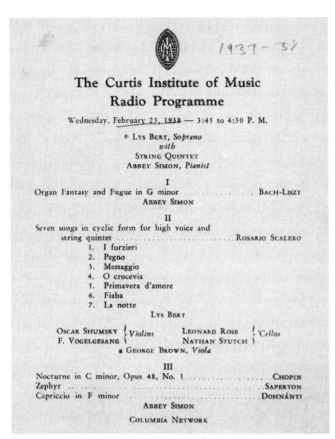

Fig. 6. Curtis Institute of Music Radio Programme, 23 February
1938, Curtis Institute of Music Archives.

register at the hotel and I asked her, "What's your table tonight?"
She gave me the number. I said, "That won't do, you're sitting
at my table!" and she never left my table. Her name was Dina
Levinson and she weighed about eighty-eight pounds. She lived
in Baltimore with her two sisters, and all three were gorgeous.
She was in the middle. I was about nineteen, she was eleven
months older, born on February 4, 1919. I used to kid her and
say I always went for older women. She said she used to play the
piano, until she heard me! I had met the love of my life.

The Curtis Institute of Music
Radio Programme

Monday, January 16, 1939 — 3:00 to 4:00 P. M.

● ABBEY SIMON, *Piano*
MARGUERITE KUEHNE, *Violin*
DONALD COKER, *Tenor*

I

Abegg variations, Opus 1 .... SCHUMANN
ABBEY SIMON

II

Lasciatemi morire .... MONTEVERDE
Spirate pur, spirate .... DONAUDY
"M'appari tutt' amor" from "Martha" .... FLOTOW
DONALD COKER

III

Siciliano .... J. S. BACH
Gavotte from Sonata in E major .... BACH-KREISLER
Romance in G major .... BEETHOVEN
Hungarian dance in F minor .... BRAHMS-KREISLER
MARGUERITE KUEHNE

IV

Sea fever .... IRELAND
Sailor's life .... OLD ENGLISH
The sleigh .... KOUNTZ
DONALD COKER

V

Music box .... GODOWSKY
Nocturne in F sharp minor, Opus 48, No. 2 .... CHOPIN
Alborada del gracioso .... RAVEL
ABBEY SIMON

VLADIMIR SOKOLOFF
EUGENE BOSSART } *Accompanists*

COLUMBIA BROADCASTING SYSTEM

Fig. 7. Curtis Institute of Music Radio Programme, 16 January 1939, Curtis Institute of Music Archives.

Chapter Three
THE REAL WORLD: 1940-1948

Curtis spoiled you to the extent that they really didn't prepare you for real life. That was the only trouble. I didn't know you needed a concert manager, and I didn't know anything about competitions—I'd never even seen or heard one. It never even occurred to me to enter a competition. Then Jorge Bolet entered the Naumburg and of course he won, so I decided I would have to win the Naumburg. The first time I entered, in 1939, I had never even played in a competition. There were two pieces in the first round that everybody had to play. One was a Scarlatti sonata in E Major and the other was the A-flat-Major Ballade of Chopin. The chief jurist was Bruce Simonds, the head of the piano department of Yale. I went out to play the A-flat Ballade and he said, "Why don't you save us a little time and start at the C-sharp minor section?" I was flabbergasted. I played badly, and of course I didn't get anywhere. When I entered it again next year, I could've played any piece on the program backward. That was when I won. Olga Samaroff was on the jury, and she was very nice to me.

They had just announced my winning the Naumburg in the morning, and I did something I never would have dared do if I wasn't drunk on myself—I went and rang Saperton's doorbell. When he opened the door, I said,

"Mr. Sa…"

"How dare you come in here?!"

"Mr. Saperton, I thought you'd like to know I just won the Naumburg."

"Oh my God."

He acted like it was the greatest disaster that ever befell him. He was giving Julius Katchen a lesson and that's when I met Julius, who was a young teenager at the time. He wasn't at Curtis, he was studying for a long time with Saperton privately.

In those days, they didn't give you eight million dollars for winning a piano competition. My Naumburg prize was a New York Town Hall debut recital, which I gave on September 28, 1940. I finished with Balakirev's *Islamey*. All the legends about *Islamey! Islamey* is not hard—you will discover there are two or three measures that are difficult. I remember one passage practically at the coda, where you play octaves in the left hand. I was having a terrible time with that, and suddenly I said, "This is a big, marvelous piece, and if I miss four notes in this passage, the world won't come to an end," and then it went out great. It was a turning point in my life. Also, those two little words are always there to tell you to play it freely: *Oriental Fantasy.* I never heard *Islamey* played as fast as it's played today and I sure as hell didn't play it that fast.

After I got these great reviews in New York for the Naumburg recital, somebody said, "Well, you have to go and take these around to the various managers. I said, "Me? I have to go and sell myself? I don't know how."

I was also in the Leventritt Competition but it took place when I was getting ready for my Naumburg debut recital. So I sailed through the solo repertoire and made it to the final round, but I did not distinguish myself with the concertos—the Brahms D-Minor and one of the Chopin concertos. Constance Keene and Sidney Foster were also in the finals, and Sidney won. The funny part about it was we were all finalists in all the various competitions, but not one of us won two.

On July 21, 1941, Dina and I eloped—our parents thought we were too young—and moved into a studio apartment at 102

West Eighty-Fourth Street in New York. It was a financially precarious time. I had to earn money, and my solo career had yet to take off. A piano career is not like an orchestral musician's. Orchestral musicians know that if they play well enough, they can get a job in an orchestra. That option did not exist for pianists, except for an occasional orchestral piano part. Back then, there also weren't any university positions that I know of, except Yale. There was no fallback job. There was the radio, however, and in those days there was far more Classical music on the radio than today. Radio producers wanted to educate listeners about serious music, and there were several shows that featured it, such as The NBC Music Appreciation Hour, The Firestone Hour, and the Radio City Music Hall of the Air. The radio also owned many theaters on Broadway and used to broadcast from theaters on Forty-Eighth Street.

I played for two radio stations, and whenever I die, it would have been a year later if not for those jobs. The first was at WQXR. We had an orchestra of about nine people, and I played the Novachord, which was a sort of electric organ. There was a fabulous pianist also working there named Jascha Zayde, who helped me tremendously. I lasted about a year at WQXR, but it would have been less if not for him. It was not a job for me. I'm well-known as a poor sight-reader, and you have no idea what it is to be a poor sight-reader in the commercial world, or a good sight-reader in the commercial world. Much of the music was in manuscript. You had one rehearsal, at eleven o'clock in the morning, and if you were like me, you came in to the radio station at nine, hoping the librarian had put out the music already. If the librarian put out the music at a quarter after ten, you were lost. Orchestral musicians say, "Well, it's easy," but they only read one line of music, whereas the pianist is supposed to know everything. At WQXR, we played with a marvelous conductor and person, Leon Barzin. I played a lot of concertos—all the Bach concertos, a Mozart concerto, etc.

My second radio job was at WOR, but there, I had a lot of solo work to do. I managed for a year until they caught on to me. Their programs were all for a live audience. I'll never forget coming to the theater once for one of their *Music for a Sunday Afternoon* broadcasts. I was always a nervous wreck because I never knew what I would find. Most of this was light music and I knew it all by ear—and I could get away with this. I came in Sunday morning and there is a piece for piano and orchestra in manuscript. It says *Biding my Time.* I was reading this manuscript and suddenly there's nothing written for twenty-four bars or something. I'm sitting at the piano and suddenly, the orchestra stops. The Polish violinist-conductor, Bob Sylvester, says, "Hey piano player, Ver's Da Biding?" Suddenly it struck me: "Biding My Time…It's a Gershwin song!" and I went frantically into the piece. The orchestra was roaring with laughter. That conductor later dropped dead. Of course, I wished it so.

Fig. 8. Early married life in New York. Photograph courtesy of Jonathan Simon.

Another time there was piece, a dialogue for piano and orchestra. The piano played twenty or thirty notes very fast, then the orchestra played twenty or thirty notes, and it went on for about ten minutes. It was a nightmare. That afternoon, a cellist friend named Leopold Teraspu-

Fig. 9. *Simon, c. 1941.*
Photograph courtesy of Jonathan Simon.

lsky had made his debut in Town Hall. I couldn't go to his concert, but I went to the reception at a friend's house. I was so exhausted from the radio ordeal, and I was sitting in a chair and took one sip of my scotch and soda, and I felt this cold starting at my toes and creeping up my body, and the glass fell on the floor, and I passed out. I wasn't unconscious for very long, but when I came to, the warmth gradually came back into my body, starting with my toes.

Another thing I did to earn money was to play for Atty Van den Berg, the star dancer for the Jooss Ballet, which was a very famous Dutch company. I played the early Shostakovich Preludes while she danced to them. That was a rewarding experience. Her husband was the world-famous photographer Fritz Henle, and they had a townhouse on Sutton Place, a couple of blocks from our second apartment on 1st Avenue between 48th and 49th Streets. She had the whole top floor of her house transformed into a dance studio.

On October 15, 1941, I gave my second Town Hall recital, with the program:

Bach-Liszt, Fantasia and Fugue in G Minor, BWV 542
Beethoven, Sonata in D Major, op. 28 ("Pastorale")
Schumann, *Kreisleriana*, op. 16

Brahms, Chopin, and Debussy, various works

Every great artist played in Town Hall—just as many as in

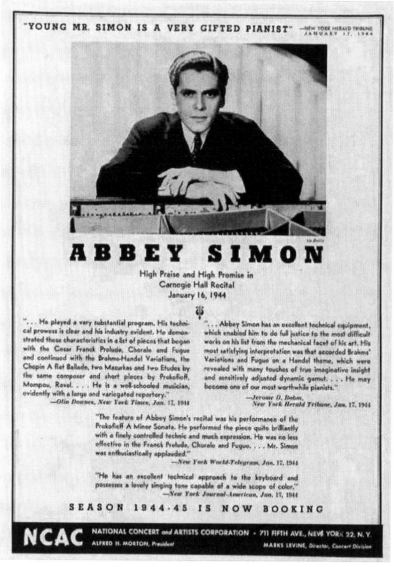

Fig. 10. *NCAC Flyer, c. 1944, showing a sampling of the different newspapers writing reviews at the time.*

Carnegie Hall. It was very prestigious, artistically on a par with Carnegie Hall. It cost 300 dollars to rent, which really wasn't much money in those days. When I think of all the newspaper ads and the printing of circulars, which were in boxes in the hall for people to see who was playing next week, and all of these things, you could put it on for very little money. Nobody thought about what it cost. It may have been poor times in the United States, just coming out of the Depression, and the war was on, but it was cheap. Carnegie Hall wasn't much more expensive.

In around 1941, my father was remarried to a wonderful woman who was a great influence in my life. She was a biology teacher. Her name was Sarah Weinraub and we called her Sally.

On December 7, 1941, I was with my wife and a dear friend of mine with his new wife, and we were walking through the Metropolitan Museum, where we used to go on Sundays. Suddenly a voice came over the loudspeaker telling all men in uniform to report immediately, and I heard people saying they bombed Pearl Harbor. It was really something to get through. During World War II, I knew about the Holocaust but I didn't have any family involved. Deen, as I called Dina, had family who were involved and survived.

In 1942, I was offered a position in the Marine Corps Symphony Orchestra and I went down to Washington to see the conductor, a captain. They were all thrilled with me, and then I didn't pass the physical because I had asthma. I went down the street to the Navy, and the same thing happened. I did pass the physical for the Army, but I decided you could get killed that way so I just said, "No, I can't, I'm too sick." The first war the American Army lost was that war with me. Instead, I enlisted in the US Army Signal Corps, stationed at Fort Dix, New Jersey. I learned every part of what was called a 6-2 radio. You went from room to room, and you were told what each part did, all these resis-

Fig. 11. Dina, c. 1945. Photograph courtesy of Jonathan Simon.

tors and everything. They gave you your final exam when you arrived, and you had to learn the material. If you didn't pass the exam at the end, you were sent out to active duty, or 1A classification. I had a 1B, which was a delay of some sort. Well, my father really passed the exam, because without his help I never would have. I was in the Signal Corps for over a year.

After my military service, I had only a short time to prepare for my first Carnegie Hall recital. Because I had played for David Saperton for so many years, I felt it was time for a change. I went to play my program for Isabelle Vengerova because I had such enormous respect and affection for her. Vengerova was a wonderful teacher, but I have the feeling that you had to study with her when you were an infant. Because if you were five years old, or fifty-five years old, you got the same lessons in the beginning: "Hold your wrist a little higher. No, a little lower. No, a little higher," etc. She had me spend an hour on the first note of the Brahms *Handel Variations*. After three lessons, I ended up writing her a letter saying, "I would be happy to become your slave afterwards, but right now I'm just a few weeks away from my concert."

I had a very close friend, a wonderful pianist named Leon

Kushner, who lived near me. One day I was lamenting the business about finding somebody to play for, and Leon, who was a student of Dora Zaslavsky at the Manhattan School, said, "Why don't you come play for Dora, she has an open class every week, and she'd be delighted to have you." Years before, Dora had been a student of Janet Schenck and had studied with Backhaus. Apparently, early in life Dora played in Town Hall, and played a great deal at the Manhattan School in chamber music with, among others, Harry (Rachmael) Weinstock, who was quite a well-known violinist in New York. I came to her class, and she was very good, completely the opposite of Saperton, and of everybody else. She knew the Schubert sonatas, the "Hammerklavier," all this complicated Classical repertoire, which I had been kept in ignorance of. I was very angry when I first met her, because I felt I had been deprived of so much.

I had practiced the *Wanderer* Fantasy a great deal in the past, but always took it off my programs at the last minute because I felt I couldn't play it. Dora said, "That's nonsense, play it for me as soon as you can get it back," and that was the first time I had a lesson on anything by Schubert.

On January 16, 1944, I played the first of many recitals in Carnegie Hall. My program was:

Franck, *Prélude, Chorale and Fugue*
Brahms, *Variations and Fugue on a Theme by Handel*, op. 24
Chopin, Ballade in A-flat Major, op. 47, two Mazurkas, two Études
Prokofiev, Sonata in A Minor, op. 28
Short pieces by Mompou, Ravel

The first time I played in Carnegie Hall, I was playing and thinking, "I'm playing in Carnegie Hall, this is so wonderful, I love playing in Carnegie Hall" and then suddenly, "Carnegie Hall? What the hell am I doing here!?"

In the mid-1940s, there were two major concert artist agencies in the United States: Columbia Artists Management and The National Concert and Artists Corporation. Sidney and I were managed by NCAC. You got long reviews in a dozen newspapers in New York—the Times, the Herald-Tribune, the World, the Journal-American, the Daily News, the Post, a Yiddish newspaper, two German newspapers, a French newspaper, an Italian newspaper…but it's a wholly different thing now.

Around 1944, I was playing a recital in northern Indiana. I was sick as a dog, and I got a call to come and audition for George Szell in Chicago. He was an autocratic and terrifying perfectionist who could play entire orchestral scores from memory on the piano. Joe Gingold, Szell's concertmaster, said he would see Rudolf Serkin's leg trembling during rehearsals with Szell, and that Serkin never finished a rehearsal—he would just get up and walk out.

You couldn't have found a worse day. I think Claudia Cassidy, the most feared critic in the United States, the scourge and the worst writer because she didn't know a thing about Classical music, had just ripped him to shreds. There were many artists who wouldn't play in Chicago because of her. One of her reviews said that Szell would be better suited to leading a marching band down Michigan Avenue. My audition for Szell was a disaster.

I had a friend, Nathan Steinberg, who kept saying to me, "You know, you have to play for Dimitri Mitropoulos, he will love your playing." I didn't take it very seriously. How he got to know Mitropoulos, I don't know, but they were good friends. One day in New York in 1945, the telephone rang and Nathan said, "What are you doing now?" I said, "Nothing, I'm home." He said, "I'm coming over with Dimitri." I went into a state of panic. Three quarters of an hour later, they came in and I rushed to the piano. Mitropoulos said, "Calm down!" He was always a sweetheart to everybody, to all young artists. We sat down, and we talked for about an hour, and had a drink, and I made some tea. I don't remember what I played for him. Then I got a letter from Columbia Artists telling me they would represent me, and I was engaged to play with the New York Philharmonic, the Philadelphia Orchestra, and the Minneapolis Symphony.

Mitropoulos wanted me to play the Prokofiev Second Concerto with him in Minneapolis. I couldn't find a copy of the score, so I called the Library of Congress and asked for two photostat copies. It cost me almost 300 dollars. Of course, a few months later, Leeds Music published it for three dollars. I started to learn it and knew it wasn't for me. Too many big chords, too much noise, and I hated the first movement, especially the cadenza, which is interminable. Then, I got a letter from the Minneapolis Symphony telling me they were obliged to change the concerto because they were being charged so much money for the orchestra parts and refused to be blackmailed. I thought, "There is a God!"

After the war, I took my first teaching position, at the Manhattan School of Music. The school had been founded in 1917 by pianist and philanthropist Janet D. Schenck. She started it with little lessons on the Lower East Side. She was an extraordinary woman, and she and Mrs. Bok admired each other. When I started teaching at the Manhattan School, it was their third home already, on 105th Street on the East Side. I told Mrs. Schenck that I had never taught children and I wouldn't know how to begin. I was given a class full of children. When she came to the school in the morning, she would take the elevator to the top floor and go down looking into all the studios. One day, she looked into my studio and there I was, teaching somebody while reading the

New York Times. She asked me to come to her office and said, "You are a wonderfully gifted pianist. You have great talent and you play gorgeously. BUT YOU CANNOT READ THE NEW YORK TIMES WHEN YOU ARE TEACHING!"

I still can't teach children. You need a special language and a special form of diplomacy, and I lose my patience too quickly. I've become a terrific teacher for people who can play. I can show them how to play better, technically, how to see what I see in a piece of music, how to hear, and I think that's all you can do for anybody.

Harold Bauer was the artist teacher at the Manhattan School. He was a marvelous, mild man. I remember hearing him play the Saint-Saëns G-Minor Concerto, and he did everything in his own modest fashion. I asked him if I could come to his performance class and he said, "Oh, with pleasure," and I played the Brahms *Paganini Variations.* He said, "Well, I have never been able to play them like that, and I could never do these things that you're doing there, and they're very interesting and very good." And then he said, "Now could you think about this one this way, and this one this way," and very nicely he showed me how to do it. He was a wonderful teacher and artist.

The composition teacher at the Manhattan School, Vittorio Giannini, was a very nice, gifted man. His two sisters, Euphemia and Dusolina, were famous opera singers. Giannini was a very well-known composer and a wonderful teacher. I ran into him in the corridor one day and said,

"Maestro Giannini, can I come to your composition class?"

"With pleasure."

"What am I supposed to do, am I supposed to do any preparation?

"What's the name of the class?"

"Composition."

"So write a composition!"

So I wrote a movement of a piano quintet. I don't have it any more. He was one of the best teachers I ever encountered.

My work with Dora Zaslavsky continued for the next several years. It was more than music study. It was life study, and our relationship developed into a long-term friendship. Dora's husband was the painter John Koch, and they turned their home into a salon of music and art in New York. I learned a great deal just being there. He and his wife changed my life enormously. They'd been married for many years, never had any children, and had lived in France for a long time. Our second apartment, on First Avenue overlooking the East River, had been their apartment. There were many musicians living in that building. Earl Wild lived there, and the famous singers Elsie Arden and Povla Frijsh. Dora and John needed a larger place and moved to a very famous building, The Eldorado, on Central Park West around Ninetieth Street. The elevator came up to their landing,

Fig. 12. *John Koch, Music, 1956-7, Ohio, The Butler Institute of American Art.*

and there was an apartment on each side. One was for his painting studio, the other was for her teaching studio.

I learned a great deal from John Koch, one of the most interesting and funny people I've ever met. He was a very cultivated man from the standpoint of literature and was a marvelous raconteur who could impersonate anybody. He played the piano and sang everything from art song to show tunes. He was used to students walking in and out, and hearing the piano all the time. Instinctively, he had the talent to like what was beautiful and dislike what was ugly, even in music.

John would suddenly get very angry for no reason and the world would come to an end. You were lucky if you could get out of the state alive. Sometimes he would start screaming, "I can't stand the sound of that fucking piano anymore!" Then, other times, Dora would say, "I'm sick and tired of all your problems with the galleries and everything." It was an impetuous life, but they seemed to be quite happy with each other and certainly very happy in their lifestyle. And, difficult as they were, I will always love them.

Fig. 13. New York, c. 1949. Photograph courtesy of Jonathan Simon.

John was a fantastic painter, and you can see what he does with light. I saw a painting of his mother that he did when he was nine years old. He was already by instinct a master. Among the cognoscenti, he is referred to as the American Vermeer. The critics were dreadful to him, though, and he never got a good review in his life. They all said, "Nobody can paint the way John Koch can, *if you like that sort of thing.*" Koch had a tremendous appreciation of the nude form and returned to it often as a subject. He was also a great portraitist who catered to very rich families: a number of governors, politicians, etc., wanted portraits from him. He once expected to be asked by the White House to do a portrait of Jacqueline Kennedy and was very upset that the commission went to a friend and former student of his who was not in the same league. It was a great blow to him.

John and I had a lot in common. We were both child prodigies, self-taught as youngsters. I think we were both acerbic in speech but generous in deeds. My own approach to music and repertoire shared much with John Koch's attitude to art, preferring romantic, traditional forms to modern abstraction. We both emphasized a strong technique and both stressed beauty and enjoying sensations, colors, and sounds as opposed to radical ideas.

Dora's students often became models for John. There is a painting called *Music* which shows me in a lesson with Dora. He painted it from memory years later, in 1956. Then there was a famous picture that he did—I was not in it because I was out of the country—called *The Cocktail Party.* It had everybody that you can think of: Virgil Thomson, Aaron Copland, Ania Dorfmann, a half a dozen other painters and musicians, some from Dora's studio.

John and Dora were maniacally generous people. There was a very famous critic on the New York Times that I knew very well named Noel Straus, and he came down with cancer. He was one of the people in *The Cocktail Party.* After he'd been in the hospital for about a week, Dora and John said, "This is not for you, you're coming to live with us," and they brought him to one of their apartments for several months, right until the day or two before he died.

Until I met Dora and John, I'd never heard of Wanda Landowska. Landowska arrived in New York on Dec. 7, 1941, the same day as Pearl Harbor. Dora was not a wealthy woman, but she was one of those people that arranged money to support Landowska when she arrived here.

In around 1945, Landowska suddenly announced a series of masterclass-recitals on Sunday mornings at her apartment on Central Park West. I think the tickets were at least fifty dollars each which, in those days, was very expensive. We went to one of her recitals on a New Year's Day when New York was covered up to the neck in snow. We met Dora and John in the lobby of Landowska's apartment and went upstairs. Landowska was playing harpsichord that day. She was a very accurate player, but something must have unnerved her terribly, because she was hitting all sorts of notes that she never meant to hit. Suddenly she

Fig. 14. *A summer concert by the Washington Symphony Orchestra at the Watergate, c. 1939. Washington, D.C., Harris & Ewing Collection, Library of Congress.*

Fig. 15. *Publicity photos, 1940s (Photographer unknown.)*

got up and said to the audience, "I must get a ham sandwich," and she walked off the stage, and nobody knew whether to get up and leave, or what. Then she came back out and announced she would play the cadenza to the Fifth Brandenburg Concerto, which she played wonderfully.

In 1945, I gave my first major orchestral performance, with the Minneapolis Symphony and Mitropoulos. In the many times we played together, he was always very discreet. Sometimes in a rehearsal, he'd come over to the piano and whisper, or after the rehearsal was over, he'd say, "I think you'd be better off trying out this idea," in a non-aggressive way.

That year, I also gave recitals in Providence and at Kimball Hall in Chicago. I wasn't known as an exponent of new music, but I occasionally gave performances of new repertoire. For example, my second Carnegie Hall recital, on January 3, 1945, contained Prokofiev's *Mephisto Waltz*, op. 96, no. 3, which nobody has heard of since, and Herbert Haufrecht's *Sicilian Suite*.

According to the review by Noel Straus, the last two pieces were receiving their first performance. In 1946, I played recitals at the New England Conservatory's Jordan Hall and the Gardner Museum in Boston, and another recital in Carnegie Hall on January 26. My program was:

Chopin, Nocturne in F-Sharp Minor, op. 48, no. 2
Ravel, *Valses nobles et sentimentales*
Brahms, *Variations on a Theme of Paganini*, op. 35
Beethoven, Seven Bagatelles, op. 33
Albéniz-Godowsky, *Triana*

In 1946, I had a very different kind of experience with Josef Hofmann. You have to understand, it used to be like buying tickets for Horowitz when Hofmann played in New York—everything was sold out. There was a gigantic portrait of Hofmann in the Steinway building. Sidney and I ran into each other in New York, and by accident, we heard about a Hofmann recital in Carnegie Hall. The concert was tragic, because the hall was empty. He had gone out of fashion. He was falling apart, drunk. It was a completely different affair.

I hate outdoor concerts because I hate the sound of the piano. It always seems like I'm not making any sound. In 1946-47, I had to play in three of them. One was at the Robin Hood Dell, a 10,000-seat amphitheater in Philadelphia, whose regular orchestra consisted mostly of members of the Philadelphia Orchestra. The Robin Hood Dell hosted the world's famous musicians—Leopold Stokowski, Eugene Ormandy, Fritz Reiner, Josef Hofmann, Jascha Heifetz, Judy Garland (in her first public concert), Marian Anderson, Benny Goodman, Artur Rubinstein, and many others. I performed the Chopin F-Minor Concerto there with Mitropoulos and got a great review.

The second outdoor site was the Lewisohn Stadium, a 6,000-seat venue in New York City. It was the athletic stadium of The City College of New York, and it was the summer home of the New York Philharmonic. It also hosted performances by the most famous musicians—perhaps most notably George Gershwin, premiering his *Rhapsody in Blue.* At Lewisohn Stadium I was going to play the Brahms D-Minor Concerto with the famous French conductor Pierre Monteux. We managed to rehearse the first movement and then the rain came in and the concert was canceled. That was my only opportunity to play with Monteux. Later on, in the summertime, they telephoned me to say I would play the Chopin F-Minor with Efrem Kurtz instead. One of my encores was one of Mompou's Songs and Dances, a piece I haven't played in many years.

The third outdoor space was the Watergate, but not the infamous hotel. It was a large outdoor amphitheater in Washington located on a raft in the Potomac River.

For a number of years, I played for Community Concerts, which arranged recitals for me in all the towns going up the river from Montreal: Québec, Rivière-du-loup, Chicoutimi, and I loved them. One of them, Arvida, is named after Arthur Vining Davis, the founder of the Aluminum Companies of America and Canada. Because all these big dignitaries came to Arvida, they built a beautiful little chateau hotel. I've stayed there several times. The last time I was there, I was sitting in front of the fire in this beautiful armchair reading a detective story, and this woman sits down opposite me. I look at her, and I say, "Rosalyn?" and she says, "Abbey?" It was Rosalyn Tureck. The next thought we both had was the same: One of us was in the wrong place. I was playing in Arvida, she was playing in Chicoutimi, and they put her in this hotel because it was such a jewel. I have no idea what it's like now.

For my encores, I would ask for four notes, called out by four different people, and improvise pieces. I would do three or four—they always wanted more. I did this a thousand times, in the style of Bach, Chopin, Mozart, Gershwin. I was known as the poor man's Alec Templeton. He was a fabulous radio star who did improvisations on the radio. He would even improvise four voices in an opera.

In 1948, I received the Federation of Music Clubs Award. For the competition, you had to play the C-sharp-Major Prelude and Fugue from the *Well-Tempered Clavier*, Book I. But I only found out about this the day before the contest, because I thought it said C-sharp-Minor Prelude and Fugue. I learned the C-sharp-Major in one day and there was no question that I was very, very, much better than anyone else! I know when I play well and when I play badly. The chief judge was Egon Petri, who came over to me and said he thought that I had totally interesting and very good ideas in that Prelude and Fugue.

That year, I was on concert tour on the train. It was my first visit to Texas and I was going to play in Graham. My wife was with me, and we stopped for a layover in Lexington, Kentucky. I picked up the New York Times and I read that I had been awarded the National Orchestral Association Prize and would be heard in three or four weeks in the Liszt E-flat-Major Concerto, which I didn't play! It was with a very, very good students' orchestra directed by Leon Barzin, who had chosen me to receive the award based on my past recitals in New York. I got into a cab and went to the nearest music store, bought the score, and studied it all the way. When we got to Texas, Van Cliburn's mother brought him to play for me—he was thirteen years old and they were living in nearby Killeen. His mother was a piano teacher, and she taught him. I never found out where her musical education came from.

When I got back to New York, I did all my practicing on the Liszt E-flat, not on the pieces I was playing on my Community Concert tours. I think I played it rather well. I had just won these prizes and suddenly, I got a letter saying, "You have been proposed for membership in the Lotos Club by Arthur Judson, and seconded by Bruno Zirato." Arthur Judson was the president of Columbia Artists Management, and Bruno Zirato was vice president. The Lotos Club was one of New York's most eminent literary clubs, and Mark Twain was an early member. It has hosted dinners for eight US presidents, eleven Nobel Prize winners, and dozens of international figures including Oscar Wilde, Maurice Maeterlinck, Richard Strauss, Saint-Saëns, Paderewski, and Caruso.

In the 1940s, Dina and I became friends with Ruth Lapham Lloyd, a well-known philanthropist. John Koch did a portrait of her. She was the mother of actor Christopher Lloyd from the *Back to the Future* movies and the TV show *Taxi*. She owned an estate in New Canaan, Connecticut called Waveny Park and always invited us to stay there. We lived there on and off for many years. The only trouble was that every time we came back to our apartment in New York, it got smaller. Mrs. Lloyd was a very sweet, unassuming, lady who lost her sight as she got older. She adored singing—and sang badly—but she was very generous and didn't think at all about money. Later, in the 1960s, I played a Carnegie Hall concert and found out afterwards she had bought four or five hundred tickets to distribute to the high schools.

The 1940s had been a decade of steady progress for my career. However, despite several high-profile performances, I wasn't having the quantity of success I sought. That was about to change.

Chapter Four
EUROPE: 1949-1959

By the late 1940s, I felt my career was being held back in the United States. At the time, the major US orchestras, which had very short seasons, were only engaging the big names—Horowitz, Rachmaninoff, Hofmann, Casadesus. I was a timid fellow and was under the spell of Horowitz. I still am. They loved me at Community Concerts, partly because of my improvised encores, but I wasn't getting any of the important engagements, and I wanted to play in the big cities. I went to my managers—I was already with Columbia Artists—and said, "Listen, it's time I did better." One of them said, "You should give introductory concerts in Europe—that would give you an international name." So, I took out all the money from our savings account and said, "Do what has to be done." Columbia booked recitals in the spring of 1949 with the leading managers in Rome, Milan, The Hague, Rotterdam, Amsterdam, London, and Paris. Lo and behold, I had an enormous success.

I was immediately engaged by all of these conductors I couldn't get in the front door to audition for before, whose names I had dreamt about: Barbirolli, Sargent, Boult. I was suddenly playing with them all and with all of these orchestras: The Concertgebouw, The Symphony Orchestra of The Hague, The London Symphony, The Hallé Orchestra. That's how my career took off. We decided to go for three or four months to Europe, and it turned out to be sixty-five years. I had no desire to get involved with anything in the US, where I was very unhappy. I rarely set foot in the States for fourteen years. I only stopped off on our way to Latin America or Australia to see my parents in New York.

By moving to Europe, I had the chance to develop my own style, to experiment with different interpretations to see what worked, and even to play badly. In the United States, one couldn't take that risk. Europe was ready to hear some new musicians after the war, and there weren't many American pianists playing there at the time. In a way, I was lucky.

On November 7, 1950, I played the Beethoven Fourth Concerto with the London Philharmonic and was engaged shortly thereafter to play with Malcolm Sargent and the London Symphony in the Royal Albert Hall. When my manager asked me what I wanted to play, I said the Brahms D-Minor, one of my four concertos. I had booked a stateroom on the *Nieuw Amsterdam*, the famous ocean liner, to cross the Atlantic from New York to England. I was looking forward to the journey, which was to take a week or so. Right before I left, I got a letter from the London Symphony saying I was going to be playing the Brahms B-flat, which is a gigantic concerto—one of the most challenging in the repertoire. I didn't know the Brahms B-flat but was too timid to admit it. So, I canceled my boat ticket and practiced forty-seven hours a day for ten days, getting every pianist I knew to play the orchestra reduction. Somehow the concert was a success, and I'll always remember that first appearance with the London Symphony. Malcolm Sargent was one of the great joys and inspirations of my life; I played with him many times. I loved playing in the Albert Hall. Everybody complains about the acoustics, but I only know that I enjoyed it because of the way the piano sounds. There are many other halls I dislike, principally because the piano doesn't sound nice to me.

In England, Harold Holt became my manager. He was one of the two biggest managers in those days, the Hurok equivalent in Great Britain. He became a great friend of ours.

On September 25, 1950, our only child, Jonathan, was born in the States. At the time, Dina was still living there when I was on tour. I remember taking Deen to the hospital, and I sat around and waited, and then the doctor brought us this absolutely gorgeous baby, and as Deen was becoming awake she said,

"For God's sake, I'm still here, when is it going to end?"

"You had a baby boy."

"I don't believe it!"

"I swear to you, I couldn't invent that!"

The following January saw more recitals in The Hague, Rotterdam, and Amsterdam, and the Schumann concerto with the London Symphony and Josef Krips in Albert Hall. A few weeks later, I found an apartment in London, and Dina and Jonathan came over to join me there.

Soon after arriving in London, I learned I needed a labor permit, which I, in my naïveté, didn't realize was necessary. I had permission to live in London, but I didn't have permission to work there. So, we left London and moved to Paris. In those days, it was a very long flight from the US to France, and there weren't many Americans there. One of them was the pianist Julius Katchen, who was the first person I called when we got there, and we became very great friends. He was remarkable for his intelligence, talent, and ability, and his French was impeccable—much better than mine. Julius, Leon Fleisher, and I used to play table tennis, but Julius was the strongest, I think—that was because I stopped playing the game for many years. We had 349 French francs to the dollar, and through Julius, we had somebody who came and gave us 520 francs to the dollar. We lived on that, that's how big the difference in the exchange rate was.

When I was in Paris I played in a masterclass for George Enescu. My wife knew him because he was teaching at Peabody, and she had met him socially in Baltimore. I brought in the Beethoven Sonata in E Major, op. 109, and he sat down and played op. 109 as well as he played the violin. He didn't know I was bringing 109, it wasn't as if he prepared himself. I was going to come back again and become a student of Enescu in Paris and the idiot went and died, which was unforgivable.

We had a terrific place in an old apartment house that had been turned into a commercial building. We were the only residents, all the other rooms were offices that closed by seven at night. The living room, dining room, and kitchen were all gigantic, and it had three very large bedrooms. Gaveau gave me a seven-foot piano, which I could play at four o'clock in the morning and it wouldn't disturb anybody. Everything was in seventh heaven for about a year. Then one day there was a knock on the door, and it was a policeman with a paper that said we had to be out of the apartment in twenty-four hours. The woman who had sublet the apartment to us had been born there before World War I, and she didn't have the right to sublet. She was living in the South of France somewhere on the money that we paid her in dollars for rent. I thought it would be another couple of days before we found another apartment. So, big shot Abbey Simon said, "Oh we'll just move into a hotel," but none of the hotels would take a baby. We had to go to a hotel that was charging us eight dollars a night, which was a huge amount, and the great Abbey Simon said, "It will only be a day or two," and the great Abbey Simon was sillier than he'd ever been in his life, and one week dragged on to two weeks and dragged on to two months. My parents were coming to see their grandson, and I was just going to have to ask them to pay the bills and take us back to New York, when I had this concert in Geneva.

The one person I knew in Geneva was Robert Weisz, who died just a couple of years ago. He had been a pupil of Dinu Lipatti and was a first prizewinner in the Geneva Competition

Fig. 16. Place du Bourg de Four, the Simons' street in Geneva.

many years ago. He said, "Move here, Geneva's empty and it's the cheapest place in Europe." It was a different type of life then. Nothing was as big as it is now, and all these places were still recovering from the war. I went with Robert the next morning to see apartments, and the first place we saw was the most perfect and beautiful place. It was in the *Vieille Ville* (old town), at 27 Place du Bourg de Four. The building had a date carved into it: 1607, and it was well within my means. Right around the corner, there was a building with a plaque that said Franz Liszt and Marie d'Agoult had lived there. I came back to Paris that night and said, "Pack the bags, we're moving to Geneva."

Right after we moved, I took my parents on a tour of Europe in my car. We went out of our way to Hamburg, to the Steinway factory, and lo and behold, there was this man who had been artistic director at Steinway's in New York throughout the war. I think he was Jewish, and came from Hamburg to New York to escape the Nazis. I had known him very well, and he was a very nice man. My parents, who were frugal, said, "Well, it seems to me that you're much better off buying a piano than paying forty or fifty dollars a month to rent one." I went into a room with at least fifteen pianos, 6' 10" Bs, to look at. They were all beautiful. I tried them all quickly and put the keyboard lid down on all the ones I disliked immediately. That brought it down to about five or six. Then I spent several hours going through those pianos and chose the one that interested me. My parents paid 2,300 dollars for that piano, to be shipped to Geneva with a cover and a bench. That was the difference in the currency. Decades later, when I picked out the Hamburg Steinway for the University of Houston, the same guy was still in Hamburg.

I had lived in Geneva for about a year when suddenly, one of the Americans that I had become acquainted with at a little café across from where we lived, said,

"Oh, I have to go get my *permis de séjour* renewed."

"What's that?"

"You don't have a residence permit?"

Once again, I was so naïve that it never occurred to me that I needed one. I went to the office, which was right across the street from where I lived in the old town, a little bit up the hill. I was practically in tears, I was so nervous. I had visions of our being thrown out

Fig. 17. Stockholm, May 1951. Photograph courtesy of Bergne Reklamfoto AB, Hamngatan 22-Stockholm.

of the country. The man said, "*Ah, vous êtes Monsieur Simon, vous habitez ici avec votre femme et votre enfant. Il n'y a pas de problème du tout.* (Ah, you are Mr. Simon, you live here with your wife and child. There's no problem at all.)" It was a different era.

I was supposed to leave on a big tour of the Dutch East Indies, but the Dutch East India Company, which organized the western music and concert life there, had recently withdrawn from the country and the whole tour was canceled. I found myself in Geneva with nothing to do, and I opened up the newspaper and there was an announcement that the Conservatoire was offering a course in conducting. I took the class, which was a disaster. The class met for approximately three hours every Friday, and the teacher spent the opening hour or so on musical dictation. I didn't make a mistake in dictation when I was ten years old, and I was the only one in the class who had it right all the time. I was in competition with the teacher, and I was determined to win all the time. One day, he dictated some ancient Greek thing, and I couldn't for the life of me find a barline. He finished the dictation, and I had it all there except for the barlines. He said, "So you see, Mr. Simon, there is something that you can learn here!" I said, "Yes, and the one thing I've learned is I don't need this class," and I got up and walked out. There were four students in the class, and Charles Dutoit was one them. He was immediately remarkable for being a gifted kid. That's where he met Martha Argerich, who was in Geneva at the time.

In the spring of 1951, my concert activities grew to Glasgow, Stockholm, Copenhagen, Oslo, and Vienna, with a recital in the Mozart-Saal. I came to Vienna, as I came to Germany, with an anti-German chip on my shoulder. I played very well, and backstage came this man with half a dozen young piano students. His name was Bruno Seidlhofer, and he was the most important teacher in Vienna. Obviously, he must have heard about me—

either I was so terrible, or so wonderful. One of the students was Alexander Jenner. When Seidlhofer introduced himself, I said, "Oh, you are the teacher of Friedrich Gulda." He said, "Yes, I'm so sorry he isn't here to hear you." I said, "Well, I'm so flattered that you came to my concert," and we went out and had coffee, and then he said a very peculiar thing: "I'm inviting you to tea tomorrow at Gulda's apartment." The next day I came to Gulda's apartment, and they were all there, and I met Gulda, and Mr. Seidlhofer said, "Oh you can't imagine how glad I am that you two are meeting, you should know each other, because Mr. Simon played wonderfully last night, and he'd heard so much about you." Then Seidlhofer said, "Why don't you play something for Gulda?" I think I played part of the C Minor Partita of Bach. Then I said to Gulda, "Well, I've heard so much

Meyerowitz

Abbey Simon and his wife are entertained by Mrs. David Ben-Gurion (center), wife of the premier of Israel, at a reception in Jerusalem following the debut appearance of the pianist in his tour of the new nation

Fig. 18. *Musical America (May 1952).*

about you, I must hear you play!" He said, "I'll play you my latest record," which was the Prokofiev Seventh Sonata, which was not very good, and I was very annoyed, and it was a very distasteful afternoon. He was very antagonistic, and I felt he was carrying anti-Semitic things in him, but maybe this is my imagination. We just didn't hit it off.

In early 1952, I returned briefly to the United States, performing the Brahms Second Concerto with the Chicago Symphony and Rafael Kubelík, a recital at the First Methodist Church in Evanston, and the Chopin Second Concerto with the Grant Park Symphony Orchestra. I also did a concerto performance in Stockholm and was invited to do a recital tour of Israel by Premier David Ben-Gurion. I think my mother and

DICK DUINKER:

Abbey Simon

STUDEERDE OP SCHIPHOL

In het Parkhotel in Den Haag ontmoetten wij Abbey Simon, de pianist die twee prachtige opnamen voor Philips heeft gemaakt (Grieg's pianoconcert op A 00689 R en Händel- en Paganini-variaties van Brahms op A 00195 L). Simon is een nog jonge Amerikaan van Russische afkomst, die al op zeer jeugdige leeftijd als pianist optrad. Ook tijdens zijn jongste concertreis door Nederland boekte hij grote successen.

De pianist ontpopte zich als een levendig verteller, vol humor en met een brede belangstelling ook buiten het louter muzikale om. De fotografie en de schilderkunst draagt hij een warm hart toe. Zelf is hij een verwoed amateur-fotograaf; de enige liefhebberij, die een reizend concertpianist zich kan veroorloven, zoals hij zegt. Hij studeerde aan het Curtis Institute in de V.S., o.a. onder Arthur Schnabel, voor welke

pianist hij nog altijd een grote bewondering koestert. Momenteel woont Simon in Genève, van waaruit hij concertreizen over de gehele wereld maakt. Tot in Argentinië en Indonesië voeren hem zijn tournees en overal waar hij komt is het publiek unaniem vol lof over zijn spel. In al deze landen ontmoet hij weer andere mensen en andere omstandigheden; ieder volk heeft zijn eigenaardigheden. Dat is de reden, waarom Simon verzot is op reizen. Al deze verschillen obsederen hem en steeds weer weet hij nieuwe anecdotes te vertellen.

Zo speelde hij twee jaar geleden in Argentinië, juist tijdens de revolutie die daar toen plaats vond. Honderden kilometers heeft hij toen per auto moeten afleggen om steeds op tijd zijn concerten te kunnen geven. Typerend voor de volksmentaliteit in Argentinië vond hij wel, dat ondanks de nogal verhitte omstandigheden toch altijd de concertzalen vol waren. Voor een pianist zijn de omstandigheden daar echter niet altijd even ideaal. Tijdens dezelfde tournee is namelijk tot twee keer toe de vleugel bezweken! Ook deze reis naar Holland verliep niet helemaal naar wens. Tweemaal moest zijn vliegtuig boven de Atlantische Oceaan terugkeren naar Amerika wegens motorstoring. **(Slot op pag. 72)**

Pianist Abbey Simon (r.) en onze medewerker Dick Duinker (foto: Smit)

70

Fig. 19. *Early publicity for Philips recordings. Disco Discussies (March 1956).*

Ben-Gurion's wife, Paula, knew each other as children. Paula Ben-Gurion was a very famous, dynamic person. But I will never forgive Israel, because I seem to be the only pianist in the world who hasn't appeared with the Israel Philharmonic. I've become anti-Semitic.

In March of that year, I began my first tour of Germany for something called America House, which the Americans built as a cultural center in every city. I played in Berlin, Nuremberg, Ulm, Frankfurt, and Essen, among other cities. Admission to these concerts was free, and I was being paid by the American government. I hadn't attempted to speak German for many years, but I could make myself understood. They always complimented me: "Where did you learn German so gut?" I replied, "Philadelphia." The first time I played in Berlin was a recital in the Hochschule für Musik, and all the manager could talk about was Glenn Gould, who had just been there. He said, "Can you imagine, he played with a glass of water on the piano." I replied, "Oh, no, I'm much stronger, I play with a urinal!" He was shocked. I'll never forget thinking to myself, "At last, you're a man."

I played seventy-eighty concerts over the next two years, and in 1953, I made my first record, the Brahms *Handel* and *Paganini Variations*, for the Philips label. Philips was the biggest electronics company in Europe and was just starting in the record business. The man who convinced them to do it was the conductor of the Philips company band. He'd never made records either, although he was obviously a man of great taste because he engaged me. He had tried to get the Philips company into the recording business, but they always said no. Then, somebody in the vast hierarchy suddenly changed his mind, and they called him and said, "You want it, it's yours. Start recording."

They gave me a contract which guaranteed two solo records

and one orchestral record a year, which was normal. Today they don't do that. The records were made in Hilversum, in Holland. They had this studio which had a common wall with a restaurant, and there was so much noise that you could never start recording until one o'clock in the morning. I had never made records or even seen how they were made, so we recorded, in one session on the first night, the Brahms *Handel Variations*. The next night, we recorded the Brahms *Paganini*. Then I got a nasty letter from Philips saying they couldn't understand why I needed so much time to record each of these works. They had only allotted me three hours each, which included setting up the microphones and doing the sound tests, and each work lasts half an hour. It would take another half-hour to listen to it and see what you liked and didn't like. So, a single performance would take a full hour. I wrote back a very undiplomatic and nasty letter, saying that if they could find somebody who could do it faster, they should get them. Executives don't know the first thing about music.

After I'd made the first record, I went to Paris for a day or two before going back to Geneva. I discovered that William Kapell, whom I had known since childhood, was staying in the same hotel as I was. I think it was the *Crillon*. We started to talk, and I told him I'd just been through a traumatic experience, recording the Brahms *Handel* one night, and the *Paganini* the next. He said,

"You're a disgrace to your profession!"

"What have I done?"

"How could you possibly imagine that you could record the Brahms *Handel* or the Brahms *Paganini* in just one session?"

"Well, this is my first record engagement, I couldn't really sit down and dictate the terms to Philips. I'm very happy I had the chance to make a record. On top of that, it's turned out to be much more than I thought—I'm also going to be making the Grieg Concerto."

"You should never have accepted it! I've been recording a Bach partita for months!"

It was true: after he died the partita was only released in part—there were a couple of movements missing. Kapell was a real nasty, snot-nosed kid. The first concert he gave—he won the Naumburg right after me—was his Naumburg recital, which I thought was stupendous. I remember him playing the Brahms C-Major Sonata, I think it was the best performance I ever heard of the piece. Of course, I didn't play it at the time. The subsequent concerts I really didn't enjoy very much.

Fig. 20. *Brochure for five Conciertos Daniel concerts. Santiago, year unknown.*

My next record, also recorded in 1953 for Philips, was the Grieg Concerto, which I learned for that record. It was done in the Concertgebouw in Amsterdam, with the Residency Orchestra of The Hague, Willem van Otterloo conducting. He was rumored to be very difficult but we got along well. I asked Philips why they wanted me to record the Grieg when there were already at least a dozen recordings of it, including Lipatti's popular version. They said, "We want you to record it because everybody buys it."

I think it was Harold Holt who arranged my first tour of Spain. My first concert was in San Sebastián, near the French border. I came to practice in the hall, and they just had a little spinet upright piano. They said, "Tonight, you will have the big piano." I walked out that night, and I had the biggest piano ever made, but the big piano was just a huge case over the spinet! But when I was young, I was timid and I wanted to get along with the managers, so I would never leave a concert. I wanted to be loved.

I also played in Gijón, Oviedo, and Madrid. I adore Spain. By the end of the first two days in Madrid, I could make myself understood in Spanish, because I already knew a lot of words. I never have problems with languages except Portuguese, which I found impossible. When I first heard Portuguese, I thought the people were speaking Russian.

When I was in Madrid, I met Ernesto de Quesada for the first time. Mr. Holt persuaded him to take me on. Quesada was the most important manager in the world—he was another czar—because he controlled music in every Spanish or Portuguese language country in the world. You didn't play there without him. In all the major countries, he had sons who ran the business, and when he ran out of sons he had nephews and cousins. In Buenos Aires, there was one of his sons. In Caracas, there was one of his sons. In Lima, there was a relative. In Colombia, there was a

Fig. 21. *Program from two concerto performances in Lima with the National Symphony Orchestra, May 19, 1954: Chopin No. 2 and Tchaikovsky No. 1.*

relative. In Mexico, there were a son and daughter-in-law. His company's name was *Conciertos Daniel.* I never found out what *Daniel* stood for, or whom it represented. I had a great success in Spain, and Quesada and his sons and I hit it off. We became old, fast friends. Now everyone I knew in the company is dead, like everyone else I know.

In March of 1954, I won the medal in honor of Elizabeth Sprague Coolidge, a patron of music in the United States. The Coolidge medal was awarded to me for the outstanding London debut of the year, which was my first concert in Wigmore Hall. It was one of the Harriet Cohen International Music Awards. That same year, Leon Fleisher received the Special Memorial Medal, another Cohen Award. These medals were created by the British composer, Sir Arnold Bax, who was a great friend of Harriet. She was very pretty when she was young, so far as the story went. I met her several times—she was a very neurotic woman and very flighty in her thoughts. She died many years ago. I never heard her play but she was apparently a very good pianist, although not in the class of Myra Hess. No one was in the same class as Myra Hess.

My first South American recital was on May 10, 1954 in Lima, Peru, and I was engaged on the spot for another recital a few

Fig. 22. *With Carmen and Pablo de Madalengoitia, July 27, 1957 (Photographer unknown.)*

days later. In South America, if they loved you, you would play another recital immediately. I had read about the South American concert scene and had some idea what to expect. I knew that Rubinstein gave some legendary number of recitals—eighteen or twenty—in one month. By then, I was an experienced performer with a large repertoire and had another program at the ready. In between the two Lima recitals, I played a recital in Caracas. On the 19th, I performed two concertos on one concert, the Chopin No. 2 and the Tchaikovsky No. 1, with the Orquesta Sinfónica Nacional in Lima, Theo Buchwald conducting. These concerts set the stage for my South American career, which lasted several decades.

For me, going to South America was always paradise, no matter what country it was. The food was great, the people were lovely, and I made very good friends. One of them, whose wife is still alive, was a media personality in Lima by the name of Pablo de Madalengoitia. He was the Johnny Carson of Peru. He was also a producer, and he and his wife would go up to New York to see musicals, and bring what they liked down to Lima.

One year, there was a famous Spanish dancer, Carmen Amaya, and she and her troupe were sort of all living backstage at the theater where I was playing in Lima. I came in to play my concert, went to the bathroom, went to zip up my trousers, and the

Fig. 23. *Teatro Elite, The Dominican Republic, May 27, 1954.*

zip came off in my hand, and here I am in evening clothes with no fly. It was Carmen Amaya, or one of her assistants, who sewed me up right before the performance.

On May 27, I performed a recital in Santo Domingo, the capital of the Dominican Republic. In those days, the capital was named Ciudad Trujillo, after the country's brutal dictator, Rafael Trujillo. After the recital, my manager said, "Well, you have to stay for an extra concert with the orchestra." The concert was announced for eight o'clock but, of course, nobody came to concerts at eight o'clock, or nine o'clock, or ten o'clock. Finally, at eleven o'clock, there were police sirens and all these cars arrived with Mr. Trujillo, his wife, the government, the army, and everything, and we finally started. Afterwards I was told, "There is a gift from the president," and I was given this big, heavy package. I thought, "Gold bars? Jewelry?" It turned out to be two volumes—one in English, one in Spanish—of his book, *The Wonders of Trujillo*. I still have them, they have gold bars on the covers.

Afterwards, I played several more recitals in Bogotá and Caracas in May and June, and a concerto with the local orchestra in Caracas. We were playing the first in a series of modestly-priced concerts in the new outdoor concert hall. We rehearsed the Tchaikovsky Concerto Monday, Tuesday, Wednesday, Thursday, and the concert was Sunday. I said, "Maestro, I don't know what you're doing, and you don't know what I'm doing, let's forget about the whole thing." I went back to the hotel, and then there was a knock at the door and in came the concertmaster. He himself was a very good conductor, and he said, "Look, you have to play. This is our first concert with a soloist, and the first concert at modest prices, and you can't give up on that. There's always difficulty with this conductor, but we know what you're doing, and we know the concerto." So, we're performing the first movement, everything is beautiful, and I'm playing the middle section of the cadenza:

and suddenly I hear the orchestra coming in two pages early: ta da da da da…The conductor accidentally turned two pages of the score, and the orchestra all came in, that was the extraordinary part about it. So, I jumped to follow the orchestra.

From June 30 to July 18, I performed four recitals at the Gran Rex Theater in Buenos Aires along with two recitals in Montevideo, Uruguay, and another concert in Rosario, Argentina. When I arrived for the first time in Buenos Aires I spent the night at my hotel, and then the next morning, a Monday, I looked up the address of *Conciertos Daniel*. I walked into the office, where Quesada's son, Ernesto Jr., ran the business. He looked around and saw me and said, "Simon, you're here!" I made light chat with him for a while and finally, I got annoyed and said, "What's happening, you act as if you don't expect me." He replied, "No, you must play here," as if my concert had never been prepared. And it hadn't been prepared. My heart sank. He said, "What are you doing Wednesday?" I said, "For heaven's sakes, I've arrived here for the first time in my life. I don't know a single soul in Argentina. I'm not doing anything on Wednesday!" He said, "I'll make a telephone call" and picked up the phone and there was a long discussion. He said, "If it's alright with you, you'll play a recital 6:30 Wednesday afternoon at the Gran Rex." So, I finally left to walk back to my hotel, but I wanted to see what this Gran Rex was. It was like Radio City Music Hall— huge, maybe 5000 seats. I went back to Ernesto Jr. and said, "Nobody will come to a hall that big to hear me, I'm unknown here." He said, "Don't worry about it, that's our problem." I had no idea how they were going to publicize the concert in one day. The next morning, I woke up, and the entire city was plastered with the announcements of *El pianista norteamericano Abbey Simon* who would be playing this and this program at 6:30 at the Gran Rex. I looked at the program, and there was a work I had never heard of by Roberto García Morillo. I ran back to the office and said, "What is this piece?" "Oh, it's the law here, foreign artists must play a work by an Argentine composer. I picked out a piece for you and you'll have no difficulty playing it. He's a nice composer and one of the leading critics here in town." So, I went to a music store to buy the piece—"Juegos" (Games), the second piece from *Esquemas*. It was a simple set of variations on a childhood theme—and I practiced it like I was at death's door.

Came the concert, and for me, a totally unknown artist, there were probably 2000 people there. I played the new piece while unintentionally adding several thousand of my own variations, and it was a great success. I was playing a pre-war piano, signed by Busoni. He played it in 1905 or something like that. It had lasted all those years, and no one took particular care of it. The ivory was starting to peel off the keys. I finished with one of my big pieces, the Prokofiev Toccata. At the end, there's this big glissando that goes up—I made the glissando, and I made a little pile of white keys on the floor. One of the audience members even tried to stick them back on. The next morning the newspaper had a caricature of me with the keys on the floor, with the caption *El Destructador del Piano*.

After the recital, my manager said,

"What are you doing next Tuesday?"

"I don't have anything to do on Tuesday!"

"You play again Tuesday afternoon."

For that concert, we sold much better than half the hall. They came expecting me to destroy the new piano and were very disappointed when I didn't. Then my manager said, "Well, we play again on Sunday morning at ten thirty." I said, "This is a Catholic country, everybody goes to church Sunday morning." He said, "They go to concerts Sunday morning," and I sold out the hall. I also did a series of four concerts in Buenos Aires for Stromberg-Carlson, a famous electronics company that broadcast their concerts on the radio every week. The concerts were open to the public and very well attended.

No city ever had a musical and cultural life like Buenos Aires. There were several orchestras, and the Mozarteum had just been created. It was like Berlin in the 1920s, with newspapers in every major language: Argentinisches Tageblatt, Buenos Aires Herald, Clarín, Crítica, Democracia, La Época, France Journal, Freie Presse, El Hogar, El Mundo, Mundo Radial, La Nación, Noticias Gráficas, La Prensa, El Pueblo, Le Quotidien, La Razón, and The Standard.

Near my hotel was a German restaurant called the ABC where I would go for lunch. One day, there was Gulda, and we started to talk and became friends. He was playing at one of the movie houses called the Ópera, across the street from the Gran Rex. When they couldn't use the Teatro Colón, they used the movie houses—some very big, some very small. There was music being performed around the clock—all the managers cooperated so that there were no conflicts. You could even go to a concert at ten o'clock at night. I went to one of Gulda's concerts, which was all Beethoven, and he was wonderful, and what I loved was the earlier sonatas. He understood, like me, the meaning and sound of the sforzando in early Beethoven: accents. I went backstage, and he said "Oh, you're here" and I said, "At last I got to hear you!"

In Buenos Aires, there was a pianist named María Rosa Oubiña de Castro who wanted to take lessons with me. At this point I couldn't speak two words of Spanish, but I spoke French, and Cucucha, as María was known, spoke sufficient amounts of French to act as my interpreter. She later became the head of the biggest conservatory in Argentina. I think she had already been divorced from the pianist Roberto Castro, whose father was the big conductor, Juan José Castro. Cucucha was a student of Vincenzo Scaramuzza, who was the big teacher in the west, and people came from the United States and Europe to study with him. Cucucha was like an older sister to Martha Argerich, who was also studying with Scaramuzza at the time.

In 1954, I met Martha Argerich in Buenos Aires. She was thirteen. There was a Jewish businessman and amateur violinist, Ernesto Rosenthal, who had fled from Vienna to Buenos Aires. His home became a gathering place for international musicians who were playing there. He had an Austrian salon in his house where there was music every night. He was a real patron of the arts and he adored Martha. He invited four of us who were on tour to his home to hear her play. There was the Hungarian violinist Joseph Szigeti, Friedrich Gulda, an Israeli pianist, Pnina Salzman—she was sort of the first artist to come out of Israel—

and me. Martha played wonderfully, and I thought she should go to the Curtis Institute of Music, Pnina thought she should study with her teacher at the Conservatoire in Paris, Szigeti said she should study with his son-in-law, Nikita Magaloff, and Gulda said she should study with him in Vienna. You never knew what Martha was thinking, whether she liked you or didn't like you, whether she respected you or didn't respect you. After sixty years, it's still that way. But Martha thought Gulda was God, and he thought Martha was God.

In between appearances in Argentina I played two recitals in Montevideo, Uruguay. Getting there was fun—you had to take an enormous sea plane, with seats for twenty or thirty people, from the port in Buenos Aires. You took off in the water in BA and came down in the water in Montevideo.

In August of 1954, I performed the Tchaikovsky Concerto with the London Symphony at one of the Proms concerts. The year ended with a Grieg Concerto with the Bournemouth Symphony, Charles Groves conducting, and a recital in Santander, Spain. In February of 1955, I recorded the Rachmaninoff *Rhapsody on a Theme of Paganini* and the Dohnányi *Variations on a Nursery Song*, again with Otterloo and the Residency Orchestra of The Hague, on the Philips label. The Rachmaninoff Paganini was the first Rachmaninoff I ever recorded. Why they picked the Dohnányi, I'll never know, but I had to learn it especially for that recording. In those days, I had the attitude: "You want it, I'll play it!"

When I was learning the Rachmaninoff for the recording, Julius Katchen was not around, and I had to have somebody play second piano. There was a Russian-Romanian pianist, Youra Guller, whom I didn't know very well, and had never heard play. I mentioned that I needed someone to play the second piano for me and Youra said, "I'll be glad to play second piano." I thought

Fig. 24. *Oslo, c. 1955 (Photographer unknown.)*

to myself, "Oh, this lady can't play worth a damn." I didn't want to be rude and turn her down, so I acquiesced and resigned myself to a wasted afternoon. We went down to the Salle Gaveau and got a room with two pianos. She sat down and read the orchestra part like she'd played it all her life. If she was sight-reading, she was the world's great-est sightreader. Even if she had been practicing it for a month, it was extraordinary. It turns out she had played with the New York Philharmonic in the early twenties. I asked her to play some more for me—she was an absolute genius, with a huge sound. Then, when you talked to her, you had to decode her. When she mentioned Igor, she meant Igor Stravinsky. She was on a first name basis with everyone.

One time, Julius Katchen, Shura Cherkassky, and I were all in London together and went to Youra's Wigmore Hall recital. She had become a drug addict, but the concert was a stunning success. The reviews were ecstatic. She was leaving the next day, and the three of us had to pay her hotel bill. Shura was leaving for Germany and Youra said, "Would you take a package for me?" and Shura, afraid it was drugs, with his usual aplomb said,

«MUSIKKENS VENNER» I FREDRIKSTAD OG OMEGN

18. KONSERT

5. abonnementskonsert 1954/55.

i Biblioteket tirsdag 1. mars kl. 8.

Den amerikanske pianist

Abbey Simon

PROGRAM:

Beethoven	Sonate A-dur op. 110 Moderato cantabile molto espressivo Allegro molto Adagio ma non troppo Fuga L'istesso tempo di arioso L'istesso tempo della fuga
Liszt	Sonate B-moll
	Pause
Dello Joio	Sonate nr. 1 With intensity Calmly With drive
Chopin	Nocturne Dess-dur op. 27 nr. 2
	Scherzo B-moll op. 31
	Vals E-moll (posth.)
	Andante Spianato & Grande Polonaise op. 22.

Neste konsert: mandag 7. mars, den polske fiolinist *Bronislaw Gimpel.*

Dette program gjelder som adgangstegn.

№ 655

Fig. 25. *Program, Fredrikstad, Norway, March 1, 1955.*

"I'll pay your hotel bill, my dear, but I wouldn't take a package across the street for you."

I've played all over Norway—Fredrikstad, Stavanger, Trondheim, and several other cities, in Finland, and in several places in Denmark and Sweden. In 1955, I played the Mozart Concerto in C Major, K. 467 with the Groninger Orchestra in the Netherlands, the Cho-

Fig. 26. Publicity photo, c. 1955 (Photographer unknown.)

pin F-Minor with the Trondheim Symphony, and the Chopin F-Minor and Tchaikovsky with the Oslo Philharmonic, then called Filharmonisk Selskaps Orkester. In Oslo, the piano started to roll away. I had to move my chair every few minutes, and the cellists started looking very nervous as I gradually drove into them.

I also undertook my second America House tour of Germany in 1955, playing in Nuremberg, Ulm, Tübingen, Freiburg, Frankfurt, Darmstadt, Berlin, Essen, Kassel, Koblenz, and Mannheim, with glowing reviews. Finally, I went to see the most important manager in Germany, who was a woman by the name of Mrs. Adler. Her son obviously hated Americans and was getting ready to hit me, but I was stuck with them. With all these great reviews from major German cities, I thought they were going to be begging to get me back, but Mrs. Adler said, "Mr. Simon, you're obviously a wonderful artist, but how am I going to get people to pay to hear you when you've played every place for free? They'll say, 'Well, we'll wait until he comes to America House next year, it won't cost us a cent.'" I was more successful than anybody in history at doing the wrong thing.

I came back to Germany a number of times. I played once with the RIAS (Radio in American Sector) Symphony and a few recitals there, but nothing really came of it. I was even thinking of giving a recital again in Berlin at my own expense, then I decided it was too expensive. Also, I hated Germany.

In April, I played the Brahms D-Minor Concerto with City of Birmingham Symphony and Harold Gray, in May, a recital in Venezuela, and then my first concert in Brazil. On my way from Europe to Brazil, the plane stopped in Dakar, which was the capital of the former French West Africa and a stopping point on the way to Recife, Brazil. I had a concert in a city called Bahia, which was a little north of Recife. We had one of the most famous English ballet companies on the plane. We were about halfway over the Atlantic—this was before jets—and an engine had a real blowout, with fire. We turned around and returned to Dakar and they put us in a brand-new hotel, which wasn't officially opened, practically in the airport. Everybody was so proud of themselves for not panicking, and we all went up to our rooms. I decided to lie down and take a nap, and I suddenly started to shake like you cannot imagine. About an hour later I went downstairs, and the others had all had the same experience. The whole building must have been shaking!

I still had to get to Bahia, so I sent a telegram to my manager and there was no answer for a day or two. Finally, I got a long telegram saying to take a flight to Recife, and change to go to Rio de Janeiro, which was hundreds of miles south, and at the Pan American desk, find a ticket to Bahia. I finally crossed over the Atlantic and changed at Recife for Rio de Janeiro, and

I went down there and got the ticket to Bahia. When I finally arrived in Bahia, I called the Donia *quelque chose*—Alexandrina, or something. She said, "You're here! That's wonderful, then we can have the concert," and I played the next night. That was the spontaneous South American concert life.

Once in Rio, I was playing some big Bach piece and these two women sitting in the front row were making so much noise I finally had to stop. I said, in French, because I didn't speak Portuguese, "*Ecoutez, Madame, c'est vous ou moi.* (Listen, Madam, it's you or me)." The men in the hall got very angry and macho, so I closed the keyboard lid, abandoned my concert, and got a taxi back to the hotel. After that night, a whole generation had to die before I could come back. I played in other parts of Brazil, but not in Rio. My manager used to say, "We put you in planes that don't even fly over Rio!" Some time later, Backhaus—I believe his wife was Brazilian, or Portuguese—was there, and he also had to stop because of the noise in the audience. So, I had a certain right on my side.

In May of 1955, I was in Buenos Aires and was scheduled to play a recital in Trinidad, and then the Tchaikovsky with Doráti in Mexico City. I found another telegram saying, "You will go from Buenos Aires and there, you will pick up a ticket to Caracas, and then you will stop in Trinidad, and then you will go to Mexico City." I went to pick up the ticket and the woman from Pan Am said,

"You can't get on that plane."

"Why?"

"Because you don't have a visa for Trinidad."

"But I have a concert tonight."

"I'm terribly sorry, it's against the law, and I can't let you go to that city without a visa."

Finally, I said, "Look at it this way: this plane is continuing after it stops. If they won't let me off to play my concert, I'll just stay on the plane and go on." So, I cajoled her into giving me this ticket and I arrived in Trinidad, and the manager was there to meet me. He said "You don't need a visa, because you're playing at nine o'clock tonight and you're leaving at one o'clock in the morning. You're only spending a few hours in the city."

I used to bring revolutions wherever I went—Argentina, Colombia, Venezuela. My friends would say that they knew where the revolutions were by looking at my concert schedule. I was in Argentina when Perón put down the revolution. Then, I was there when Perón was not successful in putting it down. I was also one of the last Americans to play in Cuba while the US was still friendly with Castro. Another time, I was flying from Santiago to Buenos Aires, and the flight had a connection in Córdoba, Colombia. I missed the connection and went to the

Fig. 27. *Aula Magna, Rome, March 18, 1957 (Photograph by Foto Diotallevi.)*

authorities telling them I needed to get to Buenos Aires. I had this card from one of the big generals in Argentina, who had told me, "If you ever have any difficulties, wherever you are, ask for the military comandante, show them this card, and they will take care of you." So in Córdoba, I said, "I am Abbey Simon, the American pianist, and I have a concert in Buenos Aires, and this

"CONCIERTOS DANIEL"
AÑO XXVI EN LIMA

SOCIEDAD FILARMONICA
SEGUNDO CONCIERTO DE ABONO DE LA SOCIEDAD FILARMONICA

TEATRO MUNICIPAL
Viernes 7 de Junio de 1957
7 p. m.
R E C I T A L
DEL PIANISTA

ABBEY SIMON

P R O G R A M A

SONATA Nº 10 EN SOL MAYOR OPUS 14 Nº 2...........L. VAN BEETHOVEN
    Allegro
    Andante
    Scherzo-Allegro assai

ARABESCA OP. 18......................................R. SCHUMANN

SONATA Nº 3 EN FA MENOR OPUS 5.......................J. BRAHMS
    Allegro maestroso
    Andante espresivo
    Allegro enérgico
    Andante molto
    Allegro moderato ma rubato

INTERMEDIO

DOCE ESTUDIOS, OPUS 10..................................F. CHOPIN
    Nº 1 en Do mayor
    Nº 2 en La menor
    Nº 3 en Mi mayor
    Nº 4 en Do sostenido menor "El Torrente"
    Nº 5 en Sol bemol mayor "Teclas Negras"
    Nº 6 en Mi bemol mayor
    Nº 7 en Do mayor
    Nº 8 en Fa mayor
    Nº 9 en Fa menor
    Nº 10 en La bemol mayor
    Nº 11 en Mi bemol mayor
    Nº 12 en Do menor "Revolucionario"

DISCOS "EPIC"

PRECIOS PARA LOS NO ABONADOS: PALCOS BAJOS: S/. 300.00; PALCOS
ALTOS: S/. 250.00; PLATEA: S/. 50.00; GALERIA NUMERADA, 1ª Y 2ª FI-
LAS: S/. 40.00; GALERIAS SIN NUMERAR: S/. 30.00; CAZUELA NUMERADA,
1ª Y 2ª FILAS: S/. 20.00; CAZUELA SIN NUMERAR: S/. 12.00

MAS LOS IMPUESTOS

Fig. 28. *Recital program, Teatro Municipal, Lima, June 7, 1957.*

card of introduction..." The guy said, "Mr. Simon, go back to your hotel and be very quiet, but above all, tear up that card, because at this moment, revolutionaries are firing bullets at the Casa Rosada (the presidential palace of Argentina)." I finally made it to Buenos Aires at four a.m., but there was a curfew in place until nine p.m. So, I had to wait fifteen hours for a taxi. Despite all these revolutions, my concerts always took place as scheduled. They knew what was important.

In late May and early June of 1955, I played in Lima six times: three concerts with the National Symphony Orchestra and three recitals at the Teatro Municipal. The first two symphony concerts featured two concertos each—the first, the Mozart in C Major, K. 457 and the Schumann; the second, Brahms No. 1 and the Rachmaninoff *Rhapsody.* The rest of June and early July saw two recitals in Montevideo, three recitals in Buenos Aires, a Grieg Concerto with the Argentine National Symphony Orchestra, and two recitals in smaller cities in Argentina.

1955 ended with performances of the Ravel G-Major Concerto with Otterloo and the Residency Orchestra of The Hague in Wetenschappen and Leiden. In 1956, I performed with the City of Birmingham Symphony in Sheffield, Cheltenham, and twice in Birmingham. The concertos were the Brahms Second, Rachmaninoff Third, and Beethoven Third. I played recitals in Chester, Sheffield, and The Hague, twice in the Royal Albert Hall with the London Philharmonic (Beethoven Fifth), and then the London Symphony (Grieg). In 1955, I also returned to the studio to record seventeen solo pieces of Brahms for Philips. These were released in various combinations, on both 45 rpm records and LPs.

In the second half of the 1950s, my concert schedule expanded to Scandinavia, with appearances in the major cities. In 1957, I gave concerto performances throughout Europe and

South America, playing with the orchestras of centers such as The Hague, Santiago, Caracas, Lisbon, Bogotá, Bournemouth, and Birmingham. I gave two recitals in London's Wigmore Hall, as well as in cities in Holland, Norway, Italy, Uruguay, Argentina, Chile, Puerto Rico, and Venezuela. I also made my second brief return to the United States, playing two performances with the Baltimore Symphony and three concerts in California.

Eduard van Beinum, the music director of the Concertgebouw Orchestra, was a wonderful musician and a very nice man. In December of 1957, he engaged me to play the Tchaikovsky Concerto, but it was with a guest conductor, George Szell. That was Szell's first time conducting the Concertgebouw, and my first time playing with them. I was a nervous wreck. I didn't want Szell to recognize me from my audition for him in Chicago, so I spent the summer growing this enormous beard. At the rehearsal, we played through the first movement and he said, "Are you comfortable?" "Wonderfully so." Then came the pizzicati at the beginning of the second movement, which the orchestra played very well together. But by the fourth or fifth time in rehearsal, the *pizzicati* sounded *arpeggiando*. Szell stopped and said, "So this is the great Concertgebouw Orchestra!" The scherzando section went like we had played it together 1000 times. The concert went very well.

At the Concertgebouw, you had to walk down approximately three flights of a circular staircase to get on stage, in full view of the audience. Each step is of a different size, and I have always been petrified of those steps. There are also no wings to the stage. When you finished, you just walked over to the side of the stage with the audience staring at you, and then walked back. Then, when the applause was done, you had to march up these steps in silence. That's the way it was built, but it's a marvelous hall.

In 1958, I recorded the Chopin concertos with the Royal Philharmonic of London on the HMV Label, and I think that record is still selling. The conductor was supposed to be André Cluytens, the conductor of the Orchestre de la Société des Concerts du Conservatoire, and the best known French symphonic conductor, but he came down with the flu. Then came Malcolm Sargent, and he came down with the flu. It was a terrible epidemic! Finally, the only one who was up on his feet was Eugene Goossens, who made the recording. I was terribly disappointed because I had been looking forward to playing with Cluytens all year, and I felt playing with him once would result in many more concerts with him.

They announced a concert with Alfred Cortot playing Chopin First and the César Franck *Variations symphoniques* with one of the orchestras at the Albert Hall. I went to the concert saying to myself, "He's a very old man, but you'll hear something that's Cortot." He played the opening phrase of the Chopin with the arpeggio going up, and every note was wrong, and every note was wrong, and every note was wrong, and he was lost after that. So, they started out again. Adrian Boult, who was conducting, put the music on the piano, and Cortot threw it into the audience. I never knew whether he played the Franck or not, I just crept out of the hall after the Chopin. After that, it took me a couple of years to find the courage to play the Chopin E-Minor, which I had already played and recorded.

My schedule continued with the orchestras of Norwich, Liverpool, Oslo, Helsinki, London (Philharmonic), and Copenhagen. After the Copenhagen concert, there was the usual reception with about twenty people present. My host and hostess brought out the drinks and began a very serious, frostbitten ritual. They filled everybody's shot glass with aquavit. Our host raised his glass and offered a toast to my good health, drank up

Fig. 29. *The Simons in London in the 1950s (Photographer unknown.)*

his glass, and said "Skoal." Of course, I thanked him, drank up my glass and said "Skoal." Next, my hostess raised her glass, drank it up, and said "Skoal." I thanked her, drank up my glass and said "Skoal." Then the conductor raised his glass, drank it up, and said "Skoal." I raised my third glass, drank it up, and said "Skoal." Another guest raised his glass, drank it up, and said "Skoal," to which I responded in like. And so on, and so on. Of course, the object of the whole exercise was to see how long it would take for me to catch on that while each person who offered a toast took only one glass, I was forced to drink a glass each time. It was all a big practical joke. I won't tell you whether I ended up drunk.

In 1958, I did a tour of Indonesia and afterwards, played recitals in the major cities of Denmark, Italy, Finland, France, Sweden, and England. That October, I was invited by the British Broadcasting Corporation to make a recording. They asked

ROYAL
LIVERPOOL
PHILHARMONIC
ORCHESTRA

(Leader, Peter Mountain)

PATRON - HER MAJESTY THE QUEEN

Soloist

ABBEY SIMON

PROGRAMME

National Anthem

Symphonie Classique in D, Op. 25	*Prokofiev*
Hungarian Fantasia	*Liszt*
Nocturne in E flat	*Chopin*
Waltz in E minor	
Etude in G flat (Black Key)	
Etude in E	
Etude in G minor (Revolutionary)	
Symphony No. 3, in E flat, 'Eroica'	*Beethoven*

Guest Conductor

EDOUARD VAN REMOORTEL

The Royal Liverpool Philharmonic Society is in association with the Arts Council of Great Britain

Fig. 30. *An unusual program, Philharmonic Hall, Liverpool, January 6, 1959.*

a group of pianists to record the Liszt transcriptions of all the symphonies of Beethoven, and I was to do the Sixth. When I said yes, I didn't even know about the Liszt transcription—I thought it would be some sort of paraphrase. They sent me the music and I opened it up and had a stroke. It turned out to be the most faithful reduction of the orchestral score imaginable. The slow movement was the toughest of the lot. The recording was done on an acetate, before tape came in, and there was no editing. I went into a panic. But I suddenly sat back and said, "Well this is what causes me the trouble and if I miss it, does it mean the whole performance is a disaster? The BBC will forgive me for one note here." I played many times on the BBC, and it is a remarkable place.

In the late 1950s, I did three more recordings for the EMI label. *Carnival of the Animals* was recorded at Abbey Road Studios with the Philharmonia Orchestra. The conductor was Efrem Kurtz, who did a tremendous amount of ballet conducting, but he was certainly a very knowledgeable musician, a nice guy, and an old friend. We had played together many times in Europe, Latin America, and the United States. Hephzibah Menuhin

Fig. 31. *Dina, Jonathan, Dora Zaslavsky, Simon, and John Koch. Bois de Boulogne, Paris, August 1959 (Photographer unknown.)*

played the other piano part. She was a charming woman and an excellent artist. We recorded it rather quickly, and it's quite a beautiful record. The only thing I dislike about it was that they should've had someone reading the poems. Later, they did issue another version, with Jonathan Winters narrating.

We were taking a break from *Carnival of the Animals* and I ran into a conductor I knew, Robert Irving. He, too, was mostly known as a ballet conductor, but a very good conductor, and he said,

"Abbey, how are you? Do you play *Un Sospiro?*"

"Yes."

"You want to record it with me? I have a fantastic arrangement of it."

"Is it the piano part changed?"

"No."

"Ok."

"We'll see you tomorrow."

That became my EMI recording of *Un Sospiro*. It was recorded with the Sinfonia of London and released on a 45-rpm record.

I also recorded Brahms's Piano Sonata No. 3 for EMI but it was never released. In 1955, EMI bought Capitol Records in the US which was to be, so far as I can remember, their big distributor. Capitol at that point was the most successful jazz and pop record label in the world and was under the impression that they were the tail that was wagging the EMI dog, even though in the Classical world, they were nothing. They thought they had to limit who was going to record Classical music. They already had Rudy Firkušný, so they didn't want to release my records, so far as I can understand. It took a long time for EMI to finally put them in their place.

In 1959, my record with the Liszt *Six Paganini Études*, the Franck *Prélude, Chorale and Fugue*, and the Schumann *"Abegg" Variations* was released on HMV. I played four different recital programs in three weeks in Derby, England, short tours with the Royal Liverpool Philharmonic, the Hallé Orchestra, and the Bournemouth Symphony, concertos with the London Symphony and London Philharmonic, and recitals at the main venues in Spain, England, Peru, Argentina, and Germany.

In June I performed the Brahms D-Minor Concerto with the National Symphony of Argentina, conducted by Juan-José Castro, who was one of the great conductors and composers. He had been Cucucha's father-in-law. The concert was at the Teatro Colón in Buenos Aires, which is a famous hall that looks like La Scala. It's where the opera is, but I've played many recitals there. I loved the hall, but I never really liked the Brahms D-Minor. I played it for years, but it's just too cumbersome. When I played it in Buenos Aires I used to kill myself playing—in the most kosher, orthodox way—those octave trills. When I heard the recording of the rehearsal, I suddenly realized, "Stupid! You can't play those trills like that. It may do your ego good, but your hands are just too small. You'll have to do it the unkosher way, otherwise it sounds ineffective." From then on, I did it two-handed. I found out years later that the recording was released and it had won a prize for one of the outstanding live performances, but I never found it.

In early July, I was in Lima playing recitals and noticed that José Iturbi, whom I knew, was conducting a series of concerts with the National Symphony Orchestra of Peru. Iturbi was from Spain and was the conductor of the Rochester Philharmonic, although he was better known as a pianist and movie star, appearing in films with people like Judy Garland, Gene Kelly, and Frank Sinatra. He was such a nice man and a wonderful conductor. I went back to see him after one of the concerts, and after warm greetings, he whispered to me, "Be a nice fellow. I'm not happy with this orchestra. Come and play something beautiful with me tomorrow night." So, the next night I played the Beethoven Fourth with him.

It was in around 1960 that my wife and I had a terrible accident in The Hague. We were hit by a car, and I canceled many concerts. After that was all over, we were contacted by a lawyer whose name was van Otterloo. I said, "Are you related to the conductor?" He said, "He's my father!" I kept screaming at my wife, "If only we'd been hit in New York, we would have gotten billions of dollars and I would have become a conductor!"

The 1950s had been a decade of great success and growth for my career in Europe and South America. Now it was time to tackle the rest of the world.

Chapter Five

INDIANA AND BEYOND: 1960-1977

In 1960, Carnegie Hall was slated to be demolished, and one of my friends called and said there was a cancelation on the last day of concerts. I would be the last person ever to play in Carnegie Hall. Of course, Carnegie Hall was ultimately saved so it didn't work out that way. That was my successful return to the United States, and I was signed by Sol Hurok, the No. 1 concert manager in the world. Mr. Hurok adored artists and really worked very hard for them.

Soon after, I was back in Europe for concerts with the orches-

Fig. 32. *Abbey Simon, Jorge Bolet, David Saperton, Sidney Foster. Saperton's inscription reads: "...taken on stage at Carnegie Hall after Abbey's enormously successful recital at Carnegie Hall March 30 of this year. N.Y., May 27, 1960."*
(Photograph by Whitestone Photo.)

Fig. 33. Hurok concert flyer from the 1960s.

tras of Birmingham, Oslo, the BBC, the Royal Opera House, and The Hague. I was in London to play in the Proms, and my stepmother called me from New York to tell me my father had just died. I flew back for all the things that needed to be done, and the BBC was furious because I was supposed to play that night. My father lived only until his sixties, so I never thought I would live this long. After he died, my stepmother moved into a large apartment on West Seventy-Third Street in Manhattan. She was retiring from teaching, and I think most of the people she knew were in Manhattan. Also, her neighborhood was changing so she decided to move. The new apartment was big enough for both of us so whenever I was in New York, I stayed there as I resumed yearly Carnegie Hall recitals.

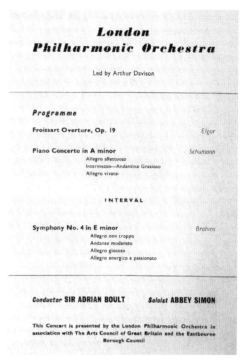

London Philharmonic Orchestra

Led by Arthur Davison

Programme

Froissart Overture, Op. 19 — *Elgar*

Piano Concerto in A minor — *Schumann*
 Allegro affettuoso
 Intermezzo—Andantino Grazioso
 Allegro vivace-

INTERVAL

Symphony No. 4 in E minor — *Brahms*
 Allegro non troppo
 Andante moderato
 Allegro giocoso
 Allegro energico e passionato

Conductor **SIR ADRIAN BOULT**   *Soloist* **ABBEY SIMON**

This Concert is presented by the London Philharmonic Orchestra in association with The Arts Council of Great Britain and the Eastbourne Borough Council

Fig. 34. Program, February 18, 1961. © London Philharmonic Orchestra.

I knew the composer Alberto Ginastera very well, I had met him in Buenos Aires. He offered me the first performance of a very complicated and difficult piano concerto. I started to think that I was no longer eighteen years old and said, "It's an honor, and I'd love to do it, but it would mean taking a year off and doing nothing else." Then, he offered it to Bolet who said the same thing. Then he offered it to a Brazilian pianist, João Carlos Martins, who learned it and played it in six weeks with the National Symphony in Washington. But Martins was young.

In 1961, I did my first tour of Australia and New Zealand, with stops in London, Calcutta, and Hong Kong on the way. The Australian tours were run by the Australian Broadcasting

Fig. 35. Rehearsing with the National Orchestra of the NZBC, Wellington, New Zealand, July, 1961 (Photograph by Tom Shanahan.)

Corporation, headed by a man named Morse. It was so well organized. You had to give your programs practically a year in advance—six different recital programs and eight concertos. You stayed and performed in the big city of each state, but you were also out into the provinces of that state every day. A car came, sometimes at seven in the morning, and you drove all day, as much as 200 miles. Everything you played had to be broadcast live over the whole country, in part because everybody in Australia paid an annual fee for their radios and TVs. The trouble is that the ABC no longer runs things. They were in a position to guarantee you performances, whereas now, it's up to you or your manager to get you a date. I have never been able to figure out what the orchestras accomplished by getting their independence of the radio.

In Australia, I heard David Helfgott, the subject of the movie

Shine. The Helfgott family was crazy. They made Orthodox Jews look like amateurs. They weren't interested in their son studying piano, they were only interested in Orthodox Judaism. I told him he should go to Curtis, but I was not on good terms with its head, Rudolf Serkin. However, Isaac Stern was close to Serkin, and he happened to be in the hotel. So, I told Helfgott to talk to Stern. Three days later, there was a headline, I don't remember if it was in Melbourne or in Sydney: *Stern Discovers Musical Genius.*

Concerts in New Zealand were run by the New Zealand Broadcasting Corporation. Right at the bottom of New Zealand, just a centimeter away from the South Pole, is Invercargill, one of my favorite places. Other people play in Paris and London. I was the star of Invercargill. It was so cold that I made them buy half a dozen heaters to surround me at the piano.

After a summer break, I was back on tour in August and September in South America. Later that year, I played several concertos with American orchestras, including the Rachmaninoff Third with the New York Philharmonic in Carnegie Hall. I came to rehearse with the orchestra, and there was Eugene Ormandy sitting in the cello section. I thought to myself, "You've had it, you've had a nervous breakdown." It turned out that Eugene Ormandy had an older brother, who looked a great deal like him and was a cellist in the New York Philharmonic. I used to run into him on the street in New York. I never even knew his name.

In those days, I never went anywhere without Dina and Jonathan. They went with me to Australia, New Zealand, Singapore, Hong Kong, and every country in Latin America. Jonathan developed friends all over South America. When he was eleven or twelve, he was already playing jazz piano. In Lima, Pablo de Madalengoitia said to Jonathan, "Come on the show with me today," and he had him on his program. Finally, Jonathan's schooling took precedence and Dina had to give up touring with me.

The manager of the Westchester County Symphony Orchestra was somebody I met on a plane leaving from Peru. Somehow or other, he and his wife saw me carrying some music. It turned out they were Americans, they sounded very nice, and we were all flying to Buenos Aires. Their daughter was with them. At that point, I had already been to Buenos Aires many times and was very well known. When we arrived at the airport, a military group marched out in front of the plane, and I was standing there thinking, "They're for me." The airplane steward threw me aside. The reception was for the daughter of this couple, because she was a college friend of the daughter one of the highest people in the government of Argentina. The Argentine daughter was getting married, and the American daughter was sort of maid-of-honor.

While we were on the plane, this orchestra manager said, "I've engaged Glenn Gould next season." I said, "I've never heard him." He said, "You will have a chance, I'll send a car to take you up to White Plains." White Plains is about twenty miles as the crow flies from New York City. When the day came, I went up there and discovered that the conductor of the Westchester County Symphony Orchestra was a terrific violist and principal in a number of orchestras, including Cleveland. He went to Curtis with me, and he was a master. So, I sat down, and out came Glenn Gould carrying a huge score. He was playing an unknown piece called the *Emperor*. He put the score on the piano, much higher than the music rack, and he sat with his legs crossed and started to conduct, and he wasn't the conductor. Gould's behavior on stage was disgraceful, and I had to go to the reception to wait for my ride back to New York City afterwards. As I was leaving them, they said, "What do you think of that *meshugganah*?" and I said, "There's only one *meshugganah* here, that's you—you signed the check!"

In 1962, against my wife's feelings, I said, "Things are going so great in the United States, I should be more on the spot and know more people in the music world there." I was playing with the Indianapolis Symphony and I went down to visit Sidney Foster in Bloomington. I met their dean at the time, a remarkable man named Wilfred Bain. The minute he met somebody he liked, he asked them to become a faculty member. That's how I joined the faculty of Indiana University. I was hired at the same time as Vlado Perlemuter, who stayed for one semester, and György Sebők, who stayed for thirty-seven years. Bloomington was already quite a flourishing place. Sidney Foster, Janos Starker, William Primrose, Josef Gingold were all already at IU when I arrived, and Bolet was to arrive in 1968. The vocal department was second to none. It was like La Scala—everybody who was getting on in years ended up in Bloomington—I mean that in a most respectful way. One of my favorite people, who also arrived there in 1962, was the great opera singer Margaret Harshaw.

Wilfred Bain was a wonderful person, an old friend, and I had the utmost respect for him. With Dean Bain, there was never any apathy, and you got an answer in the blink of an eye. I'm not saying that the dean of a music school should be autocratic, but sometimes you say, "I heard this boy in Hong Kong, and we can't make him a tape for an audition." Bain would have said, "If you think he's up to our standard, then you can bring him along." Every teacher had cases like that. Charlie Webb was Bain's assistant. If you couldn't see the dean, all you had to do was tell Charlie something, and he'd speak to the dean, and it was done.

Dina visited Bloomington several times, but finally said, "We've traveled too much, I'm not moving again. We've moved three times in New York City, we moved to London, Paris, and Geneva, we've been in Geneva a very long time. No." So, I was taking the taxi route between Geneva and the United States at least once a month. It was very stressful.

Sidney, Bolet, and I were the doctoral committee at Indiana, and we had no problems in selecting admissions and never had any complaints. The minute they insisted we add two more people to the committee, everybody was admitted on probation. The old axiom—bigger the committee, the less it accomplishes—was certainly true there. Part of the reason for the conditional admissions was that we'd have auditioning students who graduated from Juilliard and played very beautifully, but they'd never given any degree recitals. Our only alternative was to say, "Well, we're delighted to accept you as a student, but you have to make up those three recitals in addition to your doctoral program." I told Juilliard, "You're penalizing your students because they'll never be accepted to a doctorate at a state school under those conditions." I'd like to think I was one of the reasons Juilliard changed their performance requirements.

Once, Janos Starker walked into my studio, and we were talking, and he said, "You do not give private lessons." I said, "What do you mean? That's what I'm paid to do here, Janos." "No, you have at least all your students of the morning together. If

Fig. 36. Concert poster, Royal Festival Hall, London, October 12, 1962.

you're teaching from nine to twelve, that means you have at least three students to each lesson, and if you teach for three hours in the afternoon, you have three students to each lesson. First, it puts the students in a pressure situation; second, there is no reason why those who are not playing at the moment shouldn't profit from the pieces that they're hearing." He is 100 percent right, and I think it's much better for the students. The trouble is that they have classes, and you can't get students at the time you want. Maybe it's possible to arrange this in a pure conservatory, but in a university, it's not that easy.

Starker sometimes came in with weird ideas. He always had more students than he could possibly handle, but one year, his enrollment fell off. It can happen to anyone, God knows the reason why. He suddenly came to my door:

"You are a gifted musician. I want you to teach my students, and I will teach your students."

"Janos, I don't know how to play the cello."

"You are so gifted you will come up with the right suggestions."

He wanted to pump up his load with piano students. Another time, he called the faculty together and turned into Al Capone: "Now, listen to this: There are two kinds of teachers at this school. We bring 'em in here, and we get paid much more than you people who teach 'em!"

Once, Arthur Loesser came to Bloomington and Sidney Foster and I were with him in a studio. He said he was making a record and sat down and played Czerny etudes. They were drop dead gorgeous. It proved that a superb musician can make something wonderful out of a banality. After we had deposited him at his hotel, I was driving back with Sidney who said, "I know what's going on in your little mind, don't even think about it! You're going to start practicing to play a concert with Czerny etudes!"

In December, I played my first recital as a faculty member at

Indiana University. Before the new opera house was built, we played faculty concerts at the IU Auditorium, and most of the time, they put a curtain across the rear half of the hall because it was 4500 seats. Starker and Sebők never played any place but in the Recital Hall, but I always played in the IU Auditorium.

That same year, I got a letter in the mail saying I had been nominated for a grant from the Ford Foundation, which was a surprise because I hadn't applied for anything. The prize was a work commissioned by me from a composer of my choice, and I would be performing it at special concerts in New York and other places. I chose Anis Fuleihan as the composer. He was my dear friend, a really terrific pianist himself, and had been on faculty at Indiana during the 1940s and 50s. I think he already had four or five piano concertos. He was from Cyprus, but he was considered an American composer—that's why the Ford Foundation commissioned him. He lived right close, so I went over there and told him that he was going to get five thousand dollars for a piano sonata. He immediately said, "I've got my twelfth, thirteenth, and fourteenth sonatas right here, let's go get the money!" I said, "Anis, you can't do that, you have to wait a couple of months, I'm supposed to be commissioning it!"

As I was practicing Fuleihan's piece one night at Indiana, Menahem Pressler came into my room. I moaned, "I'll never be able to do it, even with the music." He said, "Don't you understand, this is not western music. You have to think of what you've heard of Middle Eastern music and if you approach it from that standpoint, you'll find it much easier." I hate to admit it, but he was right.

Fuleihan used to come to visit us all the time in Geneva when he was passing through. He was a conductor too and taught piano and composition at Indiana for a while.

In 1963, I continued to give concerts around the world and

was engaged to record a number of Chopin works for RCA, including the B-flat-Minor Sonata, for a set of Reader's Digest records. That was when I met Max Wilcox, who was the producer. He said,

"We'd like you to record the waltzes in Rome."

"Why?"

"They're sending a piano for Rubinstein, who will be performing and recording in Rome, and you'll probably like the piano."

"I know I'll like it, because we always like the same pianos!" So, the records were recorded there.

One day, Max called me and said, "Oh, by the way, you're invited to lunch by Artur Rubinstein." This is the way the lunch went: We all had dry martinis. Then we had an *hors d'oeuvre* dish, *foie gras* or something like that. We had wine galore, and then coffee and dessert, and then we were drinking cognac, and then out came the cigar, and I'm sitting there totally drunk. Rubinstein was being the grand seigneur all around. He was a man of enormous culture—and a no-nonsense man. He was also one of the most competitive people I ever met. He said to me, "I'm getting to be old, and you have to sit down and play my repertoire. Why am I taking you to lunch?" But he was very nice, very hospitable. When he moved to Geneva we ran into each other many times and became good friends. One time, a group of piano faculty and students drove up from Bloomington to Indianapolis to hear him. He was a remarkably erratic performer. Sometimes it would be wonderful, sometimes it would not be so.

I first met Marc Aubort when he was the engineer for the RCA recordings. I've known his wife, who died a couple of years ago, and their daughter, who's married to the violinist and conductor Peter Oundjian. When I was in Rome, I also saw that Barbirolli was conducting at a summer concert series at the Baths of

Fig. 37. *Dina, unidentified, Jonathan, Simon, Buenos Aires Television, 1964 (Photographer unknown.)*

Caracalla. I went backstage after his concert to say hello, and he greeted me effusively. He said, "It's a shame I didn't know you were here, you could have played with me." That was very nice. I had played with him in Manchester, and I think in London also. Barbirolli was a lovely man and a marvelous musician.

In 1963, Dina and Jonathan were accompanying me on a tour with the Scottish National Orchestra. I had played Beethoven 4 with Alec Gibson in Edinburgh and Glasgow, and was playing it a third time in the London Festival Hall on Sunday afternoon. Jonathan came backstage and I asked him what he thought of the performance. He said, "Well, two out of three is pretty good." A good friend of mine, the Spanish pianist Joaquín Achúcarro, was also backstage. He had just become a father that weekend, and he turned into a Spanish grandee from 1492: "How dare you speak to your father that way?" Jonathan was very upset—he had never thought he would be hurting me. He stopped coming to my concerts after that until finally I was playing in Geneva

Fig. 38. Concert program, February 27, 1964. Courtesy of The Philharmonia Orchestra.

with the Orchestre de la Suisse Romande. He had no excuse not to go to that concert. Fortunately, I lived up to his expectations.

For my first two years at Indiana, my rank was resident pianist. One day in 1964, I got a phone call in my studio, which was in the main building, right near the hall entrance: "Saw the article, congratulations, great!" I hadn't a clue what they

Fig. 39. Orquesta Sinfónica de Colombia, Teatro Colón, Bogotá, June 18, 1964. With Olav Roots conducting Beethoven's Piano Concerto No. 4 and Rachmaninoff's Piano Concerto No. 3 (Photographer unknown.)

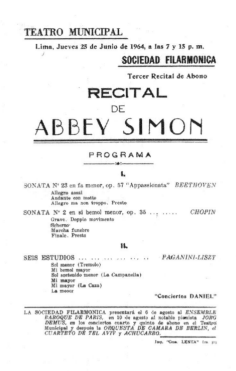

Fig. 40. Lima concert program, Sociedad Filharmonica de Lima, June 25, 1964.

were talking about. Then I got several more phone calls from different people congratulating me. Finally, I got the *New York Times,* and there wasn't a word about me in it. I was sitting at the bar, having my drink before sitting at the table for dinner, when there was somebody sitting next to me with the Bloomington newspaper, and there was my picture. I had been named to a full professorship. I hadn't even inquired about it, I didn't know anything about professors. At that moment, I was even debating whether I was going to stay the whole semester. Committee work at IU was very time consuming. One year they asked me to attend a committee meeting at seven in the morning. I said, "I don't normally stay up that late!" I was living in the faculty dorms, and mine was all painted battleship gray, and I was thinking, "If I stay here one more hour, I'll commit suicide."

In 1964, I played recitals and concertos in Spain, throughout the US, and South America, including five recitals in Buenos Aires. I played the Second Rachmaninoff with Giulini in London at the Festival Hall. That was deadly. He just went through the motions and was just not interested. He's not a man with whom you made great contact.

After another tour of South America, I performed a recital for the first time in the Peoples' Symphony Concerts. They were held at Washington Irving High School in New York City, which has a beautiful concert hall. They had low-priced tickets, and there were never fewer than 1500 people in the audience. Everybody loved the artists playing there and the artists loved playing there, because there was no press. I played there four or five times. People always said that the artists sounded at their best, their most uninhibited in those concerts, and it was all very *gemütlich*.

When John Ogdon came to the United States in 1964, my manager under Hurok, Harold Shaw, said, "Come along with me," to Ogdon's first recital in New York. This lumbering thing with this huge beard came out— he looked like he was fifty years old even though he

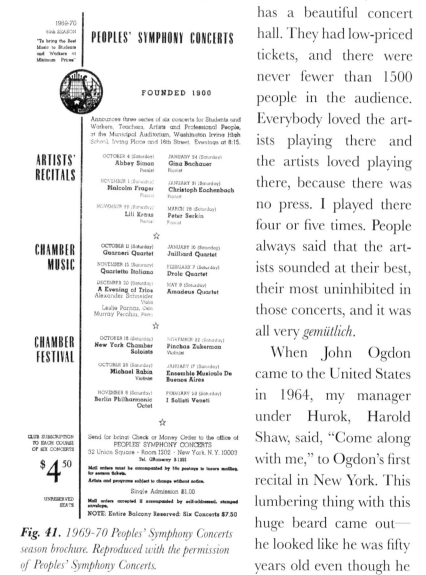

Fig. 41. *1969-70 Peoples' Symphony Concerts season brochure. Reproduced with the permission of Peoples' Symphony Concerts.*

El pianista Abbey Simon. (Dibujo de María Valencia).

Abbey Simon spiller Chopins konsert nr. 2 f-moll opus 21.
Tegnet av Thurmann Nielsen i Aulaen i går.

Fig. 42. *Caricatures and sketches: (top row left) Caracas, June 2, 1954. Newspaper and artist unknown; (top row right) Newspaper unknown, Lima, May 1955; (middle row left) Oslo, Oct. 3, 1955, Newspaper and artist unknown; (middle row right) Source unknown; (bottom right) Francisco Ugalde, Abbey Simon, 1970, Spain, Museo ABC de Dibujo e Illustración.*

was in his mid-twenties. There's a story from when John Ogdon was a student at the Northern Conservatory in Manchester. Yvonne Loriod was coming to the conservatory to play a recital of her husband Messiaen's works. The whole place was very excited, but there was some sort of accident, whether it was the rain, or the snow, and she couldn't make it. Ogdon said, "Listen, I'll be very happy to read the music for you," and he played the whole recital. He also wrote a very good piano concerto, which he recorded himself. Ogdon was so young when he died, for heaven's sakes. I don't think he was fifty. He was a remarkable and gifted person. His loss was a great musical and personal tragedy.

One day in the mid-sixties, I was sitting in the Dandale restaurant in Bloomington with some students. I ran a tab there that I would pay off once a month or so. I called for the bill, and I was making out a check, saying the date as I wrote it—the 16th. The

Fig. 43. *With Seiji Ozawa, Lincoln Center, March 1965 (Photographer unknown.)*

waitress said, "No, Mr. Simon, today is the 17th." I said, "No, I have a concert on the 17th." She said, "You lost it." I had missed my concert at Morehead State University in Kentucky. Practically in tears, I called the man in Kentucky, who said, "We've never had such a big public, what are we going to do?" I said, "I've never done anything like this before in my life, I guess I'm losing my marbles. I'm sorry. I'll do anything to make it up to you. Make any arrangement, I will come down to play at my own expense with no fee." Finally, he called me back and said, "We've found another date for you. There's only one other thing we ask: that's to meet with some of our students." I said, "With pleasure." Came the date, I played my concert, and I had to go and talk to the students. I thought I would be meeting with the music department. It turns out I was addressing the total assembly of the university—3000 people. I just didn't know what to do, I'd never spoken to an audience that size. I remember starting by saying, "A funny thing happened to me coming to Morehead State University," and I have no idea what I said after that.

That same year, I saw Anis Fuleihan again while playing at a festival outside of Tunis, in one of the most beautiful places you've ever seen. The next year, in 1965, he said, "Hey, I've got a little orchestra here, would you come and play the Mozart Concerto No. 21 and the Beethoven Fourth with me?" I said, "Fine." I was wondering what sort of an orchestra I was going to find. I came to the rehearsal a little early to get myself ready, and I heard marvelous violin and cello playing in the corridors. When they started to play the *tutti* of the Beethoven, I thought, "Geez, what kind of an orchestra is this? They're good!" It turned out that he had been able to recruit players on sabbatical from all the big European orchestras. I don't know how he got all these people.

On March 5, 1965, I premiered Fuleihan's sonata at the Met-

Fig. 44. *Publicity photo from the 1960s (Photographer unknown.)*

ropolitan Museum as part of a recital series sponsored by the Ford Foundation. Later that month, I played the Mozart K. 467 Concerto with the New York Philharmonic on Thursday night, Friday morning, Saturday night, and Sunday afternoon—but when that was over, I ran to Carnegie Hall to play with Richard Corn and the Orchestra of the Americas that night. We were giving a first performance of a Capriccio by a Canadian composer who lived in Vancouver, Murray Adaskin. I think I played it very well, with the music. I don't think anybody ever had a two-week period like I did, with two world premieres plus playing with the New York Philharmonic. There were magazines interviewing me, and I thought I was going to be the hottest thing in the world. Then HE announced he was coming back. Vladimir Horowitz came of retirement, and it wiped out all my publicity. Nevertheless, God bless him.

That year, Harold Shaw called me at Indiana and said, "I

Fig. 45. *With Erich Leinsdorf, Spring 1966 (Photograph by Phil Lowry.)*

have a date for you with the Boston Symphony for the Bartók
Third." I said to myself, "You've become old, seven hundred and
twelve, and you've become honest." I ended up playing between
forty-five and fifty works for piano and orchestra, but I couldn't
face up to learning any more. I went next door, where Sidney
Foster was teaching, and I said, "Call Herbert,"—his manager
was a man by the name of Herbert Barrett—"and if you want
to play the Bartók Third, tell him you just found out the Boston
Symphony doesn't have anybody for it." He got the date, and
ended up playing it with Aaron Copland conducting.

That May, I happened to be in New York when Horowitz
made his big return. Carnegie Hall, because I had played there
so many times, found me a ticket. I had never met Horowitz.
After the concert, they weren't admitting anybody backstage,
except the man I was with, who was the manager of Carnegie
Hall. We went up this little old famous flight of stairs—this was
before the hall was renovated—and walked in the door of the
artist room. There was little Volodya—as his intimates called

him—lying on the sofa like an Egyptian Queen. He looked at me and said, "Abbey Simon, how nice of you to come!" I almost dropped dead. It turns out this manager of Carnegie Hall had been running a series at one of the universities in New Jersey and had been trying for years to get Horowitz to come and play. He thought Horowitz would be happy playing in their beautiful hall. I had played a concert on that series, and that manager had brought Horowitz to hear the hall when I was practicing there. That was how Horowitz knew me.

In September of 1965, my wife, son, and I were involved in another car accident. My wife broke a bone in her back and I broke a bone in my right hand. We were driving in France at the time. Fortunately, seat belts helped save us, and both injuries healed well.

Soon, I was performing again, with a fifteen-concert tour of South Africa and, as it was known then, Rhodesia. I went from Bulawayo to Salisbury, as the capital of Zimbabwe was called then. I went to practice on my piano, and I noticed that everybody was rather sad. I played my concert, and then I went out to dinner with the various people involved, and I said to myself, "Well, you've really blown it this time." In the morning, I got the newspaper by my door, and there was nothing but black redacted lines on the front page. That was November 11, 1965, the day Rhodesia announced their independence from Great Britain. It was a momentous political occasion.

Around this time, I ran into Rafael Druian on the street, and he told me he had just recorded some Mozart violin sonatas with Szell. It's very interesting to look at that album cover—Szell's name is first, and on the recording, you can barely hear Rafael.

In the spring of 1966, I played the Brahms Second Concerto four times with the Boston Symphony and Erich Leinsdorf. I played with him many times and never had a moment's difficulty, but he was one of the conductors that drove me mad in the Brahms B-flat. I heard buummm buuummmm buuuuuuuummmmm… half tempo. Every time the theme came back, he made an enormous *ritard* beforehand, and he wouldn't talk to me about it. I called our mutual manager, Mr. Hurok, and said, "I have one foot and a knee out the window…what should I do?" He said, "Play slow or jump."

In the spring of 1966, I did a four-concert East Coast tour with the Boston Symphony and made my second visit to India. I've been there a number of times and never enjoyed it. The first place I played in India was Bombay, or Mumbai as it's known now, and I was playing for something called the Bombay Madrigal Society. I was staying in one of the best hotels, and I came in one night around eleven o'clock, and there was somebody lying across the threshold of my door. I had to nudge him with my foot to open the door to let me in. That was their way of life. I remember another horrible experience in India. They gave a terribly British, very nice tea party for me at someone's house,

Fig. 46. *Melbourne, 1967 (Photographer unknown.)*

Fig. 47. *With Malcolm Sargent, Beethoven 5ᵗʰ Concerto, Melbourne Symphony, 1967 (Photographer unknown.)*

with these enormous carpets rolled out on the lawn. At the end, the hostess said, "Shall we take you back to the hotel?" I got into this Rolls Royce and she said, "I have to stop at the market for one minute." We stopped and were immediately surrounded by deformed children. The beggars used to buy newborn babies, and deform them surgically to gain sympathy. It was absolutely a nightmare.

May all the pianists I know play in Calcutta—it's the most horrible place in the world. I was going out to a restaurant with some people after the concert, and there was slot parking, facing the curb. As we drove in, there was a husband and wife and two children, sitting in this parking slot cooking their dinner on a little coal burner. They paid no attention to us, and we practically drove over them. In India, the rich get richer and the poor get poorer, but there's just so much poor they can have. It's not for me.

In June, I performed the Rachmaninoff Third Concerto with the Japan Philharmonic Symphony Orchestra in Tokyo's Bunka Kaikan Hall, Akeo Watanabe conducting. They finally released that recording in the year they celebrated the fiftieth anniversary of the Japan Philharmonic, and it was one of their favorite records. As I mentioned, I always had a talent for languages, my son Jonathan has also. By the time I got to my hotel from the airport in Tokyo, I could recognize sounds. If I put my mind to it, I'm quite convinced I'd be able to learn Japanese.

In July, I played the Brahms B-flat again with Leinsdorf, this time at Tanglewood. We had played the concerto together several times recently, and I got a letter saying, "Mr. Leinsdorf insists that you be present for a rehearsal." I came down at ten o'clock in the morning, and he rehearsed other things on the program for two hours. Finally, at twelve o'clock he says, "Piano." So, I run to the piano, prepared to play my opening chords at half tempo, and he says, "Ten bars before letter S!" By the time I could figure out where he was, he stops and says, "Four bars before R!" I didn't play a single note during the whole rehearsal. He made a complete jerk out of me in front of the Boston Symphony, plus the shed was already full of audience members. I knew the first horn player—he went to Curtis—and after the rehearsal he said to me, "Abbey, why don't you just not show up to the concert and see if Leinsdorf notices?"

1966 continued with another large tour of South America, several performances with American and European orchestras and, for the first time, performances in the Soviet Union. That year, I began my association with George Mendelssohn, the founder and president of Vox Records. First he was George Mendelssohn, then he was George de Mendelssohn, then he was George H. de Mendelssohn-Bartholdy. He knew the timing of

МОСКОВСКАЯ ГОСУДАРСТВЕННАЯ ФИЛАРМОНИЯ

Концертный зал им. П. И. Чайковского

(пл. Маяковского, 29)

ПИАНИСТ

Эбби САЙМОН

(СОЕДИНЕННЫЕ ШТАТЫ АМЕРИКИ)

БЕТХОВЕН	— Соната № 30 ми мажор, соч. 109
ШУМАН	— Вариации на тему «Abegg»
ШОПЕН	— Соната си минор, соч. 58
РАВЕЛЬ	— Ночные видения
АЛЬБЕНИС — ГОДОВСКИЙ	— Триана

Начало в 7 час. 30 мин. вечера

Билеты продаются

Fig. 48. *Moscow State Philharmonic solo recital poster, December 16, 1967.*

every piece that had ever been written and he was a very considerate man, although some people say he was the world's biggest crook. They said that if he threw all his money up on the ceiling, whatever rested there was your royalties—but I found him to be a generous man who adored artists. I did make a lot of money from the recordings we did together, and he was always concerned about my career. We remained very close friends.

Around this time, I also began appearing at the Music Mountain Summer Festival in Falls Village, Connecticut, where I performed chamber music regularly with the Berkshire String Quartet and others. The spring of 1967 was taken up with another big tour of Australia and New Zealand. I was playing the Ravel G-Major in New Zealand with a marvelous conductor with whom I'd played in Australia—Alceo Galliera. After the New Zealand tour, I went to see Mr. Hurok and said, "You know, I just played with a marvelous conductor, this guy would be fantastic. Very tall, with flowing platinum blond hair like all the pictures you've seen of Liszt."

Walter Prude, who was a Hurok right-hand man, said, "How old is he?"

"I'd say, in his mid-fifties."

"He's no good to us. We want them in their eighties, or fourteen."

Prude was a resolute enemy of mine.

The next year Galliera engaged me to play the Tchaikovsky with him in Strasbourg, in Northern France.

I had played several concerts with the Dallas Symphony with great success, and in the fall of 1967, I finally got the plum—I was going to play all five Beethoven Concertos and the Choral Fantasy with them. The conductor was a nagging rehearser and he would waste time in conducting things that didn't have to be rehearsed, and during the rehearsals he wouldn't let me play the cadenzas, saying, "Oh, it's not necessary. We can't waste time." At the first concert, we were doing the Third Beethoven Concerto, which every orchestra knows very well. I knew we were in trouble the minute the concerto started because I heard "wuuuuuhhhhh…wuuuuuhhhhh…wuuuuuhhhhh." Oy! We get to the cadenza—in the middle of which there are these four trills, but it's got a long way to go to the end. He heard trills, so he brought in the orchestra. I was so stunned, I suddenly shouted, "OH NO!" At the concert, there was a wicked critic, John Ardoin, who had always been very nice to me. His headline the next day said, "Oh No, Mr. Simon!"

In November, I appeared on CBS Camera 3 TV, playing Schumann's *Arabeske*, Chopin's Impromptu in A-flat Major, and Ravel's "Alborada del gracioso." December was occupied with my second Russian tour, consisting of a dozen appearances. I brought the Chopin F-Minor, Brahms Second, and Beethoven Fourth Concertos to play with the Moscow and Leningrad Orchestras, among others, and three different solo programs.

Fig. 49. *With the Leningrad Symphony, Edouard Grikurov conducting, December 19, 1967. Music and Artists (September, 1968).*

Dina and Jonathan went with me, and in Moscow, we were entertained by Emil Gilels and his wife. Conversation was a lot in sign language because Gilels was not fluent in English. He lived in a fairly luxurious apartment and we were served caviar by the spoon. That was in 1967, the fiftieth anniversary of the Russian Revolution. Dina had a cousin who lived in Moscow, who was one of Russia's most famous poets and authors. Deen tried to reach her on the phone and all she got was somebody who said, "Don't call" in English.

I played everyplace in the Soviet Union: Moscow, St. Petersburg (then Leningrad), all the places down near Asia, Armenia, Minsk, Kiev. I was expecting all these negative things about Russia, but whenever we complained about something in the room, the next time we came back it had been repaired. We were treated as guests of the country, which was different from the experience of the citizens there.

They had someone traveling with us twenty-four hours a day and staying in our hotel. One cold, bitter day, we were coming into a town which was supposedly a resort, called Kislovodsk. I was developing a very sore throat—there were nine thousand feet of snow on the ground—and we passed a cinema. I couldn't read the Russian but saw the blurb and said, "I think that's an American or European film" to our guardian, the woman who was with us all the time. "I'd like to go to see that movie." She said, "No, that's not for you, we'll go to another movie." We got to the hotel and put our bags in the room, and I said to our guardian, "That movie looks to me like it might be a foreign movie, that's why I want to see it, I don't speak Russian." "No, you'll be better off in this movie," and she took us to another movie, it may very well have been *Sophie the Tractor Girl* for all I know, it was all Russian. I finally lost my temper. I said, "Now. We are going to the other movie." It turned out to be the French version of the *Hunchback of Notre Dame*. We came to this little theater and walked in, and the chairs were all moveable. In the center were three huge armchairs with high backs, arranged specially for us. Nobody behind us could see the film.

Our companion was sort of a tragic figure. She was very sweet, and her husband was writing this great book on the Indonesian dictator, Sukarno. When we left, she took us to the airport and was in a terrible mood. Then we discovered a few days later that Sukarno had been deposed, and her husband's work was useless, and she said to us timidly, "If you see any articles about Sukarno, please send them to me."

I enjoyed playing in the Soviet Union; there were no problems. The playing conditions were wonderful, the instruments were gorgeous, and the audiences were very large and appreciative. It was the nineteenth century that the Soviet Union wanted to hold onto. Playing Chopin and Brahms with the Leningrad Symphony was something I'll never forget. The marvelous conductor was an old man, Edouard Grikurov who, apparently, was one of the top conductors of the opera. He was a sweetie, and wonderful to play with, and I was in seventh heaven with the orchestra and the hall, with those unbelievable chandeliers. After one concert, we went to a restaurant for dinner, and I was in my evening clothes. We always got special service because our companion would say we were guests of the government. We sat down at the table and this guy, who's sitting at the next table by himself, was smiling and talking to me and he looked at my clothes and said, "What do you do?" I said, "Pianist." He said, "Pianist also." It turned out he was saying a word in Russian, *пьяный*, pronounced "piani," that means "I'm dead drunk."

In March 1968, I had been on a long tour and returned to Bloomington on a Sunday. Immediately upon my arrival, I was going to teach all day, starting at one o'clock. After only a few minutes of teaching I got a call from my agent, the Sol Hurok Office in New York. He said Claudio Arrau was sick and had to cancel a Beethoven concerto cycle in Caracas, and they needed a replacement. I cut short my teaching, flew to New York, picked up my ticket to Venezuela, and started rehearsals that Monday evening. I spent a week playing the concertos and then returned to Bloomington the next Sunday. I started the lessons by saying "As I was saying last Sunday, before I was so rudely interrupted…"

One day, when we were living in the old town in Geneva, the great Abbey Simon and his brilliant brain woke up and said, "You know, Jonathan's room is too small for him, he's in university now." Instead of saying to him, "Go get yourself a studio," I said, "It's time we moved to a place where you have room to work and study." We found a beautiful two-story penthouse in a modern building with a mountain view. There was nothing antique-y about it, and we loved it when we saw it. The new

ABBEY SIMON
by arrangement
with Harold Shaw

Photo: Christian Steiner

"A MASTER PIANIST...
A DAZZLING PERFORMANCE."
The New York Times

Fig. 50. *Flyer, Harold Shaw Concerts, c. 1970.*

apartment is wonderful for playing piano and making music. The only trouble is that it's not in a part of Geneva that I like.

We bought beds, but everything was so expensive, we couldn't afford much else. I said, "We have to buy some furniture and live like human beings." On the way back from Moscow, we had to change planes in Copenhagen, and I knew that the Danes were famous for furniture. I said, "Kiddo, I've been to the department store here before, and they have perfectly useful and attractive furniture, and it's not going to be antique." We bought all this furniture in one day and had it shipped to Geneva. It cost about 10 percent of what anything comparable would have been in Geneva. The Swiss were not famous for furniture, except their marvelous antiques. People shipped their antiques to be sold in Switzerland because the prices were much higher. We had no sooner moved into the new place when Jonathan very intelligently said, "I need my own place." He never came closer to death as on that day.

In 1969, Hurok's health was beginning to fail, and his whole office split. Shelly Gold started his own thing, and Harold Shaw, who was one of Hurok's right-hand men, formed his own artist management agency, taking with him, among others, Maureen Forrester, Julian Bream, the guitarist John Williams, John Ogdon, Stephen Bishop, Garrick Ohlsson, Peter Schickele, and me.

Around this time, I was being considered for a university position in Chicago. The director said,

"We'd like you to play for us."

"That sounds like I'm auditioning."

"Well…yes…"

"Come to Orchestra Hall on Sunday. I'll be playing a recital."

Obviously, their search committee had nothing to do with music and didn't know who I was. Another time, I got this call in Bloomington: "Would you be interested in teaching at The University of Southern California?" It was the dead of winter and I said yes—I would have gladly taken the job. "Well, we'd like you to come in and play a recital for us and give a masterclass." I said, "I'm a little too old to audition. Either you want me, or you don't." The dean at USC, Grant Beglarian, was furious with the committee: "You don't ask Abbey Simon to come and audition!" I never asked for a teaching job in my life. I was hoping against hope, quite honestly, when I gave a masterclass at the Royal Academy, that they might ask me to teach there. I would have said goodbye to whatever school I was teaching at in thirty seconds. They didn't ask me in Geneva either.

My new recordings on Vox began to come out in quick succession: Schumann *Carnaval* and Fantasie; Chopin sonatas; and Ravel *Valses nobles et sentimentales* and *Gaspard de la nuit*. They were recorded in Rutgers Presbyterian Church, just down the street from my West Seventy-Third Street apartment in New York. Rutgers was a functioning church and a center for the neighbor-

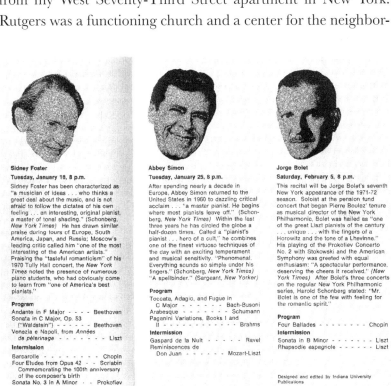

Sidney Foster
Tuesday, January 18, 8 p.m.

Sidney Foster has been characterized as "a musician of ideas ... who thinks a great deal about the music, and is not afraid to follow the dictates of his own feeling ... an interesting, original pianist, a master of tonal shading." (Schonberg, *New York Times*) He has drawn similar praise during tours of Europe, South America, Japan, and Russia; Moscow's leading critic called him "one of the most interesting of the American artists." Praising the "tasteful romanticism" of his 1970 Tully Hall concert, the *New York Times* noted the presence of numerous piano students, who had obviously come to learn from "one of America's best pianists."

Program

Andante in F Major - - - - Beethoven
Sonata in C Major, Op. 53
  ("Waldstein") - - - - - Beethoven
Venezia e Napoli, from *Années
de pèlerinage* - - - - - - - Liszt
Intermission

Barcarolle - - - - - - - - Chopin
Four Etudes from Opus 42 - - Scriabin
  Commemorating the 100th anniversary
  of the composer's birth
Sonata No. 3 in A Minor - - Prokofiev

Abbey Simon
Tuesday, January 25, 8 p.m.

After spending nearly a decade in Europe, Abbey Simon returned to the United States in 1960 to dazzling critical acclaim ... "a master pianist. He begins where most pianists leave off." (Schonberg, *New York Times*) Within the last three years he has circled the globe a half-dozen times. Called a "pianist's pianist ... hero of a cult," he combines one of the finest virtuoso techniques of the day with an exciting temperament and musical sensitivity. "Phenomenal. Everything sounds so simple under his fingers." (Schonberg, *New York Times*) "A spellbinder." (Sargeant, *New Yorker*)

Program

Toccata, Adagio, and Fugue in
  C Major - - - - - - Bach-Busoni
Arabesque - - - - - - - Schumann
Paganini Variations, Books I and
  II - - - - - - - - - - - - Brahms
Intermission

Gaspard de la Nuit - - - - - Ravel
Reminiscences de
  Don Juan - - - - - Mozart-Liszt

Jorge Bolet
Saturday, February 5, 8 p.m.

This recital will be Jorge Bolet's seventh New York appearance of the 1971-72 season. Soloist at the pension fund concert that began Pierre Boulez' tenure as musical director of the New York Philharmonic, Bolet was hailed as "one of the great Liszt pianists of the century ... unique ... with the fingers of a Horowitz and the tone of a Lhevinne." His playing of the Prokofiev Concerto No. 2 with Stokowski and the American Symphony was greeted with equal enthusiasm: "A spectacular performance, deserving the cheers it received." *(New York Times)* After Bolet's three concerts on the regular New York Philharmonic series, Harold Schonberg stated: "Mr. Bolet is one of the few with feeling for the romantic spirit."

Program

Four Ballades - - - - - - - Chopin
Intermission

Sonata in B Minor - - - - - Liszt
Rhapsodie espagnole - - - - - Liszt

Designed and edited by Indiana University
Publications

Fig. 51. *The Trio from IU play three concerts at Lincoln Center, early 1972. Reproduction courtesy of Indiana University.*

hood, and one time, my producer called to say there would be a coffin beside the piano at the next recording session. I declined to record that day.

My recording team was a company called Elite Recordings, composed of two highly trained musicians, Joanna Nickrenz and Marc Aubort. Joanna had wonderful musical instincts, was apparently a very good pianist, and was the pianist of the

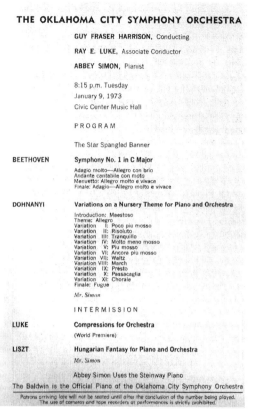

THE OKLAHOMA CITY SYMPHONY ORCHESTRA

GUY FRASER HARRISON, Conducting

RAY E. LUKE, Associate Conductor

ABBEY SIMON, Pianist

8:15 p.m. Tuesday
January 9, 1973
Civic Center Music Hall

PROGRAM

The Star Spangled Banner

BEETHOVEN	Symphony No. 1 in C Major
	Adagio molto—Allegro con brio
	Andante cantabile con moto
	Menuetto: Allegro molto e vivace
	Finale: Adagio—Allegro molto e vivace
DOHNANYI	Variations on a Nursery Theme for Piano and Orchestra
	Introduction: Maestoso
	Theme: Allegro
	Variation I: Poco piu mosso
	Variation II: Risoluto
	Variation III: Tranquillo
	Variation IV: Molto meno mosso
	Variation V: Piu mosso
	Variation VI: Ancora piu mosso
	Variation VII: Waltz
	Variation VIII: March
	Variation IX: Presto
	Variation X: Passacaglia
	Variation XI: Chorale
	Finale: Fugue
	Mr. Simon

INTERMISSION

LUKE	Compressions for Orchestra
	(World Premiere)
LISZT	Hungarian Fantasy for Piano and Orchestra
	Mr. Simon

Abbey Simon Uses the Steinway Piano

The Baldwin is the Official Piano of the Oklahoma City Symphony Orchestra

Patrons arriving late will not be seated until after the conclusion of the number being played.
The use of cameras and tape recorders at performances is strictly prohibited.

Fig. 52. *An unusual program from 1973.*

Pittsburgh Symphony. She and Marc did a fantastic job, they had several Grammys. Joanna's daughter Erika Nickrenz later studied with me at Juilliard. She is the pianist for the Eroica Trio. Of course, I've known Erika since she was six or seven years old. She studied with a very good teacher in New York, a guy who died last year by the name of Hernandez. She is quite gifted, and I always go hear her play when I can.

In June of 1971, I had an interesting experience playing with the Orchestre de la Suisse Romande in Geneva. I was just about to go on stage, and was taking everything out of my pockets. I went to take my wallet out but hooked my finger

Monday Evening, December 15, 1975 at 8:00

The Walter W. Naumburg Foundation
in association with The Carnegie Hall Corporation

presents

The Fiftieth Anniversary Celebration of
The Walter W. Naumburg Foundation

All performers in this celebration are Naumburg Award winners

Opening Remarks by Robert Mann, President

BACH	Concerto in D Minor for Two Violins and String Orchestra, S. 1043
	Vivace
	Largo ma non tanto
	Allegro
	SIDNEY HARTH (1948)
	BERL SENOFSKY (1947)
	JOSEPH SILVERSTEIN, *conductor*

MENDELSSOHN	Octet in E-flat Major, Op. 20
	Allegro moderato ma con fuoco
	Andante
	Scherzo
	Presto

JOSEPH SILVERSTEIN (1960)	ROBERT MANN (1941)
NANCY CIRILLO (1955)	JOHN GRAHAM (1972)
JOYCE FLISSLER (1951)	HARVEY SHAPIRO (1935)
YOKO MATSUO (1952)	RONALD LEONARD (1955)

LISZT	Réminiscenses de Don Juan de Mozart for Two Pianos
	JORGE BOLET (1937)
	ANDRÉ-MICHEL SCHUB (1974)

INTERMISSION

Address by Aaron Copland

BACH	Cantata No. 54, "Widerstehe doch der Sünde"
	CAROL BRICE , *contralto* (1944)
	JOSEPH SILVERSTEIN, *conductor*

BACH	Concerto in C Major for Three Pianos and String Orchestra, S. 1064
	Allegro
	Adagio
	Allegro
	ABBEY SIMON (1940) ADELE MARCUS (1928)
	CONSTANCE KEENE (1943) JOSEPH SILVERSTEIN, *conductor*

Orchestra: LEONID HAMBRO, *continuo* (1946)
AMERICAN STRING QUARTET (1974)
CONCORD STRING QUARTET (1972)
MEMBERS OF THE MENDELSSOHN OCTET
JULES LEVINE, *Double Bass (Guest Artist)*

Jorge Bolet, André-Michel Schub and
Adele Marcus play the Baldwin piano.

Abbey Simon and Constance Keene
play the Steinway piano.

Fig. 53. *Another interesting program, December 15, 1975.*

in the pocket, and I knew I had injured my hand. Everybody said, "Oh well, run it under some water and it will be fine." I went out on stage, and when I played the first chord of the Second Rachmaninoff Concerto, I saw stars. I suddenly knew the little finger on my left hand was broken. I played the whole concerto anyway, probably very badly. It was being broadcast on the radio, and I didn't know how to stop! We had a friend who was the doctor in charge of medicine in the whole Haute-Savoie region of France, near Geneva. When she looked at my finger, she said, "Let's go to the hospital."

In 1972 came the release of the four Chopin scherzos along with the Mendelssohn *Variations sérieuses* on Vox. That same year, Bolet, Foster, and I each gave a recital at Alice Tully Hall as a fundraiser for Indiana University. Around that time, I had a troubling experience with Steinway's artist director, David Rubin, who had a wide reputation for being difficult and was a thoroughly deceitful man. One day, he said to me, "You're so troublesome about pianos. Why don't you come down here in September and pick the piano you like, and we'll use it whenever it's necessary for you." So I picked out my piano. Two months later I was playing in Carnegie Hall. I came into New York and I went down to the basement of Steinway to see my piano and it wasn't there. I called David and said,

"Where's my piano?"

"Your piano? What do you mean, your piano? You can't expect us to hold pianos just for you."

"I'm just doing what you told me to do. I picked a piano in September, and this was to be put aside for me."

"We can't do things like that."

So I had to find another piano for my concert. Months later, I got a letter from Rubinstein. He said, "Mr. Simon, please, I would never take a piano from another artist. They had no business telling me that piano was available for me to take to Washington DC. It's that horrible David Rubin." I think one of the reasons Rubinstein didn't like him was that if Horowitz said,

"Jump out the window," David would say, "Should I open the window first or not?" He was the most unbelievable sycophant.

I was playing shortly before that, or right after, in the Peoples' Symphony Concerts at Washington Irving High School, and I came down there on the morning of the concert. I was practicing on the piano and a damper was stuck. I called David at home and said,

"Listen, would you leave word for the tuner that he should look out for the damper on this D flat?"

"I don't see why you don't pay for the tuner to come with you!"

"There's no reason for a tuner to come with me. I'm just alerting you, in case he doesn't see that this damper should be fixed."

"Well, from now on you have to pay for a tuner to come with you when you practice."

I couldn't figure out a way to kill him. I kept driving up and down Fifty-Seventh but he was never crossing the street. That's when I left Steinway and became a Baldwin artist.

In 1973, Vox released my recording of the entire works for piano and or-

Fig. 54. Shawnigan Festival Piano Faculty, August, 1978.

chestra of Chopin. I also recorded the Chopin préludes, but they were never released. George Mendelssohn was always looking for a cheaper way to record, and this guy in London was going to be much less expensive than Marc and Joanna doing them at Rutgers Church in New York. The minute I walked into the hall in London, I knew it was going to be a wreck. The hall was a perfect circle—that would never produce good recorded sound. I was right, and the préludes couldn't be released.

That same year, I played a three-concerto concert in Carnegie Hall on the twenty-fifth anniversary of my concerto debut with the National Orchestral Association and Leon Barzin, playing with the same orchestra and conductor Mozart K. 467, Beethoven Fourth, and Brahms B-flat. For me, the more concertos, the better. The conductor said, "Two," and I said, "How 'bout three?" After the concert, out of nowhere came a telegram: "I remember the beautiful Beethoven Fourth we played together in Lima, Peru. From Iturbi." I always loved playing more than one concerto in a concert. They did it in Europe all the time. I did it with the Shreveport Symphony, with the Beethoven Third and both Ravels. Nobody does it anymore.

In 1974, the complete Ravel solo repertoire record was released, and in 1975 the Chopin études, Barcarolle, ballades, and waltzes; and Ravel concertos. That year, I played six concertos in six cities in ten days. I played the Beethoven Third, the Gershwin Concerto in F, *Rhapsody in Blue,* and the Beethoven Fourth. Also in 1975 was an eleven-concert tour of South Africa.

One day, when we were all teaching in Bloomington, Bolet got a call from the New York Philharmonic: "Mr. Watts is sick, can you play the *Totentanz?*" Bolet was famous as a Liszt player, but he didn't know the *Totentanz,* which meant he had about a week to learn it. This sort of thing everybody does, you never

Fig. 55. *Brahms Concerto No. 2, Bergen, Norway, January 27, 1977.*

admitted there was a piece you didn't know. That is fine when you're eighteen, but it's quite different when you're sixty two. We had four piano concerto competitions a year at Indiana, and each one was for one work—a student couldn't play anything he wanted, and the next competition was for the *Totentanz*. I felt pretty sure that my student Charles Fugo would win, but he didn't bother playing in the competition. Instead, he spent all day and all night playing the second piano part while Jorge learned the *Totentanz*. Charlie Fugo is one of the most talented people you've ever met. He's still teaching in Columbia, South Carolina.

We all went with Bolet to New York because I was playing there a week later. You've never seen such a huge hulk of a man so nervous in your life. At the concert, he started out and never stopped—he even played through all the *tutti* sections. It was as if he was saying, "If I stop, I won't be able to start again!" It was probably the poorest concert he ever played in New York, but he never had such a success! His whole life changed. I don't know if he ever played it again. There was something that was sort of lacking in his playing, this hysteria. He was marvelous in a small studio—when he played for you, you were totally awestruck, but in the hall, it wasn't the same. Bolet used to complain that pianists never take chances, but when he played the Schumann Fantasie, he didn't even try to do the faster tempo at the end of the second movement.

The week after he played the Liszt, I played the Ravel Left-Hand with the New York Philharmonic and Pierre Boulez. It was like playing with a doorpost. We did the Ravel four times, and every time we came off the stage, it felt like we should be introduced to each other.

In October of 1975, Horowitz came to Indiana University. He wanted me to come listen to him in IU Auditorium before his concert, since I was the only one at IU who knew him. He was in great form then. Horowitz played on one of the three recital series on campus: A, B, or C, which had nothing to do with the music department. Only the major, number one artists you could find played on the major series. Those concerts were all well attended. We had a tremendous musical life on campus. Now, I believe, there's only one series in the school, and it's mostly pop. Every US university had a big commercial concert series, but there is nothing like that left.

Years later, I woke up one morning and, as usual, turned on CBS for the news. I said, "Gee, that looks like the Tchaikovsky Hall in Moscow, and that looks like Vladimir Horowitz walking out. Vladimir Horowitz in Moscow!? When the hell did this happen? He didn't consult me!" My next thought was, "Oh dear God, let him play well. Let him play at his best," and he did, he played very well.

Later in 1975, I played Rachmaninoff's Second Concerto with Leonard Slatkin and the St. Louis Symphony. That was around the time when John Ogdon came to Indiana. He was there from 1976 to 1980. Harold Shaw said, "You think you can get him a job at Indiana?" I said, "I can always try." I spoke to Dean Bain about it, and he said, "Honored, delighted, he'd be welcome." Ogdon was a tremendously talented fellow and a delightful person. He spoke in a whisper, his mouth and lips hardly moved. I arranged an elegant faculty lunch for the whole piano faculty to meet him.

Jorge Bolet was very unhappy with Ogdon's recital at IU, because Ogdon played well and Bolet felt threatened. Bolet was a terrible teacher—all he did was play for you. You got a piano recital. He had no patience with your problems.

In May of 1976, I did another South American tour, gave performances of the Rachmaninoff Third with the St. Louis Symphony, and started teaching at the Shawnigan Summer Festival in British Columbia, which I did for three summers. I did several summer festivals in the US, and one in France. Many of them I turned down because when I came home to Geneva, I didn't feel like going back to the US.

In the fall of 1977, I recorded the complete Rachmaninoff works for piano and orchestra with the St. Louis Symphony. I made one of the biggest mistakes in my life. I thought I had learned the First and the Fourth Rachmaninoff Concertos, and I agreed to perform them both on one concert the night before the recording. I had never played either of them, so I was performing two works that I didn't know, and it sounded like I was performing two works that I didn't know. I got lost in both of them and could barely get through them, so that was a terrible fiasco and it was all my fault. Only a ridiculous egomaniac could have done such a thing, but it's amazing how suddenly "I can" takes over, and you can't. Or maybe you could, at a different time in your life. Slatkin acted as if I didn't appreciate the mistake that I made, and he was very cruel and embarrassing with other people listening, at a private dinner party with the board of directors. After the recording I said to him, "Look, we did the Second with no problems, we did the Rachmaninoff *Paganini* about as fast as anybody could record it, and we did the Third Rachmaninoff in less than one session," because he was able to record two small orchestral pieces like the *Vocalise* and another piece in the same session.

Another instance when I overestimated my abilities happened shortly after I read an article about Godowsky getting on the 20th Century Limited, the great train of the period, which went from New York to Chicago overnight. He had with him the Liszt A-Major Concerto, I think it was. He had never played it, and he learned it on the train, all day and all night, and when he arrived he went straight to Orchestra Hall, and played the Liszt A-Major Concerto rehearsal. I was pissed off. I didn't like Godowsky. He really didn't make a great impression on me when I was a child. I had a concert in Flint, Michigan, and one of my closest friends, Jack, who is retired now out in California, decided that he would drive me there, and then after my concert we would run up to Toronto to see an old friend of ours. This was just when I had read that article about Godowsky, and I said, "I'm gonna learn the 32 Variations of Beethoven in the car." It was really unfair that I picked that, because while I might never have played the 32 Variations, I'd had students who played them, and I had heard them in concert. It wasn't as if I had to go and peruse every note to memorize them. Anyway, we arrived in Flint, and I sat down, and I played the 32 Variations, extremely well. I knew them. So I said, "Well, at least I can do that." Came the concert that night: I played six hundred and seventy-five variations. Nobody ever dreamed of so many variations. The more I played, the more I improvised before I could find the last one, because I wanted to end with the proper variation. That's the difference of being under pressure. I still have my doubts about Godowsky learning the Liszt A-Major, having never tried it at the keyboard.

1977 was a year of upheaval in my life. Bolet was resigning

from Indiana, and my dear friend Sidney Foster passed away in February at the age of 59. While Sidney had devoted more and more time to his teaching post and stayed at Indiana until the end, I was concerned about teaching and committee responsibilities encroaching on my career. The trio had been reunited in Bloomington for nine happy years, but it was breaking up. I resigned from my position at IU that spring and never returned to Bloomington.

Chapter Six
HOUSTON AND JUILLIARD: 1977-2004

Milton Katims, who had recently become the director of the University of Houston School of Music, had been asking me for two years to join their faculty. Katims was Music Director of the Seattle Symphony for twenty-two years and had been Arturo Toscanini's assistant conductor. He also conducted the New York Philharmonic, Philadelphia Orchestra, Boston Symphony, London Philharmonic, Cleveland Orchestra, and Montreal Symphony. He was one of the top violists in the country, played with Casals many times, and was principal in the NBC Symphony. He was one of these detestable players who could put the viola down for six months and then pick it up and play like he'd been practicing like a fiend all day long. It used to drive his wife Virginia crazy, she was a cellist. In 1977, I accepted Katims's invitation and began teaching at of the University of Houston, where I was given the Hugh Roy and Lillie Cranz *Cullen* Endowed Chair.

When I first came to Houston, I had a student who was from Russia whose husband was a doctor who had to requalify there. He was at the Cleveland Clinic, and she was scraping out a living teaching. She said, "Mr. Simon, we are going to a Russian restaurant." I said, "Great," and we got Milton and Virginia, and at least two carfuls of people, and we drove and we drove, out of town, and finally we came to a corner. The cross street was little more than a dirt road, and there was the Russian restaurant. It was all cinderblock. We went in, and the head waiter saw me and said, "Mr. Simon, what are you doing here?" He was Colombian, and he had a restaurant right next to the Tequendama Hotel in

Bogotá—I used to eat there all the time.

In 1977, I also accepted an invitation to come to Juilliard. They had one of the great people then, the actor John Houseman. If you ever see his memoirs anywhere, buy it, you will enjoy it. He talks about the 1930s, the parties that went on in New York City, the theater and music, and how there was this young teenager who was playing jazz at all these parties, and it was Leonard Bernstein. I found out all these things were going on AND I DIDN'T KNOW A THING ABOUT THEM. I was furious.

That year, I had another stab at the Rachmaninoff Fourth, with the Atlanta Symphony, but I always get too nervous in it because of my performance in St. Louis. The conductor for that concert was Sung Kwak, who lived in my building in New York. I persuaded him to play it with me and he was interested because he didn't know it. I also played the Rachmaninoff First with the Philharmonic-Symphony Society of New York in Avery Fisher Hall. I still think it's the most beautiful and the best of all the Rachmaninoff concertos. I don't know why it's not played more often. But once things become fashionable, like the Second or Third, that's all anyone plays. I played the 1st with several conductors, including André Kostelanetz, who was one of the great radio stars, and had the Coca Cola Hour with Kostelanetz. He was in the same class with Kurtz and half a dozen other Russian conductors. They were all serious, and if they ended up in lighter

Abbey Simon

SHAW CONCERTS, INC.
1995 BROADWAY
NEW YORK, N.Y. 10023

Fig. 56. Publicity photo, Shaw Concerts, 1970s (Photographer unknown.)

Fig. 57. *A Recording session with Joanna Nickrenz and Marc Aubort, c. 1979. American Record Guide (November 1980).*

music, it was just how their life worked out.

George Mendelssohn and I remained very close friends, and then in 1980, because of his health, he sold Vox Records. The new owner was some guy from Brooklyn who didn't know anything except business, and he was very pretentious. One time we were having lunch after he'd moved to this beautiful village in Connecticut. He said,

"Well, you probably wouldn't know it, it's called New Canaan."

"I know New Canaan."

"Oh, you know New Canaan? Have you seen that house? My daughter's graduating from high school and they're having the graduation party there." He was referring to Waveny Park.

"I've lived in that house."

He was out to impress me and make me feel lowly. I got pleasure out of destroying him.

In 1980, I had the idea to do a big Chopin festival in Alice Tully Hall. It was all worked out with my manager—one concert was going to be chamber music (with the trio and the cello sonata), one concert was the two concertos with orchestra, and then there were three solo recitals. The chamber concert was a big job for me because I didn't know those pieces. My friend, Yuri Krasnapolsky, was going to conduct the orchestra in the concertos. Yuri was conductor of Des Moines and Omaha, and had been Leonard Bernstein's assistant at the New York Philharmonic. One Saturday night, Yuri and I were walking,

Fig. 58. *With Dina aboard the SS Rotterdam, 1979. Simon played two recitals onboard (Photographer unknown.)*

talking very seriously about whom we would get to play. We stopped to buy the Sunday edition of the Times, and we opened to the music page, and there was an article about Anne Schein doing exactly the same thing, so it killed the whole idea for me.

In 1981, I was a judge at the Leeds Competition in England, and Deen was with me. I picked up the newspaper, and as I was reading through, I said, "My God I hope we're free on Sunday, because Oscar Shumsky is playing in London at the hall right next to the Festival Hall. I'd love to take up two seats, nobody knows him here." We couldn't go—there was something for us to attend to—but on Monday, there was a review of the concert. Every violinist within a hundred miles of London had come. It was sold out, everybody was ecstatic about him, and he signed a contract with EMI.

That year, I was going to play the Beethoven No. 4 with the Asheville Symphony. On the way from the airport, the driver started talking about how much everyone was looking forward to the Brahms No. 1. I hadn't performed the Brahms First in twelve years, but since it was what concertgoers had paid to hear, I knew I'd have to play it. I asked to be driven directly to the hall, obtained the score from the orchestra, borrowed a piano and began refreshing my memory. There was time for only one rehearsal with the orchestra, but it seemed to be enough. When I concluded, the audience—unaware of what had happened—gave me an enthusiastic ovation.

In 1982, I was playing at the Ambassador Auditorium in Pasadena. My Baldwin was on stage, and after a few measures of the Schumann Fantasie, the pedal apparatus started to fall off. I walked off stage, my technician came on to fix the problem, and I started again. This time none of the dampers worked, and it was a tremendous blur. They rolled the Baldwin off the stage and wheeled on one of their German Steinways. This time, everything worked. My technician, who traveled with me, had just worked on the Baldwin piano, and everything was perfect when I practiced on the piano that afternoon. My technician was a genius with the piano, and everything was always perfect with him. I couldn't understand how suddenly the whole piano fell apart on stage. I felt I was sabotaged, because they were proud of their German Steinways and were upset that I wouldn't play them.

In 1983, I went to visit Alberto Ginastera in Jonathan's hospital in Geneva. Jonathan took care of him, and he knew that Jonathan was my son. Jonathan knows everybody: the mayor, all the big politicians, they're all his patients. Ginastera passed away soon afterwards. In 1984, I created the University of Houston International Piano Festival, which continues to this day, and I play the opening recital every year. One year, I brought Earl Wild to the festival. He was a very good musician, a very nice person, certainly funny, but very unpredictable. I was

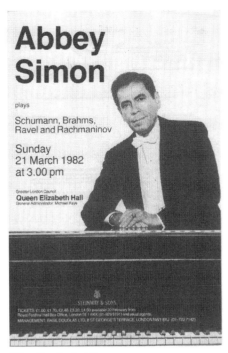

Abbey Simon

plays

Schumann, Brahms, Ravel and Rachmaninov

Sunday
21 March 1982
at 3.00 pm

Greater London Council
Queen Elizabeth Hall
General Administrator Michael Kaye

STEINWAY & SONS

TICKETS: £1.00, £1.70, £2.40, £3.20, £4.00 available 20 February from Royal Festival Hall Box Office, London SE 1 (XXX (01-928 3191) and usual agents. MANAGEMENT: BASIL DOUGLAS LTD, 8 ST GEORGE'S TERRACE, LONDON NW1 8XJ (01-722 7142)

Fig. 59. Recital flyer.

worried about his behavior so before his masterclass, I said, "Earl, we're in Houston, Texas. I don't want you lynched!" For the last twenty years of his life, he had his own recording company, Ivory Classics. It became quite successful. Some of his records were quite beautiful. The five Rachmaninoff Concertos go by so fast that you won't realize you've missed them. Harold Schonberg never wrote a nice word about him.

In the spring of 1984, I judged the Geneva and Montreal International Competitions. I was to continue judging several others, including the Geneva again in 1990 and 1996 as well as the Van Cliburn in 1989 and 1993. The Geneva Competition is going down the tubes. Like everything Swiss, it's quiet, nobody makes a big deal about it, and it's not what I think it should be. When I judged it again in 1990, one of the other jurors was this famous old Russian lady pianist, Tatiana Nikolayeva. She was evidently a living legend in Russia. She played the total Bach, total Liszt, total Shostakovich, total everything. She could apparently learn everything for a performance that morning. She was the first one who played all of the Shostakovich Preludes and Fugues. She was touring in the United States and made a big stir playing them in New York and Chicago. She had hundreds of Russian pieces dedicated to her.

Fig. 60. *With Dina and Jonathan, Vevey, Switzerland, 1985 (Photographer unknown.)*

She apparently had three or four husbands. She died, more or less on stage, in San Francisco, playing the Shostakovich Preludes and Fugues. When I met her she had to be at least seventy. We had a lot of fun together. We agreed that "Feux Follets" should not be permitted in a contest because it's always marvelous. Only an idiot would include it if they can't play it, and for some strange reason, that year, most of the "Feux Follets" were being played by Asian girls. They were knocking it off like you couldn't imagine. Every time one would walk out, Tatiana would lean over to me and say, "Feux Follets."

Fig. 61. *Abbey and Dina (Photographer unknown.)*

Through the 1990s, my career continued uninterrupted. In 1991, I was playing the "Emperor"

Concerto with The Hungarian Symphony Orchestra in Madison, Wisconsin. They had just arrived from Hungary to Chicago and gone by bus from Chicago to Madison. We practically played without rehearsal. In the concert, we got through the whole concerto, and to the last eight bars where the timpani has several solo notes. I played my chord and didn't hear anything from the timpani. The conductor looked at me and frantically gestured for me to go on. So I played the timpani part myself. It turns out the timpani player just fell asleep from jet-lag. That was the first time in any performance of the "Emperor" that the *ritardando* at the end worked out perfectly.

After I retired from Juilliard in 2004, I was forced to leave my West Seventy-Third Street apartment because I was no longer paying taxes on employment in New York City. I thought I should contest it in court but people said, "No, everybody's contesting it on the same grounds as you, and you will lose. There's no reason to waste the money." But make your own mistakes, don't make other people's mistakes. I still feel I should have contested it. That was one of the great losses of my life. Not that they were giving the apartment away. It was

Fig. 62. *Recital, Koninklijk Conservatorium, The Hague, January 9, 1998.*

Fig. 63. *Carnegie Hall, 2001 (Photographer unknown.)*

Fig. 64. *Frederic Chiu, Karen Shaw, Abbey Simon. Silvermine Artists Series, Connecticut, November 2002. Photograph courtesy of Karen Shaw.*

still very expensive at that time, over three thousand dollars a month. That may seem like nothing today, but twenty-five years ago, it was a lot of money. I could have bought it, but astute businessman that I was, I decided that 290,000 dollars was too much. Whereas 290,000 dollars would be a month's rent now. Yuri Krasnapolsky lived down the street; Lynn Harrell lived in the building, but I didn't know him at the time. All sorts of singers from the Met lived there. It's still a terrific building. Now when I'm in New York, I stay at the Lotos Club or the Athletic Club most of the time.

I continue to teach at the University of Houston to this day.

Chapter Seven
MUSINGS: 2004-PRESENT

There is a part of me that is dreadful: curiosity. I realize I have something wrong. People ask me questions such as "What do you do?" But I never ask them the same question. I don't consider it not knowing niceties, because it's not that I'm being rude, it just wouldn't occur to me to pry into somebody else's life. If he wants to tell me how things are going, then I am delighted to know. Jonathan gets very annoyed with me, but he's furious with me all the time, so it doesn't make any difference.

I have never spoken out about political matters. I don't understand politics and I'm not always for the good guy. But so many good guys have disappointed everybody that it's very hard to be serious about that. There are too many phony things. The first thing you do when you're elected is you think about the next election. That's all that counts. It doesn't make any difference whether it's in Europe, Australia, or anyplace. It's the same nonsense.

When Milton Katims retired from the University of Houston School of Music, they asked me, "Why don't you take over as head of the school?" I said, "I don't want to get involved with paperwork. In the first place, I'll get it all wrong, and in the second place, it's not my mentality. I'm not a good person to talk about these things." Nancy Weems does a very good job for the piano faculty. All these meetings she has to take with the scholarship committee, with the board members, with the social club members, with the people from the state legislature—I wouldn't do it. At Juilliard, the chairmanship of the piano department rotated every year to somebody else in the department, and I always skipped out on it.

New York had one of the richest mayors of the world, Mayor Bloomberg. He once said in a speech, something like, "Make no mistake, this whole city is just going to be for the super-rich, and there's nothing we can do to stop it," and he is one of the super-rich. He is an entrepreneur worth many billions of dollars, and I have the impression he was a good mayor, because there was no way you could bribe him.

I have silly nightmares, and I have discovered that my musical dreams are always very strange. They're about music most of the time, and very often, I see my fingers moving. One night, I was supposed to play, within a few days, a recital in New York and I was playing both volumes of the Brahms *Paganini*. There was one variation that had always caused me a lot of trouble. I saw it in my dreams with a different fingering, and it worked. In your dreams, you're a listener, and I've had many, many dreams involved with hearing myself playing something in a different way than I usually play it.

Fig. 65. June, 1999 (Photographer unknown.)

I also have many funny dreams. I once dreamt that I was playing in Carnegie Hall, and there was the same little man who opened the door to the stage, and he opened the door and I went out on stage and somebody gave me the violin, and there I was playing the piano at the same time.

Jonathan has a gorgeous apartment and a gorgeous chalet in the mountains. I finally, after a couple of years, went out there one weekend. You couldn't get me to live there for all the money in the

Fig. 66. In his studio at the University of Houston, c. 2014 (Photograph by Pablo Milanese.)

world. He's become a country gentleman—I don't know where he got it from. I cannot understand how anyone can sit on the side of a mountain and do nothing. It mystifies me. Maybe at birth, they give you an injection, which is the "love the mountains" injection. I think that's what they do in Switzerland.

My beloved wife, Dina, passed away in 2014, and we were preparing to celebrate seventy-three wonderful years together.

Now, I'm what they call at best a weekend practicer. I don't really feel like playing the piano after I've listened to three hours of piano playing. Not only that, but in my old age, I, who used to practice the piano till one o'clock in the morning, can do it no more. Too tired. I discovered that I'm just repeating and not doing anything. Whatever work I have a chance to do, if I do it in the morning, I can work from nine until twelve. But I sure as hell can't play from nine until twelve at night. The great periods of my life, when I learned the Brahms B-flat or the Rachmaninoff Second, are in the past.

I have to re-establish myself because I want to give a New York recital within the next two years if I'm still hanging around,

Fig. 67. *At home in Houston, May 2015.*

and I don't want it to be any of the music I'm playing currently. I must practice. I can't let myself disintegrate the way I'm been disintegrating. I will spend the summer practicing complicated etudes.

When you get older, you lose your sense of perfect pitch. You play op. 110 of Beethoven in A-flat Major, but you hear it in G. If you're used to hearing the Mozart A-Major Concerto, and suddenly, you hear it in A-flat or G, it comes as a shock to you. Lately, my sense of pitch is even less accurate—off by a fourth or fifth. Relative pitches are no problem, but when I start a recital program, it's just horrible. During the course of the concert you begin to get used to it, but it takes quite a while. It's nothing you can do in four seconds.

A few years ago, I was doing a public service, playing with the Doctors Orchestra of Houston. We had rehearsed the Chopin F-Minor several times. All was going well—it was a Sunday afternoon concert. I got out of the car and was walking to the stage door when I tripped on a piece of broken pavement, and I fell. This time, I really broke my hand. By the time I'd gotten on my feet, my hand had gotten twice the size. They were already finishing their overture, and I had to say, "I can't, I just fell, I can't play."

There is no human being that suffers more from the cold than I do. I've always been like that. I used to be able to play two sets of tennis in the summer heat and finish with ice cold hands. I'm even

Fig. 68. *Chapman University. Orange County Register (April 2, 2015).*

cold in Texas, and I didn't come to Texas to be cold.

I'm clinically depressed. They only dream about writing about depressions like I have. At times, I just lie down in bed, curl up, and that's that. They give you all sorts of pills, which are nonsense. I have this terrible back problem, sciatica. I'm practically crippled, and then I had a pneumonia attack, so I was stuck in bed for several days. Pain is fatiguing—after a while, you let go and fall apart. I'm trying out a new back pain remedy which has a small amount of morphine, and I said to my son, "You're trying to make a junkie out of me." Jonathan said, "There isn't enough there to do anything, and you'll have to see if there is any effect." I have no desire to become an addict. It's too expensive. Then you have to go to these snazzy hospitals and private places that get you off it, and then you start all over again.

I guess people have admired me, but it's small potatoes. I never thought I would have a legacy, except seven dollars and twenty-five cents or something like that. I suppose it would be nice if my records were heard, and I have always been very close to my students. Their success is part of my contribution to the world.

In 2015, I played in the Orpheus and Bacchus Festival in Bordeaux, France. There's a chateau every fifty yards. They would take everybody on a wine tour. I didn't go—it was because I couldn't stand that long. It was in a very beautiful place, and it turned out that it was more English than French, and many of the pianists who were invited I had known over the years, and so we were delighted to see one another. They had two concerts a day, a morning concert at eleven-thirty, with mostly very talented young pianists; and in the evening at seven-thirty, another piano recital, all us old timers. The English pianists I knew were all at the least close to fifty or something. They were all quite well-known and had played in the United States. Kathryn Stott made a great impression. She said, "You once threw me out of a competition." I said, "It did you good."

I was the closing concert, the distinguished event. Everybody kept saying I was a living legend. It's all right if you hear it once, but every day, I was introduced as a living legend. I finally lost my temper: "You know, there's no such thing as a living legend. If you're a legend, you're dead!" The director said, "We want you back next year." I said, "Well, you better hope that I'm not a legend."

Later in 2015, I was involved in yet another car accident, in Houston. I was blinded by the lights of an oncoming truck and wrapped my car around a light post. Several bones in my arm and hand were broken. But I went through all the agonizing physical therapy and was back on stage in January 2017 for my University of Houston Piano Festival Recital. I played the Mozart F-Major Sonata, K. 332, Beethoven's Sonata op. 110, Chopin's four impromptus, Ravel's *Valses nobles et sentimentales.* I was happy with the recital, except for the Chopin. I have more concerts coming up in Los Angeles and New York.

My only goal in life now is to continue what I'm doing, hoping that I have some impact on audiences and people in my life. I never want to retire, because that's when they put you in the ground. I can't imagine what I would do besides play the piano. I'm now planning a series of concerts for my 100th birthday—January 8, 2020—in London, New York, Geneva, Amsterdam, and The Hague. As long as I can crawl out on stage and make it to the piano, I'll be happy.

Chapter Eight
PLAYING AND TEACHING

Being on Stage

Solo recitals are more revealing of an artist's abilities than concertos. You're on stage for longer, with more variety of repertoire, and everything you do is heard. You might make a big impression with concertos, but I think artists are really judged by their recitals.

I'm sure there was a time when there were great differences in audiences throughout the world but now it's more or less the same, whether you're playing in Australia, Buenos Aires, or New York. I always played for large audiences, and they were always pretty responsive.

There is a trend that says we must humble ourselves in front of the great composers, but when we walk out on stage, we have to be the final authority. We have to feel like the greatest musician in the world. I can feel if I have the audience's attention. It's something that goes through the air, an indication of contact with the listeners, who suddenly know something different is going on. There is a spirit that takes over the performer, enters his body, and makes him a different being. If I were a religious man, I would say it was the Holy Spirit. Often, though, the audience's reaction doesn't correspond to how I feel the concert went. I have the feeling that, when you feel like you're flopping, there's a desperation that somehow transmits itself to the public. Audiences might respond even more warmly knowing that a performer is human, that he is trying to overcome something. It can bring a new intensity to the performance.

Sometimes, however, you really do play badly and suddenly hope for death, but death never comes because when you're going through that thing, you don't deserve death! That would be too easy. I don't think there is an artist alive who hasn't finished a concert wishing he could drop dead. Everyone tells you how wonderful it was, but that's nonsense. I'm always there with the best, or worst, critic in the world—myself—and I remember every wrong note I've ever played. But in retrospect, if you miss a note or don't play as cleanly as you want, the world doesn't come to an end. As for the good things, you take them for granted because they were supposed to be good, that's what you were working for.

I'm a Nervous Nelly when I perform and, like everybody, I sometimes rush. Even Horowitz and Rubinstein did that. I'm not really affected by how big or small the audience is, but I am unnerved by noisy audiences. It's scary enough to play in Carnegie Hall, and I've had problems twice there. The first time, I heard this wild whistling. It turned out there was a gentleman sitting in the hall and his hearing aid was right below the microphones. Finally, somebody had to move him to a different seat. That's not to admit that there were any seats vacant! The other time, I sat down at the piano after the intermission. Before I played a note, a voice screamed out, "Somebody stole my mink coat!" It turned out that this woman was in the wrong box. Everybody was roaring with laughter.

I had a dear friend, an English doctor who immigrated to the US. His name was Bernard Jaslowitz, and he became head of a big department at Sloan Kettering. When beta blockers first began to be used for performance anxiety, I went to him and said I had to have them. He told me that he had heard me play many times and that I didn't need them, and he wasn't going to prescribe them. Ever since then I've been against taking beta blockers and never used them.

I've never had a problem sustaining my energy in recitals, but I hate intermissions. I think most artists do. That's the worst moment of the concert, because you have to start all over again after the break. I always leave word that NO ONE is to be admitted backstage during the intermission.

I think I'm like most performers in that, if I'm not feeling well, I manage to forget about it on stage. There have been times when I've thought, "Oh I can't play tonight, I just don't feel well enough." Then you stagger out on the stage to the piano, and suddenly, everything turns out perfectly. Then you feel just as sick afterwards. One very bad winter in 1951, when the Tchaikovsky Concerto was at its apogee, I got a call saying one of the pianists was ill, and asking if I would play it with the London Students Orchestra at a benefit concert for the British Students Tuberculosis Appeal. The concert was in Albert Hall, conducted by Boyd Neel. Everybody calls me when they want a benefit concert. I said, "Yes." I was as sick as a dog with colitis, and I was on all sorts of medication. I thought, "I'll walk to the Albert Hall," which was about four miles away. I remember arriving thinking, "I think I feel better." Other times, when you feel very gung ho, everything goes wrong.

Making a Career

In the 1940s and 50s, engagements were hard to come by. We needed to make a living as performers, and we didn't have university jobs to fall back on, which would have given us performing opportunities in addition to a salary. Today, young pianists are more interested in getting degrees.

During and after the Depression, you couldn't find anyone who would risk any money to put on a series of concerts. So

Columbia Artists had Community Concerts, and the guys who worked for them received training. Each agent got a territory in the US and went to see the mayor and the banks, and he ran a week-long campaign in the town to raise money for, say, four recitals. When that campaign was over, they counted the money that they had and selected the artist to suit their budget. There was a period when Columbia Artists had 1500 towns in the US and its rival, the National Concert and Artists Corporation, had about 1200. All these towns had concert series, which was a great thing. We have nothing like that today.

It was very hard to be invited back to the same town because Columbia Artists didn't want you to think you were important. If you came back a second time, you had a reason to expect a higher fee. Once I was playing in a suburb of Chicago. The man who engaged me, Carl, was a very distinguished man of music in Chicago and became a lifelong friend. He liked my playing and insisted that I be reengaged for the next year. I was getting 250 dollars a concert and paying a 15% commission to Community Concerts, which was really Columbia Concerts. Columbia sold me to Community, and Community sold me to the town. Out of that 250 dollars, I was billed for every time they made a phone call on my account, or every time a letter was sent. I was lucky if I had twenty-five dollars left out of my 250-dollar fee. When I came back again the following year, Carl and I went out to lunch and he said,

"Your career is going so great, I'm so glad to see your fee go up."

"My fee go up?"

"Yes, that's a big hike—we paid 1100 dollars for you."

So Community Concerts sold me for $1100, which meant they were making 15 percent of my 250 dollar fee, plus 850 dollars in overages. That was more than they would have made from

Heifetz or Horowitz! They were such racketeers; the Mafia was kid stuff in comparison. There was a famous violinist, Mischa Elman, who had a very high fee. He discovered that he'd been sold someplace for more money, and he went to his congressman and raised bloody hell, and congress finally put a stop to the whole practice.

The days when managers sent somebody out to sell an artist are gone. Today a big manager like Columbia Artists will have forty or fifty pianists, and three are busy all the time. They'll have people like Martha Argerich—artists that they really don't have to work very hard for. They wait for the mail to arrive, asking for Martha.

Once, there was some hotshot young pianist who had just been signed to record the Second Prokofiev Concerto, and Jorge Bolet was about to record the same piece for RCA. I said to Harold Shaw, "I'm worried about my friend, Bolet. Do you think this will ruin…" and he really laid into me: "There's always room for two geniuses on a manager's list. Bolet can only play one place on one night, and it's a big country!"

My manager called one of the orchestras and said, "You know, Mr. Simon used to play with you sort of every two to three years, it's now five years since he…" This young boy said, "Abbey Simon, he's still alive?" You can laugh about it, but when you've been living with it for many years, the laughter sort of dies. I know the woman who is the big manager in San Francisco, and my manager Jimmy Murtha said that he had sent her my records and spoken to her on the phone. She said, "Yes, but those are old records…can he still play?" That's why Jimmy says I've got to make another record.

I never paid too much attention to managers. I was a very bad politician, and I didn't know how to schmooze. But later all my managers—Dutch, South American—they all became like family and we stayed together, but then they all did the incredible thing of dying. Maybe the guy passed away and his secretary is now running the business, and his secretary may not know very much.

Critics

My friend, Ernest Ulmer, who retired from the Manhattan School, started a new hobby, which was to go through the turn of the century reviews of famous artists. At the first concerts of Josef Hofmann when he was eight or nine, the critics said, "Well, he plays marvelously but there isn't a drop of music in him." Then, the Society for the Prevention of Cruelty to Children stepped in. There was a millionaire patron who said, "Go to Russia and study with Anton Rubinstein, and that's all you have to worry about." Hofmann came back at eighteen, and the reviews were the same. They said the same thing with Rachmaninoff: "All fingers, but no music." The one who got the best reviews in those days was Harold Bauer.

The critic's role is to inform the public as to how little he knows. Critics have been around since the dawn of time. Someone once wrote that the first time an animal bayed at the moon, the animal next to him said, "I don't think you bay so hot." Reviews can wound me, and I can think of times when I thought I played marvelously and got bad reviews. I try not to read the papers, but whenever I played in New York, the day after a concert I would come out of the elevator at the Windsor Hotel, and the concierge would say, "Mr. Simon, the New York Times is crazy!" It was a tragic moment, but then I would think, "Maybe the concierge hated my concert and the Times loved it!" Or else he would say, "What went wrong?" or "We did it again!" He was the most important critic in New York City!

Everybody has received great reviews and bad reviews. Whether you get a rave review or a terrible review, you're allowed to be happy or unhappy for twenty-four hours, but no longer. I always liked a good review better than a bad review, but in twenty-four hours I had forgotten them both.

I'll never forget playing a recital in London, and I had the Schumann Fantasie and all the *Paganini Études*. I was hot that afternoon—I couldn't miss a note if I tried. The critic of one of the papers wrote a wonderful review of the concert, saying that the frightening end of the second movement of the Schumann seemed to hold no fears. Then he editorialized: "But was it meant to sound that flawless? Don't you lose a little bit of the excitement if everything is coming out perfect?"

Critics are very rarely performers. I knew only two who were, and they were both in Cleveland. One was Arthur Loesser, the brother of the Broadway composer, and the other was Beryl Rubinstein. Both were consummate pianists and big teachers. They were about the only critics I know who dared go out on stage and perform, and they did so quite often. In general, though, reviews are not by anybody who's sweated through the learning process. They just haven't devoted their life to it. You never find Artur Rubinstein writing a review; it's always Luigi Goldberg who does it.

The critic Harold Schonberg made the excuse, "Well, there just wasn't enough in playing for me. I had to write." I never heard so much caca de vaca in my life. I'll never understand what he had against that young Russian tragic pianist, Sultanov, who played marvelously in Carnegie Hall. I received an invitation to Sultanov's reception at the Cosmopolitan Club in New York. I arrived, and behind me was Harold Schonberg. I thought he'd be bananas about Sultanov and I said, "That was really something, Harold, wasn't it?" He said, "A national disgrace."

From then on, I thought, "I don't want to go near you, you're too dangerous a person for me." It's better to be far away from critics, because getting involved with them means you have to talk a lot about yourself, and they have to talk a lot about themselves, and you can't possibly agree with them, because they're two different fields.

Years ago, you had at least a dozen critics coming to review your concert—you had something to show for it. Now fewer and fewer concerts are being reviewed. The last three or four times I played in New York, I had no review at all. You get the critic who says, "Well, there are so many things, you can't expect me to review all of them." I say, "But in five years, I expect you to review me!" Young pianists don't get reviewed, either. When they win a competition, they are given a recital in the small hall of Carnegie Hall, and this is the big moment of their lives. But there's no press.

The critic Anthony Tommasini once called me and said I was mentioned in David Helfgott's book. After our conversation, I said, "I have played many times in Boston, and you have never reviewed me. I hope one of these days, you will come to my recital." He said, "I promise to come to your next one." He did come to my next concert, and wrote a rave review.

Competitions

Competitions, along with edited recordings, have put too much emphasis on being note-perfect. We have a level of piano playing that never existed before. We've had a couple of Van Cliburn winners in the University of Houston Piano Festival. With one, you could put him in front of the piano at eight o'clock in the morning, and at eight o'clock at night, he would have been playing all day and not even come near a wrong note. You just hear perfectionist playing, but it really doesn't say anything to you. It's totally devoid of personality and human contact. We had a pianist who played as if somebody was saying to him, "Now, the next bar, you raise your arm higher, and you go above there, and you play this phrase this way." It was all learned, not inspired. There are too many competitions, and last year's winners are quickly forgotten. I've heard a number of people who, after they've run their course through the competitions and are now well into their thirties, don't sound good at all. Even that sleek polish is gone.

The prizes are enormous. In the founding years of the Van Cliburn, I think their top prize was twenty-five thousand dollars. Today it's a hundred thousand. Kids today even look down on a prize of ten thousand dollars.

I told off someone after a competition because she came to play one of the concertos in the finals and just didn't know it. I said, "What do you mean, you didn't expect to get to the finals? Why did you bother entering? You took the place for somebody else who might have been there. You proved you can't be depended on to do anything." Every time she walks out in another competition and one of those same jurors is there, all they will think is "Oh, that's that girl who couldn't play in the finals." I had that happen with one of my own students. She entered a competition, got to the finals, and didn't know the last movement of her concerto. She said, "Well, I didn't think they would ask for that."

There was somebody I know who played wonderfully in the Geneva Competition, and I thought she would go to the second round, and she didn't make it. We judges were all sitting on the dais, and all of the participants who didn't go to the second round were invited to talk to us. She talked to this Swiss juror from Geneva whom I knew quite well, and I heard her ask him, "Well, what was wrong with my performance?" and he said, "The Liszt"—and I thought the Liszt was terrific—"wasn't Japanese enough." I will let you cogitate about that.

When I was on the jury of the Van Cliburn Competition, I think I was the one who suggested they do away with required pieces. I thought having to play Baroque, Classical, Romantic, Contemporary was nonsense. Since the age limits have gone up to thirty-six or something like that, I said, "If somebody enters a contest at thirty-six, they are what they are already, they are mature players, and they should play whatever they want. This is not the time to make them play a graduation recital."

Counterpoint

When I was a child, there was never a melody I heard with which I didn't hear, in my mind, a counter-melody. That was always part of my life and still is today. It's at times distracting, a sort of a curse that I bear, and it doesn't make any difference whether it's a four-voice fugue in Bach, where I would hear a fifth voice, or a Chopin mazurka. It gives you a different approach to the piece of music. Once I was talking to a pianist—this was shortly after I played volume one of the Chopin études in Carnegie Hall. He said, "I heard voices that I've never heard anybody do in those Chopin études, it's beautiful." Chopin himself sometimes adds extra stems to suggest a counter melody.

Editions

Who cares about faithful editions? I've always been amazed at the contempt people have for the famous Schirmer von Bülow edition of the Beethoven sonatas. Von Bülow was supposed to have been a great conductor and player—and a direct descendent…Beethoven…Czerny… Liszt…von Bülow…so why wouldn't it be interesting to see what he has to say? If Liszt came to you and said, "I don't like the way you're playing op. 111. I think you should think about this," wouldn't you take it seriously? But the Schnabel edition is a travesty: a tempo every bar, all these footnotes—it's just silly, especially when he says "Many people do this thing, but I don't."

Editions are supposed to give you the inside word on interpreting a certain work, but all they're saying is, "Sam says play it this way, and Luigi says play it this way, and Gaston says play it this way." Everybody is printing his own edition. They're all supposed to be straight out of the horse's mouth, and the horse says, "Neigh."

The last music store in New York City just closed. It's a company called Frank Music, on West Fifty-Fourth Street in an office building. The Franks were famous, and I've known them since they opened in 1937. Whenever I'd come to New York, whether I was buying a piece of music or not, I'd always stop in to say hello. If there was something you wanted but couldn't find it at Patelson's, the Franks found it for you. They had everything. Sometimes, if the music was very old, Mrs. Frank would say, "I'll photocopy it for you, we just won't touch the original because it's just not going to survive the real air." My heart really went out to them. I always thought they had to be much older than I am but they can't be—NOBODY is older than I.

Exercise

For exercise, I was an avid tennis player up until about fifteen years ago. When I was at home in Geneva, I belonged to this tennis club and in Houston I belonged to one on top of a huge garage when you come off the Allen Parkway. Also, a block away from the School of Music are the university tennis courts.

The Hofmann Bench

Josef Hofmann created what I remember being called *The Ultimate in Piano Benches*. It weighs about 700 pounds because the legs are filled with lead, and after all these years, it still doesn't squeak. Steinway had it, and I don't even think they knew what it was. I foolishly told them it was Hofmann's chair and asked to buy it, whereupon they started cloistering it and would only let me use it in New York.

Hofmann's bench slants forward. I carry two little blocks to be placed under the back legs of whatever bench I use, but that is not to imitate Hofmann. Many years ago, when you bought a Steinway, it came with a little wooden chair with a short back. If you look carefully at these chairs, you will see they slant slightly forward, and I was used to this as a child. So I have continued that. If I play on a non-slanting bench, I feel as if my feet are in the air.

Hofmann also invented a piano action, and many people didn't like it. Others, like me, adored it. I never quite knew what he did that was so special, but the key came up as fast as it went down. It was much faster. Some of my earlier records were made on the old pianos with the Hofmann action in them. I don't know why Steinway never took it up, but all you ever had to do was suggest something to Steinway, and it immediately went out the other ear. They only made about half a dozen pianos with that action.

Listening

The fingers are the least important part of playing piano. It's the ears that separate an artist from a student. You hear everything just before you play it to create the sound that you want. Each pianist has a unique sound, which is why if you had Rubinstein and Horowitz playing on the same piano, they would sound like Rubinstein and Horowitz.

I never have stories or images in my mind when I perform, just the sound. Remember that most of the time the composers never intended the subtitles to their pieces; the subtitles were given by other people.

Pedaling

It's very important to practice with no pedal for the sake of clarity and hearing all the lines. I don't know why nobody interests themselves in the sostenuto pedal. When I got my first piano with a middle pedal, I was like a kid on Christmas morning. I invented a technique of turning my left foot inward to cover the *una corda* and *sostenuto* pedals simultaneously. I still like to use the middle pedal, especially since the accidents when my fingers were broken, because there are several things I can't do with my hand that I can manage to do with my foot, such as holding down notes as organ points. I'm very upset with the third pedal on the Yamaha—it's too sluggish. I don't know why it's not as fast as the Steinway.

When we have an accompaniment that consists of a low bass note and then chords above it, it's important to make it all one sound, with the chords emerging out of the pedaled bass.

Phrasing

Students indulge themselves too much in small phrases. You have to think of the long line. Most performers today tend to lavish too much on the little things to sound musical.

Saperton was very difficult about *Islamey*. He said, "First of all, what's the subtitle? Oriental Fantasy. You are playing it as a series of trials to overcome. You're not trying to master this piece, you want to conquer it. You're not enjoying the Oriental Fantasy, you just want to beat the hell out of it. That's not going to work with this piece."

You shouldn't try to go out and play a piece the same way twice. You experiment and discover new things. Rubato should be spontaneous. If you do the same rubato over and over again, it's not rubato, it's a hat.

Long notes that are suspended over the bar need to be played a bit louder, so we can continue to hear them.

Pianos

I began my career playing mostly Steinways, then became a Baldwin Artist, and am now a Yamaha Artist. I'm never bothered by the brightness of a piano. If you have any music inside of you, you can always control it. If it's dead, you can't do anything. I always prefer bright pianos, especially if they can have a long sound, not just a percussive sound that disappears immediately. Every piano company has its own conception of sound, and you can easily hear the difference. It's not that one sound is better than the others, but different pianists prefer different things. My main concern is how much color I can get. That's what I enjoy.

I've had things go wrong with the piano during a concert many times. Weather can change pianos. I remember once when I came down to Florida to play (this was in the past seven or eight years), and they told me at Yamaha that they had shipped a new piano down for me. When I came to play, it sounded like it was in Argentina. There was nothing I could do.

I had one concert on Martha's Vineyard—my wife was with

me—and we had to take a boat early in the morning. It was so cold that every time we tried to dock, the ice would push us out. When we finally landed, I went to the hall to try the piano. They told me it was the piano of James Cagney, the great movie actor. The piano sounded perfectly beautiful. Came the concert, and I was beginning with a soft, religious sort of piece. I started to play, and the keys didn't go down. I hit it much harder, and they went down, but they didn't come back up. I said timidly to the public, "Is there a piano tuner in the house?" After that, I was always afraid to meet James Cagney, because he would kill me for ruining his piano! I ended up playing the concert on an upright.

There is a man now in Pennsylvania who manufactures narrower keyboards. Ten years ago, they were over ten thousand dollars. I went down to Dallas where there was a very nice piano teacher who had one. It was fantastic. I was suddenly playing all these things that I can't play anymore. She had a case manufactured so that she could carry it with her. The only problem is that you need to have different keyboards manufactured for different sized pianos. A keyboard manufactured for a concert grand will only work in a concert grand. If you have a seven-foot piano, you need another action. Yamaha also manufactured a smaller keyboard but nobody wanted it, so they stopped.

Jonathan has a Steinway B just like me. It's a beautiful piano, there's only one thing wrong with it—it's too easy to play on. I quarrel with Jonathan all the time because he says, "Why don't you install a *Dampp Chaser* to keep your pianos in tune? You see, my piano's always in tune." I said, "Yes, your piano's always in tune because you play your little progressions and your little inventions, which are very attractive, but you don't play the way everybody else tries to play, with more *fortissimos* than anybody else in the world, and that's what knocks your piano out."

Hamburg Steinways are just as uneven as New York Steinways. There were years where everybody raved about the Hamburg, and nobody wanted to play the American, but I think it's come full circle. The last time I was in London going to Steinway was about seven years ago, and Deen was with me. She said, "NOW DON'T YOU DARE BUY ANOTHER PIANO!" because I used to be ecstatic when I was in the showroom. But the last couple times, I didn't see anything that was speaking to me.

We have two new Steinway Ds in Dudley Hall at the University of Houston. Pieces of the case have already fallen off, because people don't care what they put on the piano. On the pianos in my studio, the lids are wide open all the time so that people don't put things on them. On one of them, there's a rim on the top broken off. I can't figure out how they did it.

I prefer ivory keys, of course. For the first thirty years of my life, I played ivory. Now they're not permitted. I had a friend who was a Swedish cultural attaché who was transferred to the United States. They'd had a big Bösendorfer for many years, and it took him months, even with his diplomatic status, to get the piano into the US because of the ivory. When Hamburg switched to plastic, there was nothing you could do about it. You simply had to get used to it. Today, however, the plastic they use is vastly superior to the old kind. It feels almost as good as ivory.

I've played two Faziolis. I liked both of them. I spent an afternoon with one in Geneva when they had sent it down for the International Competition, and I found the sound wonderful but I didn't like the fact that it was a very heavy piano to play. But I played another one at a college in Memphis which was marvelous—it was perfection.

Practicing

Over-practicing is very dangerous. We all do that up to a

point. Playing for people is a different experience entirely. I tried out new pieces for friends, even if it was only one person, and most of the time, it was very bad.

Pre-concert Routine

When I was still young, I established a pre-concert routine that I continue today. On a concert day, I avoid as many people as possible. In the morning, I play from nine to twelve. Without the three hours in the morning—although I might not use all three—I can't play a concert. I eat a good lunch, then I go back to my hotel room and cry. In the old days, I would go to bed with a book and read. Today, most of the time, I watch T.V. That's it until I walk out onstage. I discovered at an early age that if you play a little piano in the artist room before the concert, the sound in the hall is too different. You're warming up with a piano that has a shorter key and a completely different action. It was painful for me to adjust to the different sound and feel of the concert piano. It took me three to five minutes to get used to the piano on the stage, and it was destructive to me. I did much better going in cold.

I'm not a believer in certain kinds of foods before I play. I'll generally have scrambled eggs, bacon, stuff like that, at lunchtime. Something that feels light, that doesn't leave me feeling bloated, because then I can't close the trousers. Everybody develops their own phobias, their own insanities. I remember seeing—I don't remember if it was right before the concert or during the intermission—Stern, Perlman, and several other people, all eating Chinese food out of containers backstage.

Recordings

The great artist always has a special quality that is easily recognizable. With the older recordings, pianists were freer and more individualistic. They took more chances. If they play five records of the "Appassionata," you'll be able to pick out which one is Horowitz or Rubinstein. That was one of the reasons I liked Van Cliburn's playing. He had a quality that was very distinctive. Today, you can't tell the difference between a dozen different interpretations of a Beethoven sonata. Everyone plays with slow tempos thinking slow is profound. Pianists play by the bar with no long lines.

Lately, things are starting to get much more inventive with repertoire because making a CD has become an easy thing. Individual artists are finding works that are not played very often, whether Baroque music, music that was finished yesterday, or even recently neglected classics.

There were many works of Chopin or Ravel that I played all the time—*Gaspard de la nuit, Miroirs, Valses nobles et sentimentales,* half a dozen Chopin waltzes or nocturnes, but I never dreamt of recording twenty-one waltzes or nineteen nocturnes of Chopin, or the complete Ravel piano music. It was difficult because it wasn't enough to learn to play the notes, you have to have the style, the color. Much of the complete Chopin was a simple matter because I had played all the Chopin études since I was a teenager, and frequently played most of the major works. I think the Chopin recordings that came out best were the études and the four scherzos. I don't know why they didn't want me to record the three Nouvelles Études—I played them often as encores.

Records have to be note perfect, but it's not possible, at least for me, to play for half an hour and not graze a wrong note. When I make a record, the first take is the best, the most spontaneous and alive. But if there are smudged notes, more takes have to be done, and the playing becomes sterile. This makes studio recordings less exciting than live performances.

Years ago, the company that recorded you had the only equipment, and they charged as much as 300 dollars an hour to edit your records, so there was just so much editing that the company would pay for. Now, we're arriving at an age where everybody knows how to edit their own records, so it's cheap and easy. I have known a number of artists who do this, which is fine with me.

I have worked with record producers who think their job is to tell you how to interpret. All the records they produce end up sounding the same. They think they know more than you do and cannot understand that you may have departed, from a color standpoint, from the printed page. In other words, it may say *piano* and you build this whole thing up to make it a *forte*, or vice versa. You have to stand up for yourself—it's your record—unless the producer has pointed out a true mistake.

When I recorded for Vox, I'd often get a remark from Joanna Nickrenz such as, "The dynamics here are totally different from what you're playing," and Marc Aubort, the engineer, would say, "Shh, shh!" I'd say, "I don't do it that way," and Joanna would say, "Well, if that's what you want." When I was recording the Chopin nocturnes, I came to play the big C-Minor, which I had played since I was a student, and there's a place in the middle with a trill. She said, "Come down, I have something to show you," and then we played the tape, and she said, "Don't you find something wrong? Listen to these bars and count." The trill was two beats short. I said, "My god, I've been doing that for fifty years." Nobody ever corrected me in my lessons or the dozens of times that pianists heard me, with two beats of the trill missing. She figured out how to extend it to the right length with splicing. How she did that, I don't know.

I entrusted all the editing, choosing takes, etc., to Joanna and

Marc, and if I didn't like the result, then we'd go through some of the takes that we didn't use. I usually liked the result, but I did find something that both Joanna and Leonard Slatkin missed in the Rachmaninoff concertos recording. The very fast one in the *Paganini* Rhapsody starts out with the solo piano part repeating, and the second time, there are some different notes on top. But on the recording, they were the same due to incorrect editing. We listened to it at half-speed to prove I was right. We had to go hunting through the old tapes to replace that passage.

Marc Aubort came over to Hamburg to do the Chopin cycle with the Hamburg Symphony. Those were the worst sessions I've ever had. They took a whole session, three hours, just to record the *tutti* to the E-Minor Concerto. I point-blank refused to come down and hear the tape when Joanna had edited it. She said,

"You've got to come down and hear it."

"I don't want to hear it, I don't want to have anything to do with it."

"You cannot reject it unless you hear it. Vox will not accept that."

I came back and it was gorgeous. I would never have thought it could be edited to sound good. Let that be a lesson to you about listening to people on records.

Marc did not do the Ravel concertos recording. It was somebody from Germany who worked for Vox. When I listened to the test pressing, I suddenly I heard a chair falling on the tape. We had a terrible time straightening it out.

Once, I saw a video of a recording session with Glenn Gould in which he had multiple microphones on the piano. I told Marc Aubort that I thought we should be recording that way. He said, "You can have as many microphones as you want. Of course, only two will be working."

Musicianship is always in a state of flux. You change from the time you approve the tape to when you receive the pressing a few weeks or months later. I never dreamt I could play as fast as some of my records. The only time I listen to my own records is when I get into a panic upon hearing somebody else's recording of a piece I've recorded. Then I become very competitive. I'll hear the record, and I will like it, and I become a nervous wreck. I suddenly think, "Is that record more beautiful than mine?" I run home and put on my record and compare it. I almost always win. I know that's childish.

It's happened several times that I'd be at someone's house talking about recordings. Suddenly, they'd say, "I have a great recording of that piece." Then they'd go and find it, and it would be mine.

In my Liszt *Don Juan* recording for Vox, the opening introduction and the first two variations sound like the greatest Liszt performance you ever heard in your life. I heard it and said, "I never knew I could play like that." But the last third, which is repeated three times, is too bloody cautious. The left hand is terribly tricky: double notes that do not stay in the same form: fourths, thirds. It's one of the few places in Liszt that I've ever found to be nasty, unpianistic. I found it a tiring piece, and I always wish you could cut out a repeat in the last part. I listened to Earl Wild's recording, which is so fast and he hits some wrong notes, but he just doesn't give a damn. He's a real artist.

I'd like to record the three Liszt Sonettos and the B-Minor sonata, and then what I've played all my life, but I've already recorded twice: the *Paganini-Liszt Études*. But I don't think I could make a third record of that, and I don't think I can do the *Transcendentals* any more although I did play all twelve of them many years ago. Then, I thought maybe I would play a Clementi sonata, the Liszt Sonata, and then, if I can record them live, all the Rachmaninoff transcriptions that I did. If I want to play the

Liszt Sonata, which I've played so many times in my life, I have to spend a few weeks seeing if I can still play it. The main problem is that I have difficulty stretching an octave now.

Repertoire

For me, pieces are always fresh, and I've never thought about how to keep them that way. Whenever I heard something I didn't know that I liked, I always ran to the store the next morning and started learning it. But it was a different era. There have been pieces that I haven't played for years, but that's because I didn't like them. There is some message that has to come to you by way of the performance, or else there's no point to it. I'm sick and tired of people who say, "Well, you have to grow with it." I don't know how you grow with something you really don't care for very much. A piece of music has to move me from the beginning.

I think that Classical, Romantic, Modern are artificial labels. The great composers are all romantics.

Bach

I played the C-Minor Partita, the B-flat, and the E-Minor, and several Busoni transcriptions. Once, as a very young fellow, I read a romantic biography of Liszt which said that he started every day with a prelude and fugue. I thought that was a very romantic idea. I was home in New York during the summer, and so every day I sat down and learned a prelude and fugue. It doesn't mean that I could play them in Carnegie Hall or anything, but I think that was a valuable experience for me and for everybody that I eventually taught.

Bartók

I like the Sonata for 2 Pianos and Percussion, but the dirtiest thing you can say to me is the second movement of the Bartók Piano Sonata. That slow movement is the most miserable-sounding piece that there is—it seems endless. I had to listen to that thirty times—it was an imposed piece in one of the competitions I judged. I can't understand the insanity about all of these pieces which do not give pleasure. Then, there's the eternal answer, "Who said they have to give you pleasure?" I say, "Well, I'm a hedonist, I'm interested only in pleasure!"

Beethoven

I played the op. 33 Bagatelles all the time. It never occurred to me that I would learn all thirty-two sonatas of Beethoven, but I've performed them all, although never in a series. The stretched-out Alberti basses in op. 90 are now impossible for me to play. I heard Gilels open one of his recitals beautifully with op. 101, which I played several times, but I was never moved by that sonata. I'm not in love with the fugue. I much prefer playing the "Hammerklavier" fugue. I've played the "Hammerklavier" three times in my life, with ten years in between each time. There are parts of the slow movement I didn't enjoy because I feel that the modulations are a little too primitive.

If there ever was an easy concerto to play and conduct at the same time, it's the "Emperor." If you can play the E-flat major arpeggio and scale, you can play the "Emperor" Concerto. It's a square piece. It's certainly uninventive Beethoven, not in the same class as the other four. If it didn't have this romantic story of Beethoven and Napoleon, it would never have been considered a serious piece. It's the Beethoven concerto I like the least, and it's the one I've played the most. The only Beethoven work for piano and orchestra I have never played is the Triple Concerto.

Brahms

I don't love Brahms. I don't believe a word that's been written or said about Brahms and his wonderful pianism. A natural pianist would never write the way he wrote. His music is so awkward, and I'm too old to play awkward. Nobody in his right mind writes a passage like the descending broken ninths from the Second Piano Concerto. The only thing I've ever liked in Brahms was the *Paganini Variations*. When I recorded them the last time, for Vox, that's probably the better version. I did an upward octave glissando at the end of the octave variation instead of jumping octaves. If I played the Brahms *Handel Variations* again I might change the order of some of them, for example, number fourteen, the one with the trill and the sixths, and then the one right after. I hate the two of those together. They're too square, too German, and whatever charm they have, they have by themselves, but not one after the other. I recorded many of the Brahms late solo pieces and the op. 10 Ballades.

The Brahms chamber music is more difficult than anything he wrote for solo piano. I have played, but never enjoyed, the viola sonatas. About the closest I came to enjoying the string sonatas was the D-Minor Violin Sonata. I played the Horn Trio once at a festival in Canada with the famous horn player from England, Dennis Brain. I found it very difficult. I played the Clarinet Trio once too, but I never enjoyed it. I've played the Brahms F-Minor Quintet many times.

Chopin

Nobody's going to play the Étude in thirds, or op. 10, no. 2, unless they know they can play it marvelously. It's kind of stupid to play it otherwise. You can play all the others instead.

In pieces like the Fourth Ballade, students think too much in small phrases. They indulge themselves and things get bogged down. If you practice in small segments, which everybody may do from time to time in a passage that's bugging you, in the final analysis you have to put the whole thing together.

Chopin's playing must have been very flexible. Apparently, Meyerbeer heard him playing a mazurka and said, "I didn't know mazurkas were in 4/4." Chopin was furious, as the story goes.

Chopin's shorter works for piano and orchestra don't get performed because they're too short. You really have to play them with another piece. The only one I knew before I recorded them was the *Andante Spianato and Polonaise*, which I had played as a solo piece. I didn't know the *Krakowiak*, and I didn't know the *Variations on Là ci darem la mano*, which is a fabulous piece. Peculiarly, the shorter pieces are much more difficult than the concertos. It's rare, at least to me, that Chopin writes anything that's awkward, but the last two variations on *Là ci darem la mano* are peculiarly un-Chopinesque. The end of the *Krakowiak* is the same. The other variation set—the *Variations Brillantes*—is the most adventurous piece imaginable and shows a side of Chopin that we've never seen before or since. That was one of his youngest pieces. I keep saying I'll have to program it as a solo piece. There's one variation that is just brutal. Nothing but single notes, all a tenth or two octaves apart, etc. But the Chopin piano was much easier to play. The action didn't go down as deep.

I once sat down ready to play the Chopin E-Minor, and the orchestra started playing the tutti from the Chopin F-Minor. It wasn't a problem—it was at a time when I was playing both of them very often, I had been recording them. It wasn't as if I performed some sort of miracle.

Copland
I've heard the Copland Variations hundreds of times. I've had

students who've brought it to me because they've had to learn something contemporary. I learned them, too—I had to play them in South America.

Gershwin

The Gershwin Concerto in F I've played many times. I remember playing it against my will with the Lamoureux Orchestra in Paris in the famous hall, it had to be at least three or four thousand seats. I said, "Alright, I'll play it, but if it goes well, I want to know that I can play whatever I want with this orchestra." It was a huge success. I never heard from them again.

Godowsky

I have played the original Albéniz *Triana*—it's much better than the Godowsky transcription. But I was brought up with the Godowsky, I knew it much before. If I was ever to play it again, I would certainly play the original.

Grieg

I played the Grieg Concerto a good number of times, in Norway, Spain, South America. I was very nervous playing it in Oslo, which is Grieg's home town. The Grainger edition is the best one to use. It's the only one I ever knew, I think it's a marvelous edition. I read somewhere that Rachmaninoff thought the Grieg Concerto was the best concerto ever written. I have the feeling that the First Rachmaninoff Concerto is modeled after it.

Liszt

When I played "Feux Follets," it never occurred to me that it was supposed to go as fast as it's played today. At the University of Houston auditions, we had this little girl who should have been made to play it with her hands behind her back, because it wasn't hard enough for her.

The first time I learned the *Don Juan Fantasy*, I learned it for one reason—because everybody said it was impossible. I think the first time I ever performed it was at Indiana University in 1973. There's a very annoying scale passage in two hands where there are different rhythms—many more notes in one hand. In passages like that, slow practice is useless. The best thing for me is to find a place in the middle of both hands, where they both come together on one note. I remember going crazy practicing that, and one night, Bolet stopped off at my studio. I said, "This is impossible!" He said, "Oh, that's the easiest thing in the world," but when he finally recorded it, it doesn't come out too well. At the time, there was only one recording—Shura Cherkassky on 78s. It had masses of wrong notes and missed passages, but it was wonderful. The BBC asked me to record it, and I was petrified because I was afraid that this would mean I would lose their friendship. I never had a Bar Mitzvah, but the closest thing to it was that day. Suddenly I said, "Get out of the panic. Out of this enormous piece, there are maybe six or eight bars that are unplayable. What happens if you miss those passages? The world doesn't come to an end." It changed my life.

I rarely played the Liszt A-Major Concerto, but the E-flat I played many times. I think the Liszt E-flat is a much more difficult piece than the Tchaikovsky Concerto. What always makes me nervous, especially in the A-Major, is the changes of tempo. But they're beautiful concertos. I never got around to playing *Totentanz*, although I started to learn it many times. It's a wonderful piece.

I think the Liszt Sonata is the greatest piece of the nineteenth century.

Mozart

Of the Mozart concertos, I've played the D-Minor, A-Major (K. 488), C-Major (K. 467), and the C-Minor. I also played the other A-Major (K. 414) with the Toronto Chamber Orchestra. Mozart concertos and solo sonatas are the hardest things to play. It's easy to rush in the Mozart concertos because you're so naked. You want to get off the stage. You can practice a Mozart sonata or concerto too much. At least for me, they suddenly become finger exercises, and you play a lot of notes meaninglessly. I recently played, very badly, the Mozart A-Major Piano Sonata. Because I hadn't played it in many years, I was practicing it like it was a Liszt transcription, and it came out sounding like that. I was very upset. The D-Major Sonata, the last one, is particularly difficult.

Prokofiev

I have never played any of the Prokofiev concertos. There were three pieces I wanted to learn but never had a chance: the Strauss *Burleske*, the Falla *Nights in the Gardens of Spain*, and the Prokofiev Third Concerto. I was too busy learning the repertoire for all these recording contracts. I have played the Prokofiev Second, Third, and Seventh Sonatas.

Rachmaninoff

The first Rachmaninoff concerto I learned was the *Paganini Variations*. Then the Second Concerto, then the Third, then the First and the Fourth. Learning One and Four was a big job—they're complicated pieces. They used to say that Rachmaninoff spent more time cutting his music than composing it. In the Third Concerto, I played it exactly how it's written, except there are six or eight bars that I cut out in the third movement. It's a very slow, lyrical passage—you could learn it in five minutes. Horowitz made those cuts, too. A lot of them were made because of time, I think, when they were recorded on 78s.

I played the *Corelli Variations* at the University of Houston. I don't know if I can play them anymore, especially that one variation with the octaves. I was thinking about playing them next season. I love the piece.

They love to dismantle Rachmaninoff, but I would say it's because of Rachmaninoff that Prokofiev became so popular. Prokofiev tried desperately to get away from the nineteenth century but he never made it, and there's still a great deal of lyricism in everything Prokofiev wrote. I really do believe the Third Prokofiev Concerto became the piece that it is because Rachmaninoff wrote so much music. A critic, I think it was Bernie Holland in the New York Times, wrote an article about somebody playing one of the Rachmaninoff concertos. He couldn't understand why people loved this music, and on and on, and then he finished his article by saying, "He will probably occupy a place with many of the second-rank composers like Saint-Saëns." As if Saint-Saëns is a second-rate composer!

Ravel

I played the "Alborada del gracioso" as a student at Curtis. After my first Ravel recording, Vox said, "Now this, and this, and this." Before that, I never knew there was a solo piano version of *La Valse*. Quite honestly, I never had the desire to learn every piece Ravel wrote.

You know Chopin and Liszt were great pianists because no matter how difficult it is, it's possible. But Ravel was a terrible player, he didn't like the piano, and much of his music is very awkward. For example, the Sonatine. The hands are too close together. It has to be rewritten, but I never got around to doing it. I rewrote the Toccata completely the day I decided to learn it, redistributing the notes between the hands. *Gaspard* is less awkward—it fits the hand, but you have to practice it a lot.

I hated the Ravel Left-Hand Concerto from the day I started to learn it. It doesn't excite me at all. It's a concerto—it sounds stupid of me to say—where I have to count, for example before each entry of the rapid descending block chords. I was never sure, instinctively, whether I was right. I'm just not interested in that distraction. Only a French composer could write a piece like that. I love the G-Major, played it hundreds of times. That's a glorious piece of music. When I recorded it for Vox, I had performed it the night before with the Luxembourg Orchestra.

Scarlatti

There are seven or eight sonatas that I've played many times.

Schumann

In many cases with Schumann, you know that he was not a great pianist. I've played the *Symphonic Études* many times. I hate them, for a very stupid reason—I've never been able to play the theme the way I want to. I have to roll too many chords. I've never played *Davidsbündler,* but I've taught it many times. I love it—it's very very beautiful—but there are a few pieces in the set that I don't like. The trouble with Schumann is that all his music sounds the same. I love the *Kreisleriana,* the *Carnaval,* the G-Minor Sonata, the *"Abegg" Variations*—these works I have played many, many times. I think Schumann was the most inventive composer that ever existed. You never get tired of playing Schumann.

Shostakovich

I loved early Shostakovich. I played the early set of preludes many many years ago. But the twenty-four Preludes and Fugues are more or less an intellectual challenge for Shostakovich.

Tchaikovsky

It's very hard to understand why Anton Rubinstein considered the Tchaikovsky First Concerto to be unplayable, because with the exception of forty-five seconds of octaves, it's a very easy concerto. Actually, the octave passages are not that hard either. The crazy, fast stuff in the second movement is all under the fingers, you just have to practice that. It's hardly a spectacular feat.

Gary Graffman used to play the Second Concerto a lot and he's recorded all three of them, and Shura Cherkassky has recorded the second, too. I wasn't particularly interested in the other two Tchaikovsky concertos, and you don't hear them played very often. Certainly, no one has ever asked me to play them.

Chamber Music

Chamber music is something I do too occasionally, usually with people I don't know. You arrive in the evening, you have a rehearsal, and then you play a concert the next day, and so I don't enjoy it for that reason. I've played the Brahms and Schumann Quintets, and the one I dislike the most, the Dvořák, at the University of Houston. Once, I played the Tchaikovsky Trio, which is very very long.

I've played with some of the best quartets, for example the Tokyo and the Orford. Once, I was going to Dartmouth College to play with the Concord Quartet, and I missed my plane connection in Albany, so I got a taxi to take me up there, maybe seventy-five miles. We had one rehearsal at six o'clock, then we played at eight o'clock, and that was the whole thing. I didn't enjoy it, although the quartet was marvelous. I much prefer playing with orchestra because I like the sounds.

I've played most of the piano quintets because in Bloomington we had the Berkshire String Quartet in residence. I played with them during the winter, and then in the summertime I would play chamber music concerts at a famous festival called Music Mountain, upstate in Connecticut. It still exists. I played the Elgar Quintet, the Franck, the Trout, and both versions of the Beethoven woodwind quintet, including the one with strings.

I play chamber music essentially from memory, even though I have the score in front of me. Because I'm a poor reader, I am very nervous every time I play with music. But in chamber music, you're not supposed to have it memorized. You're supposed to be delving deep into the meaning of the music. Plus, when the others are playing with the score, it would be non-collegial to play from memory. What would it be like for Anne-Sophie Mutter to come out and play with music and her pianist without?

Concertos

When I was growing up, the major orchestras had shorter seasons, yet they had much more variety in their programs. Now with longer seasons, you'd think there would be more demand for unusual works, but it isn't so. It takes many years for a new work to sneak in as a standard of the repertoire, like the Prokofiev Third, and more recently, the Second.

When you teach a student to play a concerto, you have to make them understand that they're the soloist, and it's very hard to learn to lead, instead of follow. The soloist should be able to indicate, just as the conductor has to, what his musical intentions are. It's a very complicated thing to do. As a soloist, you can't try to be too consistent just for the sake of ensemble. You're never going to do things the same way twice, and there has to be room for spontaneity. When you're playing a concerto, you have to have a private rehearsal with the conductor. I don't care how many times he's conducted the concerto, and how many times you've played it, it will save you both lots of time and problems. The best concerto conductors don't necessarily have the best conducting technique, but are gifted as accompanists. These are very hard to find. The two best ones were Mitropoulos and Sargent.

Three quarters of my orchestral repertoire was learned overnight. I never said no, I always said, "Sure, I'll play it tomorrow," and I could learn works very quickly. My repertoire is large because it was forced on me. But it's still not to be compared with the repertoire of people like Barenboim, Ashkenazy, or Pollini.

Sense of humor

I think artists have to develop a sense of humor to be able to live with the rebukes and the nasty moments, and everything else. I don't think it's a sense of humor in my case, it's just a self-defense mechanism. I'm not consciously funny.

Students

You should sell each student. Then you get a good price for each one, and you don't have to bother with them anymore. That's the logical thing to do. You raise them, you feed them, and then you sell them.

Students should not listen to other performances of the work they're learning at the beginning. That lets their imagination get lazy, and they won't discover as many new things in the work. They have to develop their own feelings first. Afterwards, they can listen to the ideas of other people.

I had the most fabulous class of ten or twelve students at Indiana. One, born in Hong Kong and raised at Juilliard, was fantastic. Pianistically, he was in the same class as Freddy Chiu, and he won the Rachmaninoff *Paganini* competition in the school. All you had to do was say something to him, and it became set in stone. There's another student who retired just this year—Joe Matthews. He is one of the nicest people under the sun and one of the most gifted.

Alice Rybak was very talented. Charles Fugo—genius. He did his masters and doctorate at IU. One of my favorite-of-all-time people, and so self-effacing. I got so sick and tired of his self-effacement! I remember when he came for his first lesson and I said, "Give me an idea of your repertoire—what you've played and what you're interested in doing," and he said, "Well, I've never played any Ravel, could I learn some?" I said, "Alright, learn the *Miroirs.*" The following week he came in with the *Miroirs*—all five of them, memorized. The first job interview he went for was in Columbia, South Carolina. He's still there.

I had one student this year who, before juries, was operating on, "Oh, well they'll never ask for that movement of that sonata," and that was all they were interested in. That lack of preparation is something I don't understand.

The University of Houston gets busier and busier. I see a good number of technically very well-equipped pianists. They come from everyplace, especially universities that don't give graduate degrees. There's a big crop from Oberlin, and we get them from China, Korea, Indiana, you name it. They play the *Rigoletto Fantasy,* which was a big trial piece when I was very young, without a drop of perspiration. We had a little Asian student audition who played the "Alborada" at the tempo that Ravel marked. It was so fast—you can hear it in the orchestra that way, but not on the piano. But I haven't heard anybody here, or in New York, or in Geneva, or anyplace, that you can say is an artist, or shows signs of becoming an artist.

Years ago, when we had the great influx of Asian girls, this little delicate Asian flower would come in for a lesson all dressed up as if she was going to a ball, and if she played a wrong note, she would make a gasping sound. As they became more and more Americanized, you heard them say, "Oh shit!" You could practically figure out how many months they'd been in the country by the change in language.

There was this seventeen-year-old Russian girl. She was on tour with the Russian Symphony Orchestra on the west coast, and she came all the way to Houston to see me and play for me. Why she picked me, I don't know—perhaps because I knew some of the great people in the Moscow Conservatory. She was absolutely unbelievable and spoke English very well. I had the whole school faculty come up and listen to her in my studio, and her repertoire was enormous. There was hardly anything we asked her about that she didn't play. I said,

"Well, do you play the first prelude and fugue?"

"Yes."

"Would you play that for us?"

You never heard it played so beautifully. She played "Feux Follets" with her hands behind her back and played a wonderful "Appassionata." I said to her,

"You don't get nervous when you play?"

"I am a nervous wreck."

"You don't seem that way."

"You don't understand. I'm not in the Moscow Conservatory. I'm in the Moscow High School of Music. I've got final exams in three weeks, and I have no business not being at home because without passing those final exams, I cannot get into any conservatory." Then I went into the office and spoke to the director about a big scholarship, and he said, "We can give her in-state fees." I said, "You don't understand, she's got to emigrate here, she's got to bring her mother, she needs to eat, she needs money to live. We should be fighting for her because this is, I would predict, a first-prize winner in the Van Cliburn." That's what Wilfred Bain would have done.

When I have a piano class, I always say, "This is the place where you can play badly. It's better in here than out in the real world." When somebody has played, and I ask the students, "What did you think of that?" they come back with, "Oh, it was better than last week," or, "It sounds ok." I finally lost my temper and I said, "You know, let's say there are two hundred people applying for a job, and three are picked for a call-back. It's not unusual to expect somebody to say, 'Would you give a lesson to one of our students?'" But they can't come up with anything constructive. All they're interested in is playing the right notes.

It's very hard to understand students today—the lack of respect, the lack of purpose in their lives. They come into lessons in underwear shirts. I try to make them understand the world doesn't run like that. I've had students decide they're not going to play any of the ornaments. I had a student here once call me saying he couldn't get to the lesson because he locked himself in the car!

I said to a student once,

"Where do you practice? I never see you in the practice rooms, and you don't seem to take part with the others."

"Oh, well, I never practice here."

"Where do you practice?"

"Oh, I have a townhouse and a D Steinway."

He was giving a junior recital and his mother finally came. She stormed into the hall before the concert and said,

"That's not a good place to put the piano!"

"But that's where we always put the piano. If you look hard enough, you'll even see some nails in the floor to show you…"

"Well that won't do for this," and she took out a video camera, "because I have to photograph this."

I gave a masterclass at the Royal Academy in London. All was going very well, and then I got who was considered the hottest talent in the school. Very arrogant. He sat down to play the Chopin Second Scherzo. I said, "Why don't you, just for my edification, play as it's written?" He said, "That's what I'm doing," and went again. I said, "Can't you play that in time? Then he said it. "I'm afraid you don't understand." That's the worst thing anybody can say to me. I said, "How you play it after you can play it properly is your own affair. When you play for me in a masterclass you play like it says on the printed page." Afterwards, his teacher came up to me and said, "I hope you've done it, I've been unsuccessful."

My student Andrew Cooperstock's first teaching job was in the sort of town where there was the university at one end of the street, and the bank at the other end. He was probably the only Jewish person in the entire city. They were crazy about him and gave him a New York recital. They were heartbroken when he left. But I used to say that the first thing you do when you get your first job is look for another one.

Philip Thomson—there was never anybody like him. Horowitz would have had a stroke if he heard Philip. I heard him in the Shawnigan Festival in Canada, on Victoria Island, and I said, "Come to Juilliard." He knew very little at the time. He would say, "I've discovered the most fantastic piece, I don't know if you've ever heard of it. It's a transcription of the Strauss *Blue Danube.*" One of the best things I ever heard him play was the *Wanderer* Fantasy, and I never heard anybody play the last movement of the Prokofiev Seventh Sonata the way he did, at a tremendous tempo. Everybody has a tendency to slow down for the last three pages, but he went straight through, totally accurate. He was always flawless. I brought him down to the University of

Houston for a recital on the Lack series. He played the "Wald-stein" Sonata in three minutes. It was just too fast. He's a very nice, intelligent, and musical fellow, and a world-class table tennis and chess player.

Karen Shaw and I speak quite frequently, two or three times a month. I knew her mother, and I know her sister very well. She and her sister have a very big music school in Connecticut which was started by their mother.

Teachers

The great teacher is one that doesn't take weak students. If you didn't play marvelously well, you didn't study with Adele Marcus. Everybody says, "Oh, she created Byron Janis." Nonsense. Byron Janis was already an enormously talented fellow. If ever there was a walking hemorrhoid, it was Adele. During my first audition period as a faculty member at Juilliard, one girl came in and played very beautifully, and Marty Canin, who is the most unmalicious person under the sun, leaned over and said, "Watch Adele go to the toilet." I looked at him as if he was crazy. As soon as the girl stopped, Adele said, "Oh, I've got to go to the ladies' room, give me two minutes."

I heard about Lang Lang before he came to the US. He was making a big stir in Germany. I'm not saying that Gary Graffman didn't have an influence on him. He was probably a good influence and got him to think about something other than all the crap he was doing onstage. He has certainly improved at least 5000 percent. The last couple times I heard him, he played very beautifully.

The French, and especially the Italians, are now beginning to produce some good pianists, and it's because all their conservatories have Russian teachers. The French don't play in any way like they used to, with a glass of water on their hand, and I attribute it to the Russians.

Stay away from any teacher that has a method because you're going to do it whether it's right for you or not. You try to play in a way which is not natural to you. Every hand is different, every arm is different. Dorothy Taubman—that's the kiss of death. I never found anyone who played marvelously because they studied with Madame Taubman.

You can't immediately decide what to do with a student. It takes time to see what they can do, and adjust your teaching to their abilities. You assign some music to him, you see if he's fast, slow, if he has any instincts, and after a few weeks you decide how to teach this child. I don't believe you can work miracles in the first lesson.

I'm totally against, especially for the talented person, the theoretical teacher who can explain everything to you, but can't do it. There are masses of them. I'm suspicious of people who suddenly become the hot teachers to study with, and nobody's ever seen them walk out on a stage. There comes a time in a talented student's life when he must come in contact with people who can perform well—and sometimes even badly. You cannot teach these gigantic, complicated works unless you know what it is to play them and even to fail with them. You cannot teach *Gaspard de la Nuit* unless you've come into physical, mortal combat with it. I certainly don't expect everyone to know everything written for the piano, but there have been many difficult pieces that I never had any desire to learn, but suddenly, a student said he was bringing it to a lesson and I had to learn it. I was teaching in Bloomington and one May a student said, "Mr. Simon, you'll be very happy to know I'm going to spend the summer learning the 'Hammerklavier,'" and my immediate thought was, "Holy moly." So I came home to Geneva and said to myself, "Well, you can't

get involved with the 'Hammerklavier' without knowing how to play it, without coming to grips with all of the difficulties."

I was giving a masterclass in Oklahoma City or Kansas City, and someone came up to play a Bartók piece I had never heard of. I said, "I must tell you the truth, I don't play this piece at all," and he played for about ten minutes,

Fig. 69. *Earl Wild, Jorge Bolet, Abbey Simon at the Baldwin Piano (Photograph and copyright by Lida Moser.)*

and then I said, "Stop. You don't know this piece either. Why don't we learn it together bar by bar?" That's what we did, and I got a standing ovation.

I know Josef Hofmann's book very well. It's a collection of articles that were serialized in *Ladies Home Journal*. He didn't know what he was talking about. He has a sentence: *The talented young pianist should never go to a bad concert.* How do you know it's going to be a bad concert?!

Technicians

They are very possessive of their profession, they're very diffi-

cult, and there are too many bad ones. You have to be very diplomatic because they don't like anybody talking about their field.
Now you've got these technicians who tune entirely by vibrations
on a meter, and you can't tune that way. If you ever see one of
these people, run. My attitude has always been: "I play them,
you fix them." I hate all of these crazy pianists who tinker with
the piano. When Paul Badura-Skoda has been there, the piano
has lost all its brilliance. Another one who always monkeyed with
pianos was Anton Kuerti, and you can hear it in his records. The
technician we have in Houston now is a real master.

With Baldwin, I had a wonderful technician who traveled
every place with me. Then the damn fool went and married a
girl and moved to Spain, and has never been seen since. I was
with Baldwin until it went out of business. The fact that they
went out of business is blamed on me, Jorge Bolet, and Earl
Wild, because we cost them so much money in technicians who
traveled with us. There was no Baldwin in Europe and so far as I
know, the only time they ever sent a piano overseas was towards
the last years of their existence, when they did it for Jorge Bolet.
I think they even shipped a piano to Japan for him. My dear,
dear friend, Jack Roman, was the artist director and a marvelous
person, and a very good pianist. He had a master's from Juilliard, and the wonderful thing about him was he could say, "No,
I can't do that." He didn't give you any nonsense. He would let
me play the Steinway piano in Europe, because Baldwin was not
operating there. An overwhelming number of people, especially
English, shipped the piano they had picked out in Hamburg to
Steinway's in London. They had the nicest man and the greatest
piano technician imaginable, Bob Glazebrook, and his brother.
When he did a piano, it was really quite extraordinary. I don't
know how true it is, but he told me he started as a kid being a
wiper in the Steinway store, then he became a technician. He

trained everyone underneath him at Steinway's, so they were all wonderful. He would let me practice at Steinway's, and when he was finally forced into retirement, they got somebody else who was very rude—he practically picked me up and threw me out of the store. Maybe it had something to do with the fact that I was playing Baldwins.

Technique

I can't play with crossed hands. Once, I was practicing the "Pathétique" Sonata at home very seriously for perhaps twenty minutes, trying to be accurate, and I suddenly threw up. Most of the cross-handed pieces I've played, I've rewritten. The first time I did it, Saperton was astonished and furious with me.

With repeated notes, it depends on the kind of *staccato* you need. If it's fast and *pp*, then I think of pulling the fingertips in. If it's *forte* you can't do it that way. If there's a passage that is written *ff*, you have to articulate it.

Hofmann said "Get your finger in the center of the key. Don't graze the sides of the keys." I try to do that when I practice. It can be unnatural because you have to lift up the other fingers to see. A good solution is to find a piano with a shiny fallboard, and watch the reflection of your fingers there.

The reason I use the music now for solo playing is because of the condition of my hands, and I've had to rearrange many fingerings. My hands suddenly cramp. For example, there are many things in *Valses nobles et sentimentales*, which I've played 4000 times, that I have to do now that I've never done. The score is just there so that I remember what I decided to change and don't revert to the old way. You'll see a page with an arrow to warn me that I'm coming to a difficult passage where I've changed my feelings about it. But there are just too many things to think about.

Travel

Jet travel has made it possible to play hundreds of times a year. A concert artist can't be a delicate person when it comes to the rigors of travel—the jet lag, the climate changes, the change in food. I envy Paderewski, who had his own private railroad car, with his own piano and food. It was leisurely. On my tours, I usually just see the hotel and the path to the concert hall. When the plane takes off, I always wish that I could have spent another day in the city as a tourist, without the pressure of a concert.

Chapter Nine
OTHER PIANISTS

Pianists are very short or very tall—nothing in between! There are so many pianists, they are flopping out of the trees, but now with the death of Horowitz and Rubinstein, we have no idols, no household names. I've heard masses of boring pianists. If you had an audiometer in front of their piano, the needle wouldn't budge. There's no great color, no great emotional climaxes. There is absolutely nobody that you can hear and say, "He really tears my heart out, or my brain out," and leaves you with an indelible impression other than basic boredom. Piano playing has become very square. Hofmann could bend the rhythm so that you didn't even know he was doing it. There isn't anyone like that now, except maybe Martha Argerich.

There was this Israeli pianist I knew in New York who lived right around the corner from me. One day I ran into him on the street, and he said "I'm crazy about your playing, you're the one pianist I admire and I want your opinions about everything. Could I come over and play for you?" So I said, "Sure, let's go." He played the César Franck Prélude, Chorale and Fugue. Horrendous. I didn't know what to say. So I said, "Well, you know, this is the way I do it." I sat down and played, and he said, "That's why I'm crazy about your playing, because you sound just like me!"

Martha Argerich

I have many of her records, and by and large, I love her playing. It's especially beautiful in the reflective parts of Schumann. The slow ones are so beautifully played, and I don't understand how she gets such a marvelous recorded sound, which nobody else who records for the same company has. I've heard her play the Prokofiev Third Concerto several times now. Charles Dutoit is a very skillful conductor, but even he has difficulty keeping up with her.

Simon Barere

I knew Simon Barere very well. He used to come over regularly. He was a very sweet and simple man. He was a remarkable pianist, but he had a tragic life. Everything Horowitz did turned to gold, everything Barere did turned to hell. The sad thing was how he died: during a performance of the Grieg Concerto with the Philadelphia Orchestra.

Harold Bauer

When he was young, if you read the reviews, he was a much bigger musical personality and star than either Hofmann or Rachmaninoff. He did everything—he played chamber music with Thibaud and Casals, he accompanied singers, he played recitals in Carnegie Hall, he played with orchestras all over the country. He was a fantastic musician, but he did not have the prodigious dexterity that Hofmann or Rachmaninoff had, so we, as young pianists, did not take him too seriously. Only later, as an adult playing for him, did I appreciate how astute he was as a teacher. He simplified his Schirmer editions with single notes in difficult passages. You should see what he does with the last movement of the Brahms F-Minor Sonata or the Schumann Fantasie.

Abram Chasins

Abram was one of Hofmann's great students. He was a very nice man, and I heard him play in Carnegie Hall when I was very young—wonderfully, I thought. But I think somehow or other he didn't really have the guts to go for the big career as a performer. He wrote some light pieces, one of which, *Rush Hour in Hong Kong*, became famous. I once said something negative about Godowsky to him, and he practically threw me out of the house: "How dare you talk that way about Popsy?!"

Shura Cherkassky

He was a remarkable pianist and a very sweet man, someone I knew from childhood on. When he played a recital at Curtis, the whole school turned out. I think it was Milton Katims who told me he once went to the airport to pick up Shura Cherkassky, and Shura said something like, "I have to stop in your house to play something for twenty-six minutes." They stopped off at his house, and Shura went in, and twenty-six minutes later he came out.

Van Cliburn

What most people don't know is that before he went to Moscow, Van had won everything there was to win in the United States. He had won the Leventritt and the Michaels Competition in Chicago, and he had played with all of the orchestras—Chicago, Pittsburgh, New York—with great success. Yet, he was dropped by his manager, Columbia. He was convinced he would have to go back to Texas and put a sign on his door: *Van Cliburn: Piano Lessons.* When he won in Moscow, he already had an engagement at Grant Park for 250 dollars, and the office said, "You can't play for that low an amount, that's ridiculous," and he said, "No, that was the only engagement I had for the whole year."

God knows I adored Van, was a good friend of his, and loved the way he played, but who ever heard of a pianist having a ticker tape parade up Broadway? Everybody acted as if he had

Fig. 70. *At Indiana University: Simon, Sidney Foster, Alfonso Montecino, Van Cliburn, Josef Battista. Herald-Telephone, Bloomington, Indiana (April 1964.)*

won the war. The only one I can remember who had anything like that was Lindbergh. Cliburn himself was very modest about it, but if anyone ever deserved it, it was he. I was already living in Geneva when Van won the Tchaikovsky. He came through Geneva to play, and our friend Robert Weisz was asked to accompany him around, because Van didn't speak French. His first performances in Geneva were remarkable.

When he started playing all these concerts at huge fees, he changed the whole fee structure of the concert world. Nobody was getting twenty thousand dollars for an engagement. When we were at Van Cliburn's house, I counted, on one floor, eleven Steinway Ds. Every time he found a piano he liked, he bought it.

I've heard him play many times and on many records. There used to be this radio program from Chicago with record critics, and you could hear it anyplace, late at night. They played several records of the same piece without identifying the performers, and the analysis and voting were at the end of the program. The one that was the most beautiful 99 percent of the time was Van's. The wonderful thing about his playing was that you could always recognize it. It was Van Cliburn.

One time, I was playing with orchestra in Carnegie Hall, and he came backstage. His hand was so enormous, it was like shaking hands with a baseball glove. I felt like I was three months old.

I think his career deteriorated because he couldn't stand the constant scrutiny of the critics. They were either ecstatic or nasty. I think he was mistreated because he played *The Star-Spangled Banner* at the openings of his concerts, and he was a deeply religious man who very often insisted on prayer before he performed.

Sidney Foster

He was one of the most talented people I ever met, and he was very gifted as a composer. He reminded me very much of myself. When he won the Leventritt, he played the first movement of the Brahms B-flat, which he had just learned, and they didn't ask him to play the second, third or fourth movements. Sometimes when he was really prepared, he could play beautifully. But something always went wrong. Every once in awhile, he would do something very musical or beautiful, but then he would do silly things to prove he could do them, and he couldn't. He would come out to play encores, to play the Étude in thirds, which everybody can play. Some play it slower, some play it faster. He would always get tangled up in it. Or he would play all sorts of weird pieces.

Walter Gieseking

Gieseking was an artist—I'm being kind—I never appreciated, quite apart from the fact that he turned out to be a real Nazi. Everything I heard of Gieseking was so surfacy, so fast, so skimmed through, that I really never enjoyed it. For example, the Beethoven sonatas are so fast. The first time I heard *Gaspard de la nuit*, it was on that famous record of his. I went out and bought the music to learn it, looked at it, and said, "Oh my god, so many notes." I started to learn it and the more I learned, the less I liked the Gieseking record. Then in my early teens, I heard the famous performance of Gieseking with the Philharmonic playing the Rachmaninoff Third. I didn't know the Rachmaninoff Third, I was just beginning to learn it by ear because Jorge Bolet was learning it, but I thought Gieseking's performance was terrible. And the strangest thing of all was an article in which Rachmaninoff supposedly said that the only one who understood his music was Walter Gieseking.

Emil Gilels

I first met Gilels when we were introduced after a performance of his at the Festival Hall in London, sometime in the late 1950s. He always used to visit us when he came to Geneva, and we were very close friends. We were invited to his home many times in Moscow.

I had an uncle who had a jewelry shop in New York on Fifty-Seventh Street and Eighth Avenue in a very fancy apartment house, the Parc Vendome. I always dropped in to say hello, and one day he said to me, "Oh, I have regards to you from Gilels." I said, "How did you meet Gilels?" "He was going back to Russia, and he stopped by here to buy some presents." Just by accident, my uncle asked Gilels if he knew me. They had a long discussion, and they both decided they liked me. Two weeks later, I opened a newspaper and read that that uncle was murdered in broad daylight in an armed robbery. My stepmother's brother was also murdered, in Florida.

Leopold Godowsky

You know what they said about Godowsky—when he practiced, he played all the scales with the same fingering. And he would transpose and play everything in different keys. I did that automatically.

Richard Goodman

When Richard graduated from Curtis, he moved back to Baltimore and became more important than Peabody. You only went to Peabody if Richard wouldn't take you. He played a recital or two every year, and he could do anything at the piano. He was the nicest guy but had an unfortunate life. He had a tragic marriage, with two children. He married a singer, a gorgeous woman, who was a hopeless drunk. He used to have to go looking for her in the middle of the night.

He was obviously quite wealthy, and any time I was near Baltimore, I went to see him. The last time, he'd had a heart attack. I found him in bed. He was doing quite well and we were talking, he said,

"You know, I have become a businessman."

"What does that mean?"

"Well you know, when my family died, they left me some little pieces of property. Minute little things, unimportant things. I've sold them for millions."

We were good friends right up until he died. He was, as far as I was concerned, a much more satisfying artist than Bolet and certainly the person who had the greatest influence on me as a young pianist. He was a very cultivated guy. He contributed far more to me than Saperton or the other students.

Friedrich Gulda

I heard him in New York. His jazz was not very good—I never took it seriously. My attitude was, "Keep your day job." Years later, in 1989, I saw Gulda on TV in the Munich Festival playing and conducting the "Emperor" Concerto with the Munich Philharmonic Orchestra. If there ever was an easy concerto to play and conduct at the same time, it's the "Emperor." I'm sure the orchestra could all have played it by heart. Gulda was going around in this African costume with draping robes, making a big todo about his conducting. He would stand up, conduct, then he'd run and sit down at the piano, then he'd get up again. It was ridiculous, like a Marx Brothers movie.

Myra Hess

She played the Brahms B-flat very often. I heard her play it in New York and the performance was gorgeous. I never even took notice of it, but when she played those two scales in double notes, she sort of just played the top notes. According to a story, this idiot in front went backstage and apparently said, "Dame Myra, why don't you play the scale in thirds going up in that movement?" She apparently looked at him and said, "I can't, and if that's all you can remember of my performance, it was a very bad performance anyway. Goodbye."

Josef Hofmann

I don't think that Josef Hofmann occupied Horowitz's level. Rachmaninoff and Hofmann were very close friends, with mutual admiration. Rachmaninoff dedicated his Third Concerto to Hofmann, who said, "Too many notes." That destroyed their great friendship. If I wrote you a piano concerto and you said, "Too many notes, I don't want to bother learning it," I'd be pissed off a little bit too. Hofmann invented all sorts of things, such as a suspension system for automobiles. I played his pianos, with the slightly narrower keys. They were very strange because of the way they were built. The corners of the keys, instead of being square, were rounded off. There was no traction. I couldn't understand that at all.

Vladimir Horowitz

Horowitz never had a greater admirer than I. There were really no other pianists that made the impression he made on both professional musicians and concert goers. When he was great, he was unequalled. When he was not great, he was just as unequalled. That's what made Horowitz so exciting in essence, because everything was either so beautiful or else an utter catastrophe. The more sophisticated a pianist you were, the more you were destroyed by his bad concerts, because when he was bad, you never knew whether he'd make it to the next bar. I love to say that that's what I have in common with Horowitz! Nevertheless, an artist may be playing on an off-night, but the qualities of his artistry will come through. A second-rate Rembrandt is still a Rembrandt.

I once said to him, "I've never heard you play the Chopin B-Minor Sonata," and he said the strangest thing, and I don't know if he was pulling my leg: "Oh no, it's much too hard." It's hard to imagine anything being too hard for Horowitz. I asked him when we were having lunch, "You've never recorded all the Chopin études. It would be wonderful to hear you do that." "Not possible." Rubinstein said the same thing, "That's just too hard. I can't practice like that."

You hear many things in Horowitz's recordings that are just rhythmically wrong. Every time there's a long note, it's too short.

Every time there's a rest, it's too short, and it doesn't make any difference whether he's playing Mozart or Chopin. The same thing goes for Rubinstein.

The repertoire that Horowitz played in Europe, before he came to the US, was vast, much greater than anything he played later. He played *Gaspard de la nuit* and the Brahms *Paganini Variations*, which I never heard him play. Plus, he played a great deal of chamber music. What he played in the US was rapidly condensed to a very small repertoire. I'm not saying that to criticize him, because he was wonderful, but in essence, he abandoned a lot of things.

I'm curious about what sort of teacher Horowitz was. I never knew anything about his teaching, and none of his students ever talk about their lessons with him. I would have jumped at the chance to study with Horowitz.

Evgeny Kissin

The first time I heard Kissin, I had turned on the TV, and there is this kid walking out with mile-high hair playing the Tchaikovsky Concerto. He was about fifteen, and it was so slow that I thought, "Well, he must have won some sort of student prize, or something." He said later on, in an interview somewhere, "I'll never forget that concert, I had to play everything at half tempo because of Karajan." Once, he and I were playing practically the same program on the same night in Houston. He was performing in Jones Hall, and I was opening the festival at the U of H. Then, I got a call the day before: "Would you change your program?" I said, "I'll tell you what we can do: you can listen to either one of us, or both of us, and compare the old man playing this Chopin sonata to the young man playing this Chopin sonata." I've still never met Kissin. He played a benefit recital for the Manhattan School scholarship fund there. I went to that concert, and he played the Brahms F-Minor Sonata and the *Carnaval*. He did something in the Brahms Sonata which, if I play it, I will do next time: when the development comes, then there's a big *ritard*, and he didn't make the *ritard*, but continued in tempo, and then slowed down afterward. I thought, that was the first time I ever heard anybody do that, it was right, and very Brahmsian. I don't remember if he did it perfectly. He hit plenty of wrong notes that night, both in the Sonata and the *Carnaval*.

Jonathan Simon

The first letter I ever received from him was when I was in South America. It said, "On Wednesday night, I went to hear the Orchestre de la Suisse Romande. A lady came out and she played the Rachmaninoff piece that you play she got all lost in the middle I went to bed at eleven o'clock." It was one sentence.

All his schooling was in French. His medical school was at the University of Geneva, but he did a full internship in the United States and so he passed the American exams. The last time he paid any attention to me, although he probably intended to do it all along, was when he interned at Maimonides, which is a very big hospital in New York City.

It's hard to believe, but he's now sixty-six years old. He's a very well-known and successful doctor in Geneva. He shouldn't have followed the family tradition and become a doctor—he's too gifted as a jazz pianist. He works very hard, but he comes home, and the first thing he does is go to the piano. God help you if you're sick and he wants to play the piano. His career as a jazz pianist is growing every day. He writes out these great chord progressions in a language I don't understand. They're sort of graphs, with chord numbers. He has a very good friend, a very nice guy and a blind Swiss pianist who's one of the most successful jazz pianists in Europe, and they play two-piano jazz as well as Jonathan playing alone.

Beveridge Webster

Beveridge was one of the heroes of music in New York City. He was a very well-known pianist, and he was considerably older than I. At Juilliard, he was one of the few teachers there that I had enormous respect for, because he knew everything about everything—he was the Britannica. Whenever I didn't know something, I would go and ask him. I once said to him, "You know, when I was very young, I was told that some of the most difficult pieces in the history of piano playing were the three Szymanowski piano sonatas. It was number two, I think, that was the most difficult one. I checked the music out from the library, and they were right." He said, "I played all three in New York, in Town Hall, during the war, at a special Polish relief concert." He was that sort of guy. He also played one of Anis Fuleihan's piano concertos with the Chicago Symphony.

He was an alcoholic—you'd find him in the street, like Josef Hofmann. That's why he had to retire. He gave a farewell recital at Merkin Hall, which is a very small, very nice hall to play in. I think he was ninety-two or ninety-three. He played very well that evening. He came out with the music, was playing and turning pages, got lost, and looked at the audience and said, "This never happens at home." It was so endearing that everyone wanted to run up on stage and put their arms around him, and he was not an endearing person—he was very withdrawn. You had to really get engaged with him to get to know him.

Chapter Ten
STUDENT RECOLLECTIONS

Being on Stage

After my years in New York, I moved to Toronto. One time, Abbey Simon was coming there to play, and of course I couldn't wait to hear him again. As I was walking along a corridor on my way to the hall, Mr. Simon emerged by chance from a door I was passing, and so we walked together. I asked him how he was, and he replied, "Terrible." He told me that he had been very sick all night and had not slept for even a moment. Before we parted, I to find my seat in the hall and he to prepare to go on stage, I sympathized with him and wished him luck. The first piece on the program was a piece of Weber, which he performed stunningly and which allayed my fears that he was not in top form. In the following pieces, he continued to prove that neither sickness nor sleeplessness would have any effect upon the magic he could work at the piano.

-Philip Thomson

Demonstrating

I marveled at his ability to demonstrate just about anything I was playing. It seemed as if he had the entire repertoire under his fingertips. Of course, for him, hearing a piece seemed to be just as good as playing it. His ear is that strong.

-Garnet Ungar

I learned the most from watching and hearing him play at my

lessons. He often played so beautifully that I felt I simply couldn't play after hearing that. It was humbling. I remember playing the Mozart C-Minor Concerto at a lesson and he was accompanying me. In the slow movement he started by playing a half-step too high. It is in E-flat and he played it in E. He apparently mixed it up with the Beethoven C-Minor Concerto. It was clear evidence of his incredible ear and how he didn't like sight-reading.

-Daniel Glover

Everything comes so naturally for him, sometimes he doesn't realize that little guys like us need time to understand what he's saying, what he wants us to do. Sometimes he'll change the fingering and just say, "Do it like this," and you'll say, "How?"

-Jerico Vasquez

Mr. Simon has a performer's personality and is capable of accomplishing any task in the blaze of the spotlights. He would always choose to be performing rather than teaching. It was with this very realistic background that I began studying with Mr. Simon. He matched my expectations in those regards, but as the lessons progressed, my expectations were exceeded as I learned in increasing detail how he worked as a pianist and musician.

-John Spradling

Discipline

One always got the feeling that he meant business and was deadly serious about great music-making and piano playing. No matter how well I played, I always sensed that he felt I could do better. This attitude has rubbed off on me in a profound way, and I have imparted this to my students. He is perhaps the only teacher who made me feel this way. My students tire of hearing his name mentioned because of the deep influence he has left on my playing and approach to music. I feel so very lucky to have studied with this legendary man and pianist.

-Daniel Glover

I learned how to prepare for a recital, how to run through the program and fix the things that need to be fixed (i.e., not the other things). I always tell my students, "You've got to RUN through your program—you can't take it apart every day."

-Jerico Vasquez

We got along very well indeed, both musically and personally, and the more I played for him, the more respect I developed for exactly the qualities that put off some of the other students—his incapacity to accept anything less than total involvement in the practice and performance of one's pieces. He was of tremendous help. I quickly came to the realization that he was my best choice for a teacher not only for the summer, but for future studies.

-Philip Thomson

Generosity

I had never known such a worldly person before and, although he could be intimidating, he was essentially a very warm and kind person, and I truly love him like a father.

-Joseph Matthews

He is as much larger than life as his stature is tiny. He is a man of great generosity. I have never paid him a penny for lessons outside of institutions—"You can't possibly afford what I'm worth" is his rationale. He has an eminently practical, straightforward, and largely non-delusional approach to life, and great personal warmth.

   -Charles Foreman

I remember many occasions when he treated his entire class to dinner at Beefsteak Charlie's restaurant in New York following studio classes.

   -Andrew Cooperstock

Musical values

I remember one small thing that may seem insignificant. Frequently, pianists are called on to play two notes at the same time with one finger. I brought in a piece and in one such place, he said, "Try to voice the top note," one of the notes I was playing with one finger. I was taken aback, I had never even considered it possible or necessary. But after a bit of experimentation, it was indeed possible. This was a small illustration of his attention to detail, something that comes across in his playing. There are no stones unturned, nothing sloppy or random.

When I returned to play for Mr. Simon during my first year as a university professor, one of the things he yelled out was, "Don't go university on me!" He was referring to my tempo, which was too slow. He pointed out something that has been confirmed over the years to me, which is that spending a lot of time working through things slowly with students often distorts the sense of tempo and makes teachers play too slowly themselves. Slow practicing, while necessary, can produce the same unwanted side effect. Since then I've adopted a habit of writing down performance tempo metronome marks for pieces I am about to learn before I started practicing them.

   -Garnet Ungar

I think I can say that I learned to adopt my own personal version of his basically simple and intuitive approach to music. He always waited to ask me to comment on performances in his master classes, because he quickly learned that I would say the one essential thing he really wanted to hear. At the same time, he never responded in a routine or completely predictable way to any performance and often had something to say that related specifically to the piece he was hearing—something (again) essential about the nature of a specific piece that needed to be the primary mode of communication in that piece.

-Charles Foreman

He was a fountain of information as well as an insightful teacher. I had never experienced the kind of infinite detail that he brought to the music. I really learned how to shape the music and be expressive without letting the music fall apart. He also worked on projection and communication.

-Joe Matthews

Once I took to a lesson a piece of Ravel. It was in a fast 3/8, and in one section there is a series of two-bar phrases that he said I was interpreting incorrectly. According to him, the phrases should begin—not end, as I was doing—on the first beats of every odd-numbered bar in the section. But the way I was playing the section made sense to me—after all, the downbeats of the even-numbered bars were the resolutions of the harmonies, and they were even marked with an accent. And there was no indication whatsoever by Ravel—no phrase marks, no crescendos, nothing. Puzzled, I asked, "How do you know?" Mr. Simon, instead of answering, burst out laughing. I wasn't embarrassed by the reaction, but still it didn't answer my question. In the following days during my practice, I tried to feel it differently, and one day, it suddenly made sense. That's putting it too lightly; it didn't just "make sense," it kicked me in the gut with a "but of course!" realization. Only then was I embarrassed at how off-the-mark my original conception was. The right way is now so ingrained in me that I think that if I had a student who played it the way I did and asked me the same question, I might react the same way Mr. Simon did. It's so wonderful the correct way, and it so misses the point otherwise.

-Philip Thomson

I learned how to listen and how to pace myself at the piano, both musically and physically. He is very good at explaining just about everything in the music that he wanted the student to address. Also, he is very generous with his knowledge of how to negotiate the music and the instrument. My impression is that he placed the music above the ego, which is rare. I was working on this concerto, and there was this really difficult part and he said, "Don't knock yourself out. Nobody will hear you."

-Hsia-Jung Chang

One time, I flew down to Houston for a lesson on Scarlatti and, following my complaining that I couldn't get a good sound out of his old pianos there, he proceeded to sit down and play the same sonata—which he hadn't touched in years—just beautifully. I learned a great deal about color, pedaling, facility, showmanship, and even the business of playing the piano professionally. He was an amazingly facile and expressive pianist. I heard him play the Chopin B-Minor Sonata in Houston to a sold-out house. He missed the fifth note, grimaced, and instead of starting over, like I might have, began to focus more and more intensely until by the end of the piece people were on their feet applauding. I use that example in my own teaching and consider it one of the finest performances I've ever heard of anyone. His playing is elegant and really from another time. It is full of personality and style. I think his playing has become even more refined. He is one of the last of the old school of playing from the golden age.

-Andrew Cooperstock

His sense of phrasing was kind of anti-gravity, so unusual and unlike any style I had heard up until hearing him play. The first time I heard him play, the tone was gripping, from the first note to the last.

-Hsia-Jung Chang

I remember Mr. Simon attended a recital at Dudley Hall at the University of Houston. He looked very dapper in a white jacket. I complimented his jacket, and he gathered up the lower side of it and admitted, "But it has a stain." I looked, and indeed there was a tiny mustardy speck there. I said, "That is not notice-able at all" and he said, "It's like a wrong note on a recording. The listener does not hear it, but I know it is there."

-Roger Wright

His playing in concerts was always a revelation, particularly hearing such repertoire as the Chopin ballades, the Schumann Fantasie and the Chopin concertos.

-Daniel Glover

Mr. Simon's was the first faculty recital I heard at IU. It in-cluded, in part, the Chopin B-flat-Minor Sonata, the Ravel *Valses nobles et sentimentales*, and the Schumann *Carnaval*. I was greatly impressed with the ease with which Mr. Simon played and how unforced his tone was. Completely fluent, relaxed equipment while at the same time possessing fingers that could do anything. Only in recent years have I had the opportunity to see and hear more videos of Hofmann, and I see the direct link to him in Simon's playing. This is an approach that is sadly disappearing. Mr. Simon often spoke of experiences hearing Hofmann, and invariably would end his reminiscences saying, "He played like a GOD!"

-John Spradling

An unforgettable pianistic revelation came one evening at Shawnigan when I heard him play a recital. In the same auditorium in which we first met, there were frequent concerts, both by the teachers and by the students. And on the day of his concert, I was of course eager to hear the actual results of his musical thoughts, which I had come, even in the short time I had known him, to so admire. And the performance, nearly forty years ago now, is still powerfully in my memory. I had never heard playing like this in my life. It was so controlled, so meticulously crafted, so clear, so wonderfully conceived, and above all, so obviously full of pure and true love for the music, that I was riveted from the first note to the last. The last piece on the program was the Chopin B-Minor Sonata, and when the theme in the last movement returned for the last time, I positively shook with excitement. I had spent the previous year in London, and had befriended one of its large paper's Classical music critics, Robert Henderson, with whom I often went to hear concerts. I had heard many of the world's greatest pianists during the year before I met Abbey Simon and was impressed by all of them in many regards. But this performance of the Chopin B-Minor sonata in an auditorium in a summer music camp was something that put more fire in me than anything I'd ever heard.

-Philip Thomson

He is always lyrical, always passionate.

-Charles Foreman

I always loved his playing. I was there for thirteen years in Houston and never missed any performance that he did. One year, the first or second year I was there, he did a magnificent program: "Les Adieux," Schumann Fantasie, Chopin op. 10—amazing playing. When he played the Schumann Fantasie, he was always on. There were also a few times he wasn't completely on, and it's good to see that. You realize that he's human. There was one time when he played *Gaspard*, played it beautifully, then he got to "Scarbo," and he just fell apart in the coda.

-Jerico Vasquez

One reason Abbey and I became long-lasting friends is that we share a wonderful sense of humor, which even in adverse circumstances, Simon retains. He has a charming and persuasive personality, and always had nice things to say about his fellow pianists. Very rarely did he criticize his professional peers—he would rather have no comment than a negative one. Through Abbey, I met many pianists, musicians, and non-musicians, as his circle of friends extended beyond the music profession!

Approaching ninety years old, he played one of his signature works in New York and Chicago among other cities—Chopin's Études, op. 10. He was still playing them flawlessly, with his usual impeccable technique and charming style!

I, as founder and director of the Silvermine Artists Series in Connecticut, have presented him several times in concert. The last event was a celebration of his ninetieth birthday in 2010: "Abbey Simon, a Life in Music." I gathered former students from Indiana, New York, and Texas where he had held teaching positions, who came from far and wide to pay tribute to the Master. I showed the YouTube interview filmed at his NY apartment. He then played a recital program and three invited speakers gave tribute to him. His wonderful sense of humor endured as we talked about our lessons with him, the Dracula poster facing us in the studio, or how we called him "crabby Abbey!" It was a wonderful and fitting occasion, with much adoration and admiration being displayed to a legendary pianist, who has left a lasting impression on so many pianists over the years.

I have had the privilege of knowing Abbey for some fifty years now, and we are still in touch on a regular basis. I have shared a friendship with him through his prime career days as well as the hard times he has recently faced in his twilight years. I have always said, "Abbey Simon lives to play—and plays to live!" What a wonderful legacy he will leave. I will always feel fortunate to have had the opportunity to know and work with him.

-Karen Shaw

Improvisation

Many think the series of chords between the scherzo and the largo of the Chopin B-Minor Sonata represents an improvised connecting passage between pieces, the kind one might hear in a piano recital a hundred years ago. Simon sometimes improvises this way between pieces in recitals.

When teaching a piece, Simon sometimes demonstrates using an improvised but highly convincing facsimile. The melody, texture, and style are the same, but the inside notes are different. He jokes that he sometimes does that in concerts, too!

-Garnet Ungar

He played the first two movements of the Chopin B-Minor Sonata as only he could, and I could not have been in a happier musical heaven. And although his tempo of the slow movement was not mine, I sat there as if in a dream, lost in the beautiful phrasings he was producing—until the moment that I realized, "Wait a minute: this isn't the slow movement of the sonata!" He had lost his place partway through the movement and, brilliant improviser that he always was, continued without losing a fraction of a beat, to play in the same style, the same tempo, and the same mood as where he had veered off track. He was on stage making things up and continued his improvisation for a few minutes before bringing the piece to a gentle and appropriate close. I was stunned—not in a disappointed way, but quite the opposite. Who could do such a thing? We have all heard pianists lose their way, and the professional ones generally can either cover up, jump somewhere convenient, or repeat the last few bars, but to suddenly compose out of one's head in the style of Chopin so that nobody but those who knew the piece would even know? That was one of the most amazing feats I had ever witnessed.

Either that movement unnerved him temporarily, or he was simply feverish, but after finishing that movement and playing the opening few introductory bars of the last one, he began the theme in the wrong register – on the B above middle C instead of the one just below it. Realizing it immediately, he continued to play it an octave too high for the first half of the phrase, and then – again, without losing a beat – jumped down to the correct one. The rest of the sonata was without incident; either the fever broke or he commanded it to stop interfering with his playing. The concert as a whole was a big success, and the next evening, a concerto performance, was a true Abbey Simon experience. As an encore, he played a Kreisler-Rachmaninoff transcription, and the way he performs it is a good example of one of the traits that I have always deeply admired in his playing: his ability to impart every aspect of music and pianism. Many pianists can, and do, play this transcription, even though it requires a virtuoso technique. But I've never heard it performed by anyone else with such playfulness, such sheer fun.

-Philip Thomson

Pedaling

One of the greatest features of Simon's playing is its clarity, in particular, of inner voices. His playing sometimes sounds like he has different damper pedals for different parts of the keyboard. In the development section of the first movement of the Prokofiev Sixth Sonata, he was having me experiment with some difficult, split-second "grabbing" of inside voices with the middle pedal, while simultaneously fluttering the damper pedal. Again, I had never dreamed such a thing was possible. One of his favorite things was suddenly to yell "No pedal!" Not that it should be performed that way, but he wanted me to hear everything more lucidly.

-Garnet Ungar

Abbey insisted on absolute clarity at all times. I won't ever forget that the first note I played for him in my lesson was the Liszt B-Minor Sonata. After the first note, a staccato octave, he came running across the room and literally kicked my foot and said, "Get your damn foot off the pedal." It wasn't dry enough for him. We spent the whole semester on the piece (interspersed with other things), and at the end he said, "Now you are ready to think about the interpretation," as if we hadn't even discussed it to that point. His first priority was getting everything under technical control and the clarity, which I apparently lacked at the time.

-Daniel Glover

His pedaling is such an influence on me: half-pedal, quarter-pedal, holding the pedal all the way through the last two pages of the Beethoven G-Major Concerto.

-Jerico Vasquez

I do remember some of his comments, for example, "What are you doing, pedaling by the page?"

-Alice Rybak

Personality

Several times during my lessons, he asked me to play something hands separately from memory. If I couldn't do it, he would get very irritated and yell, "Oh, you're all too perfect!" I still don't feel satisfied unless I can play my program this way.

-Garnet Ungar

Crusty New York guy—I was a pretty naive kid who grew up in California, so Abbey was exotic to me, with his abrupt manner, quick (often acid-tinged) judgments, etc.

-David Korevaar

Looking back, I have only gratitude for both his teaching and his playing. Mr. Simon was suave, debonair, yet intimidating—he was especially tough with the Rachmaninoff Piano Concerto No. 2 in C Minor: "Oh for God's sake, if you cannot play this whole damn thing, left hand alone, no pedal, by memory, I don't want to hear it." That was over twenty years ago. Now, having lived with it for over twenty years and performing it with orchestras, I will once again perform this "whole damn thing" with the New York Concertos Sinfonietta. I think I know it pretty well by now, and a big part of my knowing this work as I do was the teaching of Abbey Simon.

-Christopher Johnson

In 1978, Horowitz played the Rachmaninoff Third Concerto with the New York Philharmonic, Eugene Ormandy conducting. Mr. Simon was not planning to attend the concert itself, but he did mention in passing that he was planning to attend the dress rehearsal. I eagerly approached Mr. Simon as he returned from the dress rehearsal. "Mr. Simon, how was the rehearsal? How did Horowitz do with the concerto?" Simon glared at me as silently as a lit fuse on a bomb before it blows everything to smithereens. Finally, he answered. It was a yell from that craggy voice he used when he was utterly disgusted with something. "HE WAS HOROWITZ PLAYING RACHMANINOFF THREE!! Is there anything else you want to know??"

Mr. Simon could be surprisingly collegial at times and at other times was mercurial and unpredictable. Mr. Simon owned a full-length bearskin coat, which he wore in the 1970s, when nobody wore a coat like that. "Nobody else has a coat like this, and if they did, they would not look right wearing it. I can wear it because I stand out from the ordinary." During the winter months of 1971-72, there was a concerto competition at Indiana University in which all contestants played the Liszt Totentanz. On a brilliantly sunny morning with snow on the ground, Mr. Simon walked from his residence to the School of Music wearing his coat and a pair of sunglasses. In his studio, already warming up, was Charles Fugo, who was playing in the competition, which was near at hand. I watched this amusing lesson from a window in a building next door, where I was serving as a Teaching Assistant. Charles had already begun with his accompanist, and they were well into the concerto as Mr. Simon entered the studio. Not wanting to be distracted from any of the performance,

Mr. Simon did not bother to remove either his sunglasses or his coat, but simply stood in a corner of the studio listening. It was a well-known fact that as performance time drew near, Mr. Simon would turn up the heat on his comments and criticisms, and he was soon gesticulating and calling—yelling—out his commentary as Charles continued to play. He got quite animated, the "fur was flying," and it was fun to watch the goings-on with no sound, either from Mr. Simon or the piano. Charles continued in his fluid, relaxed method, and Mr. Simon certainly burned a lot of calories on his "encouragements." I knew Charles to be implacable, and whatever Mr. Simon was commenting about was used in the proper way.

-John Spradling

When I played Rach Three for him, my friend, Garnet Ungar, came to my lesson to accompany me. Mr. Simon was demonstrating a passage from the first movement; he sat at the piano and I stood above him to the side. I believe he was approaching seventy-five years of age. He blundered the passage somewhat, and as he started again, I reached for the rack (supporting the score) and pulled it out towards him, as if to let him see better. Garnet laughed to himself, while Mr. Simon looked up at me with a look on his face that could only mean "How dare you?"

-Roger Wright

The first time I played for him, he told me, "When I'm quiet, you need to be afraid of me. But when I'm yelling at the top of my lungs, you're doing a good job." He is always very blunt, but for the most part I wasn't offended by him. I would just laugh. Sometimes maybe he would be too blunt. For example, "My students are all idiots," or "Oh, she's a mess," or "Did you get it into your little brain?" or "You can't teach an old monkey new tricks!" I remember going into the lesson of a friend of mine—she was working on the Ravel G-Major Concerto. After she played through the second movement he said, "Dear, if you play it slower than that, I'll be dead before you get to the end." There was one year I did not study with him—we had a falling out, because of his random temper. I went in one time after working on the Tchaikovsky Concerto all summer, and I had the piece memorized. There was another student in the room waiting for her lesson. Somehow during the lesson he was showing me something I could not figure out how to do immediately, and he started just shouting at me, and I thought to myself, "You don't have to embarrass me in front of someone else, and I am a very responsible person, you let me know what I need to do, let me work on it, I'll come back." I calmly took my score and went out of the studio. I did not go back for a year. That was the second semester of my doctorate. We tried to avoid one another for a year. That was about the only time I didn't get to work with him. I've had a great relationship. One time, I was working on Chopin's Second Sonata. He was picky as hell, and he just started yelling at me again, so I did the same thing, picked up my score, went out the door, and then the following day, knocked on the door, and said "Are you going to yell at me again?" He said, "You know what? That lesson sounded really good, you should play it at the student recital!" He's a gentleman when you're not in the studio, when you're not playing.

-Jerico Vasquez

His personality struck me as gruff at first, but after I got used to it, I found a very sincere and gentle quality that isn't apparent at first. He was never lovey dovey, or grandfatherly, as Eugene List could be.

-Daniel Glover

He is a typical New Yorker. Very gracious, a very pleasant man to talk to, and has a way with words. Once, a fellow student, Lois Leventhal, was playing the Ravel Left-Hand for one of her recitals, and Abbey went backstage, held her left hand and said, "Remember, this one." I think it was in his weekly class where somebody played the Bartók Sonata, a piece that he wasn't fond of, and when they finished he said, "You know, this piece grows on you. Like a fungus."

-Alice Rybak

My first impression was that he was quite unimpressed with me. One on one, he seemed quite reserved, I even felt that he did not like me. But in studio class and other groups, he always made me laugh.

-Roger Wright

Every Sunday morning, he held workshops in the old Recital Hall at IU, and these were exceptionally valuable. Abbey was a very direct person, but also very supportive, and his impressions of your effectiveness in the concert hall were very important in your training.

-Joseph Matthews

After I finished my undergraduate studies, I took a bit of time off from school. I knew I wanted to continue to study, but I didn't know where nor with whom. One day, I was talking with a former university classmate and friend, Kerry McShane, who told me that there was a pianist by the name of Abbey Simon whom he thought I would like and who taught during the summer at a camp called Shawnigan in British Columbia. I decided to go there that summer. On the first day, all of the students met in a large auditorium and were asked to play something short. So one by one, we all played for a few minutes until we were asked to stop. There were four or five teachers present, one of whom was a raspy-voiced fellow who laughed when I said that since I hadn't known I would be asked to play something on the first day there, I hadn't really prepared anything for performance. But I chose the first Mephisto Waltz of Liszt and played several minutes of it before he stopped me, saying good-naturedly, "Yes, you should have practiced something." He had the occasion to laugh again when I was given something to sight-read. Sight-reading was never a strong point of mine and being nervous made it even worse. But he delivered his comments in a jocular way, and I took no offense. I liked him right away. Each morning, one of the teachers gave a masterclass in the auditorium, so I had a chance to hear comments from all of them. All of them had strengths, and all were knowledgeable. But my favorite by far was that fellow with the raspy voice. Abbey Simon had boundless energy, amazing ears, and a seemingly profound knowledge of every piece in the repertoire. He was not diplomatic in his comments: in his classes, instead of saying to a student with less than meticulous pedaling, "Be careful in this section; it's a little blurry," he'd be just as likely to bark, "What are you doing with your stupid feet?" I want to be quick to point out, though, that never did I witness a personally disparaging remark from him. He was direct, even blunt about his opinions regarding the playing of the piano, but never even then was there the slightest hint of insult in them. We could have private lessons with the teachers of our choice. During the first few weeks of that summer, I played, I think, for all of them, but the biggest help by far came from Abbey Simon, and for the rest of the summer, I played only for him. Many of the students at the camp were intimidated by him, being unused to the unsparing approach that was his hallmark. This was fine by me, because it gave me the opportunity to have all the more lessons with him. Near the summer's end, I asked him if it might be possible to continue to study with him when the camp was over. At the time, I had no idea where he taught, but I didn't care: wherever it was, I would go if he would accept me as a student. I was delighted when he told me that he would be most pleased to continue to teach me. It turned out that he taught at The Juilliard School in New York, so that's where I went. My studies at Juilliard remain some of my life's most pleasant memories. I had good friends among my classmates, all pianists, and all studying with different teachers. Stories abound concerning students of one teacher not speaking to those of another, or even of teachers themselves keeping their distances because of heated rivalries, but I personally did not have such unpleasant experiences there. Nor did Mr. Simon have such philosophies. One day, I went in to a lesson to tell him that a Canadian orchestra had asked me to perform the Gershwin Concerto in F and the *Variations on "I Got Rhythm"* with them in the coming season. He told me that he was very familiar with the concerto but not with the variations. But he added that one of the other piano teachers on the faculty, Earl Wild, had played the variations many times, and maybe that teacher could help me with them. He called Wild, who said that he'd be happy to listen to me and give my some suggestions, which he did.

  -Philip Thomson

I worked with him when doing my DMA at Juilliard, 1998-2000. By the time I studied with him, we'd been acquainted for nearly twenty years, so I had a pretty good idea what I was getting into. On the other hand, we had to establish a different kind of relationship, going from acquaintances, quasi-collegial, to teacher-student. It took a few months for us to find the right rhythm, but then we had what I felt was a productive and warm relationship. He has always been quite positive after my recitals, and after my recital last fall, he gave me a big compliment (I think), including the potential backhand "You're learning how to be a human being."

   -David Korevaar

He was acerbic, yet charming, and intensely devoted to his students. He is outwardly gruff, but really caring and good-humored underneath. He was charismatic. I admire him greatly.

   -Andrew Cooperstock

Recordings

On one occasion, Simon asked me to be his producer on a new recording of Schumann: *"Abegg" Variations, Kinderszenen,* and *Kreisleriana.* I was immensely flattered—overwhelmed, really, that he would want my help. The recording began. On the first take, he played the *"Abegg" Variations* note-perfectly. Over the intercom, he said,

   "How was that?"

   "Well...perfect."

   "Oh, no, no, we have to do it again and again."

   "Ummm, ok, if you like."

He didn't need me there. The first take of every piece was flawless. He could have done the entire recording in an hour, without any editing. He can summon concentration when it counts, the first time, when inspiration is at its strongest for him. But when the pedantry of repetition began, things went downhill fast. His performances got worse and worse, with wrong notes and tightness gradually taking over. For various reasons, this Schumann recording was never issued. There were many distractions that made the recording sessions a somewhat comical experience. The recording engineer, whom we had just met, wouldn't stop talking about his newfound homosexuality. There's nothing wrong with homosexuality, it's just that he talked about it incessantly. He also didn't appear to have any experience with Classical music. We were recording in a large church and the bells were constantly ringing, and the wooden roof kept creaking loudly with temperature changes. To add to that, we kept hearing the loud shrieking of some sort of wild beast outside. It turned out to be the neighbor's peacocks.

-Garnet Ungar

I knew only that his recordings of the complete works of Ravel was superb and I felt compelled to study with him. I wasn't disappointed!

-Andrew Cooperstock

I had a recording I really respected, which was released as one side of a four-record set (vinyl, of course, in those days) on RCA Victor called World's Greatest Piano Music. I still own it. All Chopin, including op. 10, no. 5, op. 66, and op. 17, no. 4. I was particularly impressed by the forcefulness of this recording, which seemed to me to be distinctly un-feminine. I thought Abbey Simon was a woman, and there was nothing in the recording notes to dispel this—and no photo. I've never admitted this to anyone before! I don't hear much of a difference in his live playing or recordings, other than the excitement of a live performance being sometimes somewhat absent in recordings, which is true for everybody, I think.

-Charles Foreman

I had many of his recordings starting when I was in high

school. My first acquaintance with Ravel's piano music was through his Vox recordings. I also owned his Ravel and Chopin concertos LPs, which remain as valued treasures. His playing was always polished and refined.

-Daniel Glover

I knew Abbey's name since I was a young boy in the Philippines—my dad was a lover of music and he collected recordings from Reader's Digest. One of those was an album of Chopin's music, and one of those LPs was a recording of Mr. Simon, and I've always heard that name. I've heard his performances since I was young. I always remember the pieces that were in that LP, which included the B-flat-Minor Scherzo, the B-flat-Minor Sonata, and the "Winter Wind" Étude. Live performances give an extra dimension, but I feel like the way he played on his records is exactly the way he played in live performances. He hears the music exactly the way he wants to hear it, and he really doesn't deviate from that. His conception of the music is exactly the same—the voicing, the rubato.

-Jerico Vasquez

I first met Abbey during my student years at the IU School of Music. I was impressed by his fluent and stylish piano playing immediately upon hearing him. He was rehearsing the Rachmaninoff Third Concerto with Sidney Foster playing the orchestral reduction, and the pianistic ease with which he journeyed through the maze of notes was nothing short of amazing. Abbey, Sidney, and Jorge Bolet had been students together at Curtis, and Sidney was responsible for getting them both to eventually join the piano faculty at IU, which I have now labeled as the "Golden Age" of the greatest pianists assembled in this budding, but not yet famous school of music! What an inspiring, and remarkable time it was at Indiana, which left its mark on me, as an aspiring young pianist, and eventually a Professor of Piano at IU to this very day.

His initial recognition came from his performances of Ravel: *Gaspard de la Nuit*, and *Miroirs* more specifically. "Ondine" (from *Gaspard*) was admired and praised for his beautiful sound and magical interpretation. His Kreisler-Rachmaninoff transcriptions of *Liebeslied* and *Liebesfreud* were simply astonishing.

Abbey's playing has always impressed me as technically effortless, musically tasteful, and in the grand romantic style, about which I gained tremendous insight through his stories about his teachers and classmates at Curtis and, of course, his performances. I have heard him play many, many times, first as a student in Bloomington. Later, I was in attendance at some of his numerous Carnegie Hall recitals (which he presented annually for many years), in Europe, where I heard him play in the huge Royal Albert Hall in London back in the mid-60s, as well as other venues in Europe and throughout the US.

-Karen Shaw

Repertoire

Abbey Simon is not the sort of pianist to get bored—or sound bored—playing a piece for many years. Instead, he delights in refining and illuminating myriad inner voices and textures through hundreds of performances. He has favorite pieces that have been with him all through his career, and these have a decided tendency toward extreme difficulty. Pieces like Ravel's *Gaspard de la nuit*, Brahms's *Paganini Variations*, the Chopin B-Minor Sonata, the Brahms Second Piano Concerto, and Rachmaninoff's Third Piano Concerto are mainstays of his repertoire. The last piece was just beginning to be heard with regularity when he began performing it in the 1950s—-the Second Rachmaninoff Concerto had eclipsed it.

Many of the pieces he has performed, like clothing tried on but not worn, have not stayed in his repertoire for any length of time. Pieces such as Ravel's solo piano version of *La Valse*, the Chopin op. 25 Études, Beethoven's "Pastorale" Sonata, op. 28, Schubert's sonatas, and Mozart's sonatas fit this description. This is even more true of some of the repertoire he has recorded. Vox, in particular, was interested in sets of "complete works." So, although Simon undertook recording projects such as the complete Chopin nocturnes, waltzes, and works for piano and orchestra, he did not perform most of these works with regularity, with the exception of the two Chopin concertos. Other pieces appeared for a season or two, disappeared for thirty years, then reemerged: Ravel's *Valses nobles et sentimentales*, Rachmaninoff's *Corelli Variations*, Schumann's *Carnaval*. Still others, such as Balakirev's *Islamey*, were retired from his repertoire early and never reappeared. What is perhaps most impressive is that the performances of pieces he played infrequently received just as glowing reviews.

Simon's live recording of the Brahms B-flat Concerto in Carnegie Hall has everything—power, passion, sweep, tenderness, mind-boggling accuracy, speed, and charm. His live *Handel Variations* at Indiana University was an avalanche of power and vitality. His early Philips solo Brahms pieces are models of maturity, intimacy, and poetry. It is a pity that these recordings are not currently available to the public.

-Garnet Ungar

Sense of humor

His wit was priceless! Some of my favorite memories of the

Bloomington days were dinners at the Dandale (a favorite Bloomington restaurant) with Abbey and students. He was, and is, such a great raconteur, and these social times were much loved.

-Joseph Matthews

We all know he missed a huge career as a stand-up comic.

-Charles Foreman

In the summer of 1978, between my two years of study with Mr. Simon, I had some lessons with him at his apartment on West Seventy-Third Street, just off Central Park West. Of Mr. Simon's various residences, this apartment, I am sure, was a secondary dwelling. There was nothing wrong with it, and I had several friends who also lived in the building, but it was not air-conditioned. On this hot day, I approached Mr. Simon's door to hear him playing the *Don Juan Fantasy* on what sounded like a Steinway M—and indeed it was an M, as I found out in a few minutes. I wanted to hear him play through to the end and was not about to interrupt him. I had already heard him play this work in a Carnegie Hall recital and knew a bit about his approach to it. I was particularly interested because he probably would have been familiar with Hofmann's legendary performance of it, which was supposed to have been staggering. The piece was a showcase for Mr. Simon's devilishly light-fingered abilities, and he was in fine shape that day. He played convincingly with a powerful accelerando at the end—so fast he actually missed notes—the M being absolutely tested to its limits. It was a volcanic ending. I waited until after he finished and finally knocked. Mr. Simon threw open the door. He was pouring sweat, stripped to the waist (Mr. Simon looked in quite good shape without a shirt.) All I could think to say was "That was a stunning performance, Mr. Simon!" He brushed my comment aside with a comment about it being a very hot day and ushered me into the apartment. I sat down at the M that had just brought forth the *Don Juan Fantasy*, Mr. Simon threw on a shirt, and we had a lesson on op. 111. Quite a contrast in a few moments!

Mr. Simon was used to projecting his personality through the music he played, and at other times, his personality projected as though he was playing even when he was not. That was just fine. You were lucky to be gaining experience from his mentoring, and you took everything he had to give. My experiences with Abbey Simon are some of the most enduring in my memory, and I am grateful for every moment I spent with him.

-John Spradling

Stage demeanor

Simon has always played from memory, and his eyes remain glued to the keyboard at all times. His stage demeanor is understated, and he moves very little. This was the way with many older pianists, possibly because they grew up in the age of radio, where sound was the only important thing. Simon is sometimes called a pianist's pianist. Perhaps he does things which only someone who is trained to hear contrapuntally—in layers—can hear. Another thing which impresses lay, non-professional audiences is sheer volume, which doesn't interest Mr. Simon.

-Garnet Ungar

Technique

I learned many technical secrets just watching him play. For example, the ease with which he tossed off rotation passages always intrigued me, and I try to imitate him to this day.

-Daniel Glover

Doing jumps in rhythms, e.g. Prokofiev 7th Sonata, in qua-druplets, then triplets, then duplets, and making sure the tempo stays constant, and using the wrist a lot, rather than the arm.

-Jerico Vasquez

I have always loved Abbey Simon's playing. He was a powerful musician and a phenomenal pianist. He has an incredibly well-oiled technique, and the sound is just so special and beautiful. He was very interested in economy of motion in regards to tech-nique, and he worked on my propensity to be a bit heavy-hand-ed. When I think of the piano music of Chopin, Ravel, or Schumann, I instantly think of Abbey Simon.

-Joseph Matthews

I gained much greater relaxation and experience in playing "big" repertoire without pounding. I had previously spent a lot of time practicing super-slowly and with very deep attack into the keys. As a result, my playing was much too "vertical" and had very little color. Mr. Simon played through many parts of the Chopin B-Minor Sonata under tempo—but not dead slow as I had done—with no pedal and using pauses and breaths. Taking my cues from the way he did it gave my playing a much more horizontal feeling and took away the "attack" quality I too often had. The lightest playing I had the opportunity to learn from him was in *L'isle joyeuse.* In the Rachmaninoff Second Con-certo, there were many places in which he told me not to force my sound. He would demonstrate, and I had serious doubts as to whether or not he would be heard with an orchestra, even though I heard him many times with orchestra. Soon thereafter, I heard him play Rachmaninoff's First Concerto with the New York Philharmonic and received a valuable lesson in cutting through an orchestra without pounding. He played in a relaxed manner, and never had a problem being heard. Simon's performance of Rachmaninoff Three was brilliant, both musically and technically.

-John Spradling

Technique to Abbey Simon is neither an end nor even an afterthought; it's simply a given. In my years of studying with him, I don't remember us discussing technique even once. I do remember him remarking once that technique is not in one's fingers, but in one's ears, adding for clarification that if you can hear something in your head, you can reproduce it on the piano. But he never said anything to me about how to play something pianistically. We spoke only of music.

-Philip Thomson

When he is "on," there is a virtually flawless level of technical mastery that is phenomenal to hear, particularly live in concert.

-Charles Foreman

As a student, I became aware that his pianistic wizardry was something I wanted to experience, and I sought his instruction, subsequently working with him both at Indiana and in Geneva, where he has called home until the present. It was there that Abbey generously awarded me lessons at no cost, sharing many of his pianistic "tricks" of his specialty repertoire such as Chopin's études, Brahms's *Paganini* and *Handel Variations* as well as other repertoire including Schumann, Beethoven, and Rachmaninoff. His addition to my natural, yet not fully developed technique was simply invaluable and most surely became a part of me throughout my pianistic career.

-Karen Shaw

Appendix A

DISCOGRAPHY

Only the first releases on record are shown here. In the case of works which were first released individually and then as part of a set of complete works, only the set of complete works is shown. Many of these recordings have been re-released several times on CD, often in different combinations. These re-releases are not shown.

Albéniz-Godowsky: Triana
from *Rarities of Piano Music at Schloss vor Husum, Vol. 2*
Live recording, August 25 1990
Danacord LP DACOCD 379

Beethoven: Quintet for Piano and Winds, op. 16 (with Richard Woodhams, Oboe, George Silfies, Clarinet, George Berry, Bassoon, Roland Pandolfi, French Horn)
Vox LP TVC 37004
1979

Brahms: Intermezzi, op. 116, nos. 2, 4, 6/op. 117, no. 2
Philips 45 rpm 400151 AE

Brahms: Ballades, op. 10, nos. 1 and 2/Capriccio, op. 116, no. 7
Philips 45 rpm 400152 AE

Brahms: Capriccio, op. 116, no. 3/Romance, op. 118, no. 5/Rhapsody, op. 119, no. 4
Philips 45 rpm 400153 AE

Brahms: Ballades, op. 10, nos. 3, 4
Philips 45 rpm 400154 AE
Brahms: Concerto No. 1 in D Minor, op. 15 (Orquesta Sinfónica
Nacional/Juan-José Castro)
Live Recording, June 9 1959, Teatro Colón, Buenos Aires

Brahms: Sonata No. 3 in F Minor, op. 5
EMI LP Unreleased

*Brahms: Variations and Fugue on a Theme by Handel, op. 24/Variations
on a Theme of Paganini, op. 35*
Philips LP A00195L
Recording Venue: Hilversum, Phonogramstudio
1953

Brahms: Variations on a Theme of Paganini, op. 35
(Issued with *Liszt: Six Grandes Études de Paganini*)
Vox LP VU 9004

Chopin: 4 Ballades/Barcarolle, op. 60
Vox LP TV34763
Recording Date: 1974-07-01

*Chopin: Barcarolle, op. 60/Étude in C-sharp Minor, op. 10, no. 4/
Nocturne in B-flat Minor, op. 9, no. 1/Scherzo No. 2 in B-flat Minor, op.
31/Sonata No. 2 in B-flat Minor, op. 35*
Part of *Chopin, Poet of the Piano*
Reader's Digest LP RDA 41

Chopin: Concertos Nos. 1 and 2 (Royal Philharmonic Orchestra/
Eugene Goossens)
HMV LP ALP 1580

EMI LP D 13175?
1958

Chopin: Complete works for piano and orchestra (Hamburg Symphony Orchestra/Heribert Beissel)
Vox LP QSVBX 5126

Chopin: Études, op. 10, op. 25
Vox LP TV34688
Recording Date: 1976-02-01
1977

Chopin: 4 Impromptus/Variations brillantes, op. 12/Berceuse, op. 57/ Fantaisie in F Minor, op. 49
Vox LP TV34777
Recording Date: 1979-11-01

Chopin: Complete Nocturnes
Vox LP 9094

Chopin: Préludes, op. 28, op. 45
Vox unreleased

Chopin: 4 Scherzos
(Issued with *Mendelssohn: Variations sérieuses*)
VOX LP TVS 34460
1972

Chopin: Sonatas Nos. 2 and 3
Vox LP TV 34272
1970

Chopin: Complete Waltzes
Vox LP TVS 34580
1974

Dohnányi: Variations on a Nursery Song, op. 25 (Hague Philharmonic
Orchestra/Willem van Otterloo)
(Issued with *Rachmaninoff: Rhapsody on a theme of Paganini*)
Philips LP G03091L also S 04022L

Franck: Prélude, Chorale and Fugue
(Issued with *Liszt: Six Grandes Études de Paganini/Schumann:
"Abegg" Variations*)
HMV LP ALP 1719
1959

Grieg: Concerto in A Minor, op. 16 (Residency Orchestra of The
Hague/Willem van Otterloo)
Philips LP A00689R/S 06097R/Epic LC-3182
Recording Date: 1953-09-06

Liszt: Six Grandes Études de Paganini
(Issued with *Franck: Prélude, Chorale and Fugue/Schumann: "Abegg"
Variations*)
HMV LP ALP 1719
1959

Liszt: Six Grandes Études de Paganini
(Issued with Brahms *Variations on a Theme of Paganini*, op. 35)
Vox LP VU 9004

Liszt: Un Sospiro, Arranged for piano and orchestra by Douglas Gamley
(Sinfonia of London/Robert Irving)

EMI/HMV 45 rpm 7EP 7087

Mendelssohn: Variations sérieuses, op. 54
Vox LP TVS 34460
(issued with *Chopin: 4 Scherzos*)
1972

Rachmaninoff: Rhapsody on a theme of Paganini, op. 43 (Residency
Orchestra of The Hague/Willem van Otterloo) rec. 12-15
February 1955?
(Issued with *Dohnányi: Variations on a Nursery Song*)
Philips LP SBL-5210
Recording Date: 1955-02-12
Venue: Amsterdam, Concertgebouw, Grote Zaal

Rachmaninoff: Complete Works for Piano and Orchestra (St. Louis
Symphony/Leonard Slatkin)
Vox LP VBX 5149
1978

Rachmaninoff: Concerto No. 3, op. 30 (Japan Philharmonic/Akeo
Watanabe)
Live Recording, June 21, 1966, Bunka Kaikan Hall, Tokyo

Ravel: 2 Concertos (Orchestra of Radio Luxembourg/Louis de
Froment)
Vox LP QTV-S 34589
1975

Ravel: Complete Works for Piano Solo
Vox LP CDX 5012

Saint-Saëns: Carnival of the Animals (with Hepzibah Menuhin/
Philharmonia Orchestra/Efrem Kurtz)
EMI LP DCL 707202

Schumann: "Abegg" Variations, op. 1
(Issued with *Franck: Prélude, Chorale and Fugue/Liszt: Six Grandes
Études de Paganini*)
HMV LP ALP 1719
1959

Schumann: Carnaval, op. 9, Fantasie, op. 17
Vox LP TVS 34432

Transcriptions by Liszt, Rachmaninoff, Godowsky, Chasins
Vox LP 8204

Appendix B
REVIEW EXCERPTS

The young pianist showed again that he is a musician of sensitivity and refinement who has a way with a songful slow movement, and who can produce a beautiful, clear, light tone in quick treble passages. But he does not yet seem to be able to come to grips with a big work. His Chopin, for instance, was gentle and charming, but it lacked the intense feeling intended by the composer for music so poignant.

R.P., "Abbey Simon in Recital," *New York Times,* October 16, 1941.

Mr. Simon made a most favorable impression in the Bach-Busoni transcription at the start of the recital. The three divisions of the work were taken at well considered tempi, and though powerfully projected were always admirable in tone quality. There was rhythmic life in the presentation and real insight into the intentions of the masterpiece.

But in the romantic variations of Mendelssohn and sonata of Chopin Mr. Simon proved distinctly out of his element. Here his decided limitations as a colorist were particularly obvious, and also his want of inner intensity. The Mendelssohn, like the Chopin, became principally a vehicle for the display of the virtuoso technic at the pianist's command, and exhibited an unfortunate absence of insight into their poetic content.

Noel Straus, "Abbey Simon Gives Fourth Recital Here," *New York Times,* January 4, 1945.

Good pianists are so numerous this season that when a new

one who is better than good comes along, the critic's vocabulary is apt to falter. Such a one is Abbey Simon, young easterner, winner of several major awards, who made his Chicago debut with outstanding success in Kimball Hall yesterday afternoon.

Upon sober reflection Mr. Simon may be placed in the front rank of the younger generation of pianists…

He can play such unaccustomed and ordinarily unrewarding concert fare as Beethoven's seven Bagatelles, Opus 33, with the meticulous sobriety of a Schnabel. He can undertake the formidable feat of performing both books of the *Paganini-Brahms Variations*, and leave the auditor not only admiring a dauntless but never overworked technical display, but basking in the rich Brahmsian warmth which underlies the glittering surface. This sort of ability does not always spell good Chopin, but when that composer's turn came, Mr. Simon dashed out four sparkling études and what is more difficult, made the F-sharp-Minor Nocturne sing with approved morbid lushness, and in encores captured the witty caprice of two mazurkas.

And his Ravel, the *Valses nobles et sentimentales* and "Alborada del gracioso," an encore, might have been the work of a specialist.

Albert Goldberg, "Abbey Simon in Top Rank of Young Pianists," *Chicago Daily Tribune*, December 3, 1945.

Abbey Simon, youthful American pianist, was the soloist, playing the exquisite and seldom heard Chopin Piano Concerto no. 2 in F Minor. Mr. Simon is an artist to his fingertips. His tone is large and of lovely quality, and his style and feeling for Chopin's music, plus his youthful and unassuming personality, earned for him one of the finest successes enjoyed so far this year. The pianist counts a fluid and facile technique among his assets. His playing of the lovely second movement was a model of sensitivity.

Max De Schauensee, "Abbey Simon, Pianist, Scores Hit in Refreshing Dell Concert," *Philadelphia Evening Bulletin*, July 10, 1946.

Rubinstein's performance of the same concerto was less accurate, tonally less alluring, and less poetic.
Glenn Dillard Gunn, "Abbey Simon, Unknown Here, Stars at Watergate," *Washington Times-Herald*, July 25, 1947.

The musician asked the audience for certain notes upon which he could improvise…The first series of four notes picked at random developed into an improvisation upon a Chopin waltz. Three others followed: a Brahms intermezzo, a Bach fugue, and last, a Gershwin tune.
"Pianist Abbey Simon Opens Concert Series," *Ludington Daily News*, October 31, 1947.

At Orchestra Hall, Abbey Simon, pianist, offered one or the most satisfying performances heard by one of the younger artists … His sense of purely musical values, of interpretive understanding, was beautifully revealed in Chopin's B-Minor Sonata and in the Intermezzo und Capriccio in G Minor by Brahms…
From the Sonata was distilled that romantic essence that still can enslave the hearing of a modern listener. Brahms was sterner stuff, but a seductive *cantilene*—particularly in the Intermezzo—and a sturdy execution on the Capriccio made the performance a delight.
That technical difficulties offer no hurdles to Mr. Simon proved in two pieces by Ravel—"Scarbo" from *Gaspard de la Nuit* and "Oiseaux tristes," the second of the six pieces entitled *Miroirs*. "Scarbo" seldom is heard in our concert halls, probably because few pianists are able to negotiate it. Mr. Simon did, and

with brilliant results.

"Pianist Displays A Blazing Talent," *Chicago Sun*, November 4, 1947.

His first demonstration was an invention in the manner of a Chopin waltz based on a theme provided by Reidy Smith who bravely sang out the first four notes of Gagnon & Frère's theme song.

The most successful improvisation [was] as Rachmaninoff might have written it, built around four notes suggested by different members of the audience...

Finally Mr. Simon applied his unique gifts to the development of a fugue, mystifying and charming his hearers by his ability to turn a random selection of notes into beautiful music.

S.F. White, "Abbey Simon Gives Delightful Concert," *Arvida News*, November 19, 1947.

Since so often young pianists make a flash debut and then develop no further, it is a pleasure to report that Abbey Simon, who played last night at Carnegie Hall, is still growing. It was his sixth local recital since his debut as a Naumburg Award Winner in 1940.

He is only 27 years old now and still needs to develop more dramatic intensity to enter the top rank. But he is already so sensitive and thoughtful a musician that he can give a recital that touches his listeners and have them leave the hall with the sense of a real musical experience.

Chopin's B-Minor Sonata was his most extended selection. The performance gave the measure of his growth. In his first recitals he showed that he had a way with a slow, songful melody, but there was little grasp of big structures, but last night his interpretative powers seemed to fill the whole work.

R. P., "Abbey Simon Plays Chopin, Prokofiev," *New York Times*, December 3, 1947.

His performances of the three pieces of Ravel's *Gaspard de la Nuit* were really quite remarkable. They required a listening ear as sensitive as his own, but the attention was rewarded with impressions of the utmost subtlety and strangeness.

R. P., "Abbey Simon Plays at Carnegie Hall," *New York Times*, February 24, 1949.

He possesses, besides an excellent technique, a certain delicate taste in touch and in choice of color. He obtained a cordial success from the large and warm audience.

Il Giornale d'Italia (Rome), May 19, 1949.

One can try to describe A. S.'s masterly playing—thereby having to exhaust all existing superlatives—but the beauty of his playing cannot be described in words…one has to think back twenty years, to Horowitz's debut, to remember an equal event.

Algemeen Dagblad (Rotterdam), May 27, 1949.

His breathtaking technique puts him above any criticism…I would not have been surprised had he played the *Paganini Variations* the other way round, or standing up, or blindfolded…It would be impossible for him to make mistakes.

Trouw (Amsterdam), May 28, 1949.

A young American pianist of great distinction…his rubato in Chopin was faultless and the variety of color effect in Ravel's *Gaspard de la Nuit* had astounding finesse.

London Telegram, June 13, 1949.

Everything in his playing reflects a profound, poetical, and thought-out sentiment. This is a name to remember.

Opera (Paris), June 15, 1949.

Simon, who is an excellent technician, is served by an eminent musicianship that impresses even when one is of an absolutely different opinion regarding the interpretation...The encores that Simon played to the enthusiastic public resembled the fine workmanship of a goldsmith.

"Music without Ballast," *Täglicher Anzeiger am Morgen* (Berlin), March 26, 1952.

The first pianist of the world...a demoniacal technique.

A. De Wal, *De Niewe Courant* (The Hague), January 5, 1951.

He has an extraordinary feeling for the inner meaning of the music.

"A Remarkable Piano Recital," *Aftonbladet* (Stockholm), May 5, 1951.

His dynamic phrasing is always perfect...This pianist certainly has a great future before him.

R.K., *Im Rampenlicht* (Vienna), May 21, 1951.

His fund of imaginative power is extraordinary and his interpretation is always fascinating.

K.L., *Weltpresse* (Vienna), May 21, 1951.

In recent weeks, through the Ruhr America House, we have come to know a series of instrumentalists of unique rank. Above all, we were deeply impressed by the young generation of American pianists. At their peak stands Abbey Simon.

Essener Tagblatt (Essen), March 29, 1952.

The young pianist Abbey Simon played last Monday for the first time in Bogotá in a recital under the auspices of the Musical Society Daniel. In it he revealed the remarkable, first class instrumental qualities which fully justify the already vast renown which he enjoys in the musical circles of North America and Europe.

"The Pianist Simon," *La Republica* (Bogotá), June 2, 1954.

Mr. Simon left this country a skillful pianist. He has returned a master. Everything on the program was played to perfection… Mr. Simon begins where most pianists leave off.

Harold Schonberg, "Abbey Simon Returns in Piano Recital," *New York Times*, March 31, 1960.

The pianism was by turns noble and brilliant, and frequently both; the singing (or humming) was deplorable. It was as bad as Toscanini's: something between a grunt, a groan, and the sigh of a heavy sleeper.

"Abbey Simon's Recital," *Sydney Morning Herald*, April 17, 1961.

The…soloist…addressed himself to the Brahms B-Flat-Major Piano Concerto with barely passable results.

Donal Henahan, "Grant Park Opens with Words, Music," *Chicago Daily News*, June 28, 1962.

The Brahms B-Flat-Major Concerto was a poor choice for Abbey Simon, who found himself frequently at the limit of his technical resources.

Robert C. Marsh, "Grant Park Concerts Open in Well-Blended Program," *Chicago Sun Times*, June 28, 1962.

His performance was...plodding along monochromatically note by note, beat by beat, with wrong notes to make you wince.

Thomas Willis, "Open Grant Park Concert Season," *Chicago Daily Tribune*, June 28, 1962.

The resplendent playing of Mr. Abbey Simon in Rachmaninoff's Third Piano Concerto at the Festival Hall last night was the focal point in the London Philharmonic Orchestra's concert, a shining light putting all else in the shade...The sheer virtuosity of his playing was exhilarating, that and the ease with which he manipulated the intricate embellishments of his solo part.

"Resplendent Playing By Mr. Abbey Simon," *London Times*, October 13, 1962.

He is that fortunate combination of probing intellect that constantly holds the music up for re-examination for new possibilities of expression and a rich, fulfilling emotional commitment to warm, illuminative playing.

Howard Klein, "Abbey Simon at Carnegie Hall Plays Liszt's B Minor Sonata," *New York Times*, December 16, 1963.

Simon should have his wrist slapped for playing, in this day and age, one of those Busoni transcriptions of Bach's organ works. Although Bach rises above everything with a sovereign genius that no amount of abuse can tarnish, it would have been much better for Simon to expend his artistry on works written, at the very least, for the harpsichord.

J.F. Goosen, "Pianist Simon Superb in University Concert," *Tuscaloosa News*, April 27, 1964.

For his *Capriccio*, Mr. Adaskin, a professor of music at the University of Saskatchewan, has employed a French-Canadian folksong as the principal source of the thematic material. It is a rather mournful theme, and the back-and-forth exchanges between piano and orchestra are not particularly eventful. Abbey Simon played the piano part from the score. It did not offer him—or the orchestra—much challenge.

Unknown New York Newspaper, March 22, 1965.

The prolix and driveless *Capriccio* was saved at times by the wonderful piano playing of Simon.

Louis Biancolli, "Americas Have Their Day in Two Carnegie Concerts," *New York World Telegram*, March 22, 1965.

Adaskin's *Capriccio* resolved from an inviting beginning into a dry workout that hardly ingratiated the listener except for admiration of Abbey Simon's piano playing.

Miles Kastendieck, "Sincere Direction by David Katz," *New York Journal-American*, March 22, 1965.

Fuleihan's…Sonata No. 9 received its world premiere. A conservative score, full of impressionistic effects and pseudo-Oriental colors, the sonata scampers about, gleefully splattering all sorts of attractive sounds. It doesn't seem actually to get anywhere, but as brilliantly played by Mr. Simon, it certainly had fun going wherever it went.

Robert Sherman, "Abbey Simon Back for Piano Recital," *New York Times*, March 22, 1965.

Hero of a Cult…Exquisite finish…perfectly equalized fingers, and…a superb ear.

Harold Schonberg, "Music: Pianist's Pianist," *New York Times*,

January 20, 1967.

American pianist Abbey Simon, resident in Geneva for eighteen years, performed Wednesday night, as soloist, the Second Concerto by Rachmaninoff, which was included in the program of the symphonic concert Radio Romande. Fifteen minutes before going down to the studio on Carl Vogt Boulevard, this artist was victim of a seemingly innocuous incident: he had twisted the little finger of the left hand seeking an object in his pants pocket. Suffering, he played anyway. To perfection, in the opinion of connoisseurs. And the public, to whom we had announced that Abbey Simon had injured his hand, applauded him for keeping to his score with such perfect control. Now, in retrospect, the exploit appears even more meritorious. At the end of the concert, a friend drove the pianist to the hospital, where radiography revealed without hesitation a fracture of the finger and where the doctor, after having provided his care, prescribed immobilization of four weeks.

A.R., "Pour un pianiste: Un doigt cassé n'exclut pas le talent," *Tribune de Genève*, June 10, 1971.

Nothing could have been more satisfying than the opening pages of the Franck work, at once expansive, thoughtful, expressive. It was a performance that sustained tension, even at its most reflective, before it went into the brilliant complexities of the fugue....

In the Chopin études, Mr. Simon provided the kind of dazzling finger-work that is rare today. The apparent ease of the fireworks, combined with a musical shaping of the material, caused the audience to erupt in bravos after individual études, even though the pianist was trying to play them without interruption. Especially memorable was No. 9 in F Minor; with its moody agitated atmosphere transformed into a work of surprising beauty through pianistic coloration.

Raymond Ericson, "Romantic Works Dazzlingly Done By Abbey Simon," *New York Times,* December 4, 1974.

Mr. Simon, that powerful technician, gave the Ravel Left-Hand Concerto an expert performance. The approach had the necessary combination of virtuosity and elegance. Here and there the pianist was obscured by the over-hearty accompaniment of Mr. Boulez, who seemed to forget that only half a pianist was at work. Not that one would have noticed the deficiency during the two cadenzas, which Mr. Simon played with extraordinary fluency.

Harold C. Schonberg, *New York Times,* March 22, 1975.

At the outset of his programme on Sunday, Abbey Simon's piano artistry reminded his audience that Beethoven's *Bagatelles* are no mere trifles but remarkably varied explorations of keyboard fantasy. He played the first set of seven, op. 33, with a keen rhythmic impetus in the more extrovert among them, some beautifully veiled soft passages, including the echo phrases in the gently rocking triple time of No. 3, and an engaging suggestion of harpsichord figuration in No. 4.

From Beethoven to Brahms was a giant leap in pianistic terms, but Mr Simon accomplished it in a warmly romantic yet musically purposeful account of the F-Minor Sonata, op. 5. Hunched over the keyboard on a piano stool specially tilted forward by legs of uneven length, his head seldom raised from its angle of close concentration and his body utterly unmoving from the shoulders to the lower limbs, he put a forceful technique at the service of imaginative feeling.

Noël Goodwin, "Abbey Simon, Queen Elizabeth Hall," *Lon-*

don Times, March 26, 1985.

Listen to Simon's account of Beethoven's Sonata in G Major (op. 14, no. 2), which opened the program, and you will hear what a master lyricist can do with the simplest of gestures. In the long-lined middle movement, Simon proved that subtle inflections and the gentlest relaxations in tempo can be supremely expressive.

One couldn't ask for more freshness and innocence in three of Mendelssohn's *Songs Without Words* (in E Major, F-sharp Minor and C Major). Simon knows that the charm of these works lies in their simplicity, thus he avoided the romantic excesses to which these miniatures are sometimes subjected.

The pianist evoked another world entirely in Chopin's Piano Sonata in B-flat Minor (op. 35). Though there probably were those in the audience who were slightly taken aback by Simon's decidedly nostalgic approach, at least one listener found it as intriguing as it was persuasive....

The pianist brought much atmosphere and color to Rachmaninoff's *Variations on a Theme by Corelli* (op. 22). That he could sustain the piece at so slow a tempo was as much a testament to his finger legato as to his understanding of how these variations cohere.

And even in three miniatures from Ravel's *Miroirs* ("Noctuelles," "Oiseaux tristes," and "Alborada del gracioso"), Simon managed to draw silken melodic lines from amid bold splashes of color.

Howard Reich, "Simon Simple Refinement Enriches Keyboard," *Chicago Tribune,* February 23, 1988.

It would be hard to imagine performances more penetrating than those Simon gave the two great works—Beethoven's op.

110 Sonata in A-flat Major and Schumann's op. 17 Fantasy in C Major—that made up the first half of his recital at the St. Louis Conservatory of Music on Monday evening.

James Wierzbicki, "Straightforward Approach Sparkles," *St. Louis Post-Dispatch*, February 7, 1990.

In the difficult and rich-in-ideas series of variations by Rachmaninoff on the Corelli theme "La folia," Simon's sheer joy in playing also became evident. Lively passages, arpeggio cascades and clown-like motifs were just as gripping as the full play given to beautiful melodic themes and the restrained interpretation of quiet, reflective passages.

Hedwig Schroder, "Cultivated Playing," *Husumer Nachrichten* (Husum), August 28, 1990.

Simon, a man of mature years, let the work speak in its own words. By no means wanting for technical aplomb or coloristic finesse, Simon employs these traits in the service of the music, demonstrating that virtuosity is in fact virtuous. The deliciously somnambulant Andante, which separates the majestic opening movement from the energetic Scherzo, was both gentle and genteel, never nervously hurried, never complacently stalled. This had the desired effect of making emotional room for the fury to follow. Such understatement is particularly well applied to Brahms, who even in his youth spoke with a canny reserve....

Of the two other works on the program, Busoni's transcription of Bach's Organ Toccata, Adagio and Fugue in C Major and the *Six Grandes Études d'apres les caprices de Paganini* by Franz Liszt, it was the Liszt that brought out the traditional virtuoso in Simon. Constituting the second half of the concert, these six stunts are among the most ingeniously difficult pieces in the repertoire. Simon brought out the fun and joy in these pieces, reminding us that for these early composer/pianists, the piano was a universe unto itself whose exploration was a noble and sublime adventure.

Michael Manning, "Abbey Simon's Intelligent, Tasteful Pianism," *The Boston Globe*, December 6, 1994.

Simon's ability to spin out evenly weighted legato lines, no matter how busy the notes are on the page, was a virtue in most settings. Beethoven's Sonata no. 31 in A-flat, op. 110, came across as a near-ideal blend of architecture and pure sound, its last-movement fugue a stimulating, lyrical celebration. In the *"Abegg" Variations*, op. 1, phrases breathed, and the smooth transitions matched the music's mercurial nature.

Chopin is a Simon specialty, and his take on the Sonata No. 3 in B Minor, op. 58, had something for every listener. Opulent tone, clean articulation and dreamily suspended chords in the slow movement showed his expert balance of resources. In the macabre world of Ravel's *Gaspard de la nuit*, Simon hummed along, disconcertingly at times, as he evoked images of irregular wave crests, tolling death-watch bells that sustained for an ungodly length of time, and a surreal dancing dwarf.

Ravel paved the way for Prokofiev's Toccata in C, op. 11, which allowed Simon to cut loose by hammering the keys and buzzing through the rhythms like a madman. True to form, there's a great deal of method to Simon's madness.

Charles McCardell, "Abbey Simon," *Washington Post*, October 9, 1995.

Simon didn't "bring out" inner voices, which suggests something artificial; instead he seemed alert to the full inner life of the music, the heart, the brain, the breathing.

Simon's pedal technique is exceedingly complex; it helps create that swirl of color, and it dramatizes both the melting and the onward march of harmony. This was particularly remarkable in the Chopin sonata, where the great melody of the Largo truly sang, and in the irresistible stride of the finale. In the Scherzo, the mists lifted as each scampering note caught its bit of sunlight and turned it into a rainbow.

Richard Dyer, "Simon's keyboard of many colors," *Boston Globe*, Mar 18, 1997.

If the opening Allegro maestoso was a model of architectural clarity, the Scherzo had a free-spirited quality that edged toward wildness. The finale combined qualities from both those movements. Hard driven as it was, it also offered a wealth of detail, including some lovely coloristic touches in the bass.

Mr. Simon's graceful, ruminative account of the Nocturne in F-sharp Minor (op. 48, no. 2) and his alternately tempestuous and introspective look at the Impromptu No. 1 in A flat (op. 29) were attractive for creating the illusion of closeness to Chopin's sound world and esthetic.

Allan Kozinn, "A Romantic Who Has A Rational Side, Too," *New York Times*, September 24, 1999.

It was not the kind of virtuosity that is most common today— loud, fast, flashy and insensitive. Instead, it combined fleetness, lightness and precision with a golden tone….

The most memorable thing about Simon's playing was its poetry, the pianist's total immersion in the music.

Joseph McLellan, "Abbey Simon & Romanticism: A Perfect Pair," *Washington Post*, November 3, 2003.

Appendix C
MASTER TIMETABLE

The majority of the information on this list comes from material compiled over the years by Dina Simon. The absence of dates toward the end of the list is in some measure due to her final illness and death. In fact, Mr. Simon continues to perform regularly at the time of publication, even though this is not accurately represented here. Additionally, there are many obvious gaps for which complete information could not be found.

1937
4-19 Recital, Shared, Curtis Institute, Philadelphia, PA

1940
3-14 Recital, Curtis Institute, Philadelphia, PA
9-28 Recital, Town Hall, New York, NY

1941
10-15 Recital, Town Hall, New York, NY
10-29 Recital, Albert Leonard High School, New Rochelle, NY

1944
1-16 Recital, Carnegie Hall, New York, NY

1945
1-3 Recital, Carnegie Hall, New York, NY
12-2 Recital, Kimball Hall, Chicago, IL

1946

? Recital, Providence, RI
? Concerto, Minneapolis Symphony, Minneapolis, MN
? Concerto, Buffalo Symphony, Buffalo, NY
1-10 Recital, New England Conservatory, Boston, MA
1-13 Recital, Gardner Museum, Boston, MA
1-21 Recital, Carnegie Hall, New York, NY
7-9 Concerto, Robin Hood Dell Orchestra, Dimitri
Mitropoulos, Robin Hood Dell, Philadelphia, PA, Chopin 2
8-6 Concerto, New York Philharmonic-Symphony Orchestra,
Efrem Kurtz, Lewisohn Stadium, New York, NY, Chopin 2

1947
7-24 Concerto, Watergate Orchestra, The Watergate,
Washington, DC, Chopin 2
10-30 Recital, Lyric Theater, Ludington, MI
11-3 Recital, Orchestra Hall, Chicago, IL
11-10 Recital, Arvida, Canada
12-2 Recital, Carnegie Hall, New York, NY

1948
4-19 Concerto, National Orchestral Association Orchestra,
Leon Barzin, Carnegie Hall, New York, NY, Liszt 1

1949
2-22 Recital, Carnegie Hall, New York, NY
4-29 Recital, Maine Township Community Concert
Association, Chicago, IL
5-18 Recital, Rome, Italy
5-26 Recital, Rotterdam, Netherlands
5-27 Recital, Amsterdam, Netherlands
5-29 Recital, The Hague, Netherlands
6-11 Recital, Wigmore Hall, London, England

6-14? Recital, Opéra, Paris, France
11-7 Concerto, London Philharmonic, Hugo Rignold, City
Hall, Chatham, England, Beethoven 4

1950
4-2 Concerto, London Symphony, Malcolm Sargent, Albert
Hall, London, England, Brahms 2

1951
1-4 Recital, The Hague, Netherlands
1-5 Recital, Rotterdam, Netherlands
1-6 Recital, Amsterdam, Netherlands
1-21 Concerto, London Symphony, Josef Krips, Albert Hall,
London, England, Schumann
2-16 Concerto, London Students Orchestra, Boyd Neel, Albert
Hall, London, England, Tchaikovsky 1
2-20 Recital, Shared with Ida Haendel, McLellan Galleries,
Glasgow, Scotland
5-7 Recital, Stockholm, Sweden
5-10 Recital, Odd Fellow Palæet, Copenhagen, Denmark
5-20 Recital, Mozart Saal, Vienna, Austria
5-25 Recital, University Festival Hall, Oslo, Norway

1952
1-10 Concerto, BBC Symphony, Malcolm Sargent, Albert Hall,
London, England, Brahms 1
1-29 Concerto, Chicago Symphony, George Schick, Chicago,
IL, Brahms 2
2-1 Recital, First Methodist Church, Evanston, IL
3-6 Recital, German Museum, Nuremberg, Germany
3-12 Recital, Freien Schule, Ulm, Germany
3-21 Recital, America House, Frankfurt, Germany

3-25 Recital, America House, Berlin, Germany
3-28 Recital, America House, Essen, Germany
5-22 Recital, Jerusalem, Israel
6-28 Concerto, Grant Park Symphony Orchestra, Nicolai
Malko, Grant Park, Chicago, IL, Chopin 2
7-27? Concerto, Yorkshire Symphony Orchestra, Leeds,
England, Beethoven 5

1953
1-15 Recital, Festival Hall, London, England
2-22 Recital, Geneva, Switzerland
12-3 Recital, Goldsmiths' Hall, London, England
12-10 Recital, Teatro Victoria Eugenia, San Sebastián, Spain
12-? Recital, Teatro María Cristina, Gijon, Spain
12-? Recital, Teatro Filarmonica, Oviedo, Spain

1954
5-10 Recital, Teatro Municipal, Lima, Peru
5-11 Recital, Teatro Municipal, Caracas, Venezuela
5-14 Recital, Teatro Municipal, Lima, Peru
5-19 Concertos, Orquesta Sinfónica Nacional, Theo Buchwald,
Lima, Peru, Chopin 2, Tchaikovsky 1
5-27 Recital, Teatro Elite, Santo Domingo, Dominican
Republic
5-31 Recital, Teatro Colón, Bogotá, Colombia
6-2 Recital, Teatro Colón, Bogotá, Colombia
6-7 Recital, Teatro Municipal, Caracas, Venezuela
6-9 Recital, Teatro Municipal, Caracas, Venezuela
6-13 Concerto, Angel Sousa, Caracas, Venezuela, Tchaikovsky
1
6-17 Recital, Teatro Municipal, Caracas, Venezuela
6-22 Recital, Teatro Municipal, Caracas, Venezuela

6-30 Recital, Teatro Gran Rex, Buenos Aires, Argentina
7-2 Recital, Rosario, Argentina
7-6 Recital, Teatro Gran Rex, Buenos Aires, Argentina
7-11 Recital, Teatro Gran Rex, Buenos Aires, Argentina
7-13 Recital, Sodre Auditorio Nacional, Montevideo, Uruguay
7-15 Recital, Sodre Auditorio Nacional, Montevideo, Uruguay
7-18 Recital, Teatro Gran Rex, Buenos Aires, Argentina
8-2 Concerto, London Symphony, Basil Cameron, Albert Hall,
London, England, Tchaikovsky 1
8-12 Concerto, Bournemouth Symphony, Charles Groves,
Bournemouth, England, Grieg
12-13 Recital, Cine Cervantes, Santander, Spain

1955
1-3 Recital, America House, Kassel, Germany
1-13 Concerto, Groninger Orkest, Jan van Epenhuysen,
Groningen, Netherlands, Mozart 21
2-28 Recital, Parkteatret, Oslo, Norway
3-1 Recital, Biblioteket, Fredrikstad, Norway
3-3 Concerto, Trondheim Symphony, Finn Audun Oftedal,
Trondheim, Norway, Chopin 2
3-6 Recital, Nuremberg, Germany
3-9 Concertos, Filharmonisk Selskaps Orkester (Oslo
Philharmonic), Odd Grüner-Hegge, Oslo, Norway, Chopin 2,
Tchaikovsky 1
3-13 Recital, Ulm, Germany
3-15 Recital, Tübingen, Germany
3-16 Recital, America House, Freiburg, Germany
3-21 Recital, America House, Frankfurt, Germany
3-23 Recital, Darmstadt, Germany
3-26 Recital, Radio in American Sector Studio 7, Berlin,
Germany

3-28 Recital, Essen, Germany

3-29 Recital, America House, Kassel, Germany

4-5 Recital, America House, Koblenz, Germany

4-6 Recital, America House, Mannheim, Germany

4-21 Concerto, City of Birmingham Symphony, Harold Gray, Town Hall, Birmingham, England, Brahms 1

4-30 Recital, Teatro do Instituto Normal for Sociedade de Cultura Artística, Bahia, Brazil

5-2 Recital, Auditorio del CIA, Buenos Aires, Argentina

5-13,14 Concerto, Orquesta Sinfónica Nacional, Antal Doráti, Palacio de Bellas Artes, Mexico City, Mexico, Tchaikovsky 1

5-18 Recital, Palacio de Bellas Artes, Mexico City, Mexico

5-? Concertos, Orquesta Sinfónica Nacional, Theo Buchwald, Teatro Municipal, Lima, Peru, Mozart 21, Schumann

5-25 Concertos, Orquesta Sinfónica Nacional, Theo Buchwald, Teatro Municipal, Lima, Peru, Brahms 1, Rachmaninoff Paganini

5-27 Recital, Teatro Municipal, Lima, Peru

5-30 Recital, Teatro Municipal, Lima, Peru

6-4 Recital, Teatro Municipal, Lima, Peru

6-7 Concerto, Orquesta Sinfónica Nacional, Theo Buchwald, Teatro Municipal, Lima, Peru, Rachmaninoff Paganini

6-10 Recital, Montevideo, Uruguay

6-14 Recital, Teatro Independencia, Mendoza, Argentina

6-18 Recital, Concepción del Uruguay, Argentina

6-25 Recital, Teatro Colón, Buenos Aires, Argentina

6-29 Recital, Teatro Solís, Montevideo, Uruguay

7-6 Concerto, Orquesta Sinfónica Nacional, Carlos Felix Cillario, Buenos Aires, Argentina, Grieg

7-28 Recital, Teatro Municipal, Buenos Aires, Argentina

8-5 Recital, Teatro Paramount, Buenos Aires, Argentina

12-21 Concerto, Residentie Orkest, Willem van Otterloo,

Gebouw voor Kunsten en Wetenschappen, Utrecht, Netherlands, Ravel G

12-22 Concerto, Residentie Orkest, Willem van Otterloo, Stadsgehoorzaal, Leiden, Netherlands, Ravel G

1956
1-7 Concerto, City of Birmingham Symphony, Rudolf Schwarz, City Hall, Sheffield, England, Brahms 2

1-29 Recital, Diligentia Theatre, The Hague, Netherlands

2-23 Concerto, City of Birmingham Symphony, Harold Gray, Town Hall, Birmingham, Rachmaninoff 3

4-6,13 Concerto, London Philharmonic, Massimo Freccia, Albert Hall, Beethoven 5

5-26 Concerto, Limburgs Symphonie Orkest, André Rieu, Staargebouw te Maastricht, Limburg, Netherlands, Beethoven 5

9-11 Concerto, City of Birmingham Symphony, Rudolf Schwarz, Town Hall, Cheltenham, England, Beethoven 3

9-13 Concerto, City of Birmingham Symphony, Rudolf Schwarz, Town Hall, Birmingham, England, Beethoven 3

10-10 Recital, Town Hall, Chester, England

10-13 Recital, Wigmore Hall, London, England

10-25 Recital, City Hall, Sheffield, England

11-8 Concerto, Norwich Philharmonic, Heathcote Statham, St. Andrew's Hall, Norwich, England, Rachmaninoff 2

12-2 Concerto, London Symphony, George Wheldon, Albert Hall, London, England, Grieg

1957
1-20 Recital, The Hague, Netherlands

1-22 Recital, Laren, Netherlands

2-14 Concerto, Stavanger Byorkester, Karsten Andersen,

Stavanger, Norway, Beethoven 5

2-21 Recital, Rjukanhusets store sal, Rjukan, Norway

2-22 Concerto, Filharmonisk Selskaps Orkester (Oslo Philharmonic), Edouard van Remoortel, Universitetets Aula, Oslo, Norway, Rachmaninoff 3

2-24 Concerto, Residentie Orkest, Willem van Otterloo, Stadsgehoorzaal, Leiden, Netherlands, Chopin 2

3-18 Recital, Aula Magna, Rome, Italy

4-23 Recital, Wigmore Hall, London, England

5-6 Recital for Asociación Amigos del Arte, Santa Fe (Argentina?)

5-10 Recital, Teatro Solís, Montevideo, Uruguay

5-11 Recital, Teatro Colón, (Argentina?)

5-20 Recital, Cine Artigas, Montevideo, Uruguay

6-1 Concertos, Orquesta Sinfónica de Chile, Víctor Tevah, Aula Magna de las Universidad Santa Maria, Santiago, Chile, Beethoven 4, Ravel G

6-3 Recital, Teatro Astor, Santiago, Chile

6-7 Recital, Teatro Municipal, Lima, Peru

6-21 Concerto, Orquesta Sinfónica de Colombia, Olav Roots, Teatro Colón, Bogotá, Colombia

6-28 Recital, Teatro de la Universidad de Puerto Rico, San Juan, Puerto Rico

7-8 Recital, Teatro Municipal, Caracas, Venezuela

7-18 Recital, Cine Texier, Concepción del Uruguay, Argentina

9-4 Concerto, Bournemouth Symphony, Charles Groves, Winter Gardens, Birmingham, England, Tchaikovsky 1

9-28 Recital, Wigmore Hall, London, England

10-10 Concerto, City of Birmingham Symphony, Andrzej Panufnik, Town Hall, Birmingham, England, Rachmaninoff Paganini

10-23,26 Concerto, Baltimore Symphony, Massimo Freccia,

Baltimore, MD, Schumann
11-5 Concerto and Recital, Compton Civic Symphony,
Compton, CA, Schumann
11-7 Recital, St. Augustine by-the-Sea, HI
11-23 Concerto, Orquesta Sinfónica Nacional, Teatro Nacional
de S. Carlos, Lisbon, Spain, Tchaikovsky 1
12-7 Concerto, Concertgebouw Orchestra, George Szell,
Amsterdam, Netherlands, Tchaikovsky 1
12-9 Recital, Tilburg, Netherlands

1958
3-1 to 5-2 Tour of Indonesia
5-3 Recital, Milan, Italy
6-7 Concerto, Norwich Orchestra, Heathcote Statham, St.
Andrew's Hall, Norwich, England, Beethoven 5
6-23 Concerto, Royal Liverpool Philharmonic, Alexander
Gibson, Liverpool, England, Beethoven 4
8-? Recital, Copenhagen, Denmark
8-12 Concerto, Tivoli Orkester, Robert Blot, Tivolis
Koncertsal, Copenhagen, Denmark, Beethoven 4
9-4 Concerto, Filharmonisk Selskaps Orkester (Oslo
Philharmonic), Odd Grüner-Hegge, Universitetets Aula, Oslo,
Norway, Beethoven 5
9-24 Recital, Helsinki, Finland
9-25 Concerto, Helsinki Philharmonic, Ole Edgren, Helsinki,
Finland, Tchaikovsky 1
9-26 Concerto, Helsinki Philharmonic, Tauno Hannikainen,
Helsinki, Finland, Rachmaninoff Paganini
9-29 Recital, Björneborg, Sweden
10-12 Concerto, London Philharmonic, Royalton Kisch, Albert
Hall, London, England, Tchaikovsky 1
11-12 Concerto, London Philharmonic, Adrian Boult, Town

Hall, Huddersfield, England, Rachmaninoff 2

11-? Concerto, Tivoli Orkester, Robert Blot, Tivolis Koncertsal, Copenhagen, Denmark, Brahms 1

12-11 Concerto, *Statsradiofoniens Symfoniorkester*, Johan Hye-Knudsen, Copenhagen, Denmark, Brahms 1

1959

1-4 Recital, Wigmore Hall, London, England

1-6,7,9 Concerto and Recital, Royal Liverpool Philharmonic, Edouard van Remoortel, Different Cities, England, Liszt Hungarian Fantasy

1-10 Concerto and Recital, Royal Liverpool Philharmonic, Zubin Mehta, Philharmonic Hall, Liverpool, England, Liszt Hungarian Fantasy

1-13 Recital, Croydon, England

1-16,23,30, 2-6 Recitals, Art Gallery, Derby, England

1-19 Recital, Royal Dublin Society, Dublin, Ireland

1-20 Recital, Waterford Music Club, Waterford, Ireland

1-31 Concerto, London Philharmonic Orchestra, William Steinberg, The Dome, Brighton, England

2-27 Concerto, Hallé Orchestra, Georges Tzipine, Sheffield, England, Schumann

2-28 Concerto, Hallé Orchestra, Georges Tzipine, Bradford, England, Chopin 1

3-1 Concerto, Hallé Orchestra, Georges Tzipine, Free Trade Hall, Manchester, England, Chopin 1

3-10 Recital, Salón Liceo del Círculo de la Amistad, Córdoba, Spain

3-11 Recital, Conservatorio de Música, Málaga, Spain

3-26 Concerto, Bournemouth Symphony, Charles Groves, Winter Gardens, Bournemouth, England, Beethoven 5

4-5 Concerto, Bournemouth Symphony, Herbert Menges,

King's Theatre, Southsea, England, Brahms 2
4-7 Concerto, Bournemouth Symphony, Charles Groves,
Guildhall, Southampton, England, Tchaikovsky 1
4-12 Concerto, London Symphony, George Weldon, Albert
Hall, London, England, Rachmaninoff 2
4-23 Recital, St. Andrew's Hall, Norwich, England
5-19 Recital, Asociación Wagneriana, Buenos Aires, Argentina
5-22 Recital, Mozarteum Argentino, Buenos Aires, Argentina
6-9 Concerto, Orquesta Sinfónica Nacional, Juan-José Castro,
Teatro Colón, Buenos Aires, Argentina, Brahms 1
6-17 Concerto, Amigos de la musica, Antonio Janigro, Gran
Cine-Teatro Opera, Buenos Aires, Argentina, Beethoven 4
6-22 Concerto, Orquesta Filarmónica de Chile, Juan
Matteucci, Teatro Real, Santiago, Tchaikovsky 1
6-30 Recital, Teatro Municipal, Lima, Peru
7-1 Recital, Teatro Municipal, Lima, Peru
7-11 Concerto, Orquesta Sinfónica Nacionale, José Iturbi,
Teatro Municipal, Lima, Peru, Beethoven 4
9-20 Concerto, Newcastle Sinfonia Orchestra, City Hall,
Newcastle, Schumann
10-4 Recital, Oundle School, Oundle, England
10-22 Concerto, City of Birmingham Symphony, Meredith
Davies, Town Hall, Birmingham, Brahms 1
10-31 Recital, Swansea Music and Arts Club, Swansea, Wales
11-8 Concerto, London Philharmonic, Hugo Rignold, Winter
Gardens, Margate, England, Beethoven 4
11-13 Recital, Musikhalle, Hamburg
11-16 Recital, Ernst Reuter Haus, Berlin

1960
3-15 Recital, Salones del Conservatorio, Santiago de Cuba,
Cuba

3-21 Recital, Tuesday Musical Club, Houston, Houston, TX

3-30 Recital, Carnegie Hall, New York, NY

7-19 Concerto, City of Birmingham Symphony, Meredith Davies, Town Hall, Birmingham, Brahms 2

8-25 Concerto, Filharmonisk Selskaps Orkester (Oslo Philharmonic), Odd Grüner-Hegge, Oslo, Norway Chopin 1

10-5 Concerto, Residentie-Orkest, Willem van Otterloo, Gebouw voor Kunsten en Wetenschappen, The Hague, Netherlands, Beethoven 4

10-7 Concerto, Residentie-Orkest, Willem van Otterloo, Dordrecht, Netherlands, Beethoven 4

10-10 Concerto, Residentie-Orkest, Willem van Otterloo, Grand Theater Gooiland, Hilversum, Netherlands, Beethoven 4

10-30 Concerto, Orchestra of the Royal Opera House, Colin Davis, Albert Hall, London, Beethoven 5

10-31 Concerto, City of Birmingham Symphony, Harold Gray, Birmingham, England, Rachmaninoff 3

11-16 Recital, Roslyn Country Club, Roslyn Heights, NY

11-23 Concerto, BBC Symphony, Rudolf Schwarz, Civic Hall, Wolverhampton, England, Beethoven 4

12-19 Recital, Carnegie Hall, New York, NY

?-? Concerts in Genoa, Italy

1961

1-21 Concerto, Emperor Symphony Orchestra, Royalton Kisch, Albert Hall, London, Tchaikovsky 1

2-18 Concerto, London Philharmonic, Adrian Boult, Winter Garden, Eastbourne, England, Schumann

3-1 Concerto, Calcutta Symphony, New Empire Theatre, Bernard Jacob, Calcutta, India, Tchaikovsky 1

3-4 Recital, Loke Yew Hall, University of Hong Kong, Hong

Kong

3-18 Recital, Town Hall, Armidale, Australia

3-19 Recital, ABC Television, Sydney, Australia

3-21,22,23 Concerto, Sydney Symphony, Joseph Post, Town Hall, Sydney, Australia, Chopin 2

3-25,27 Concerto, Sydney Symphony, Joseph Post, Town Hall, Sydney, Australia, Tchaikovsky 1

3-29 Recital, Vanity Theatre, Lismore, Australia

4-5,6 Recitals, Albert Hall, Canberra, Australia

4-8 Concerto, Queensland Symphony, Rudolf Pekarek, Brisbane, Australia, Beethoven 4

4-10 Recital, Newcastle, Australia

4-12,15 Recitals, Conservatorium Hall, Sydney, Australia,

4-19,20 Concerto, Victorian Symphony, Georges Tzipine, Town Hall, Melbourne, Australia, Rachmaninoff Paganini

4-22,24 Concerto, Victorian Symphony, Georges Tzipine, Town Hall, Melbourne, Australia, Brahms 1

4-26 Recital, Assembly Hall, Melbourne, Australia,

4-28 Recital, Memorial Hall, Sale, Australia

5-1 Recital, Civic Hall, Ballarat, Australia

5-5,6 Concerto, West Australian Symphony, John Farnsworth Hall, Capitol Theatre, Perth, Australia, Brahms 2

5-9 Concerto, West Australian Youth Orchestra, John Farnsworth Hall, Capitol Theatre, Perth, Australia, Rachmaninoff Paganini

5-11 Recital, Capitol Theatre, Perth, Australia,

5-13 Recital, Town Hall, Broken Hill, Australia

5-16 Recital, Town Hall, Adelaide, Australia

5-18,19,20 Concerto, South Australian Symphony, Tibor Paul, Town Hall, Adelaide, Australia, Chopin 2

5-23 Concerto, South Australian Youth Symphony, Rudolf Pekarek, Town Hall, Adelaide, Australia, Tchaikovsky 1

5-26 Recital, Star Theatre, Shepparton, Australia

5-30 Recital, Horsham, Australia

5-31 Recital, Hamilton, Australia

6-2 Recital, Geelong, Australia

6-6 Concerto, Tasmanian Symphony Orchestra, Kenneth Murison Bourn, City Hall, Hobart, Australia, Chopin 2

6-7 Concerto, Tasmanian Symphony Orchestra, Kenneth Murison Bourn, National Theatre, Launceston, Australia, Chopin 2

6-14 Recital, Civic Theatre, Albury, Australia

6-15 Recital, Plaza Theatre, Wagga, Australia

6-18 Recital, Sydney, Australia

6-19 Recital, Bathurst, Australia

6-22,23 Victorian Youth Symphony, Clive Douglas, Town Hall, Melbourne, Australia, Beethoven 4

6-26 Recital, Whanganui, New Zealand

7-1 Recital, Christchurch, New Zealand

7-4 Recital, Palmerston North, New Zealand

7-8 Concerto, National Orchestra of the New Zealand Broadcasting Service, John Hopkins, Town Hall, Wellington, New Zealand, Beethoven 4

7-11 Concerto, National Orchestra of the New Zealand Broadcasting Service, John Hopkins, Town Hall, Christchurch, New Zealand, Beethoven 4

7-15 Recital, Invercargill, New Zealand

7-18 Recital, Dunedin, New Zealand

7-20 Concerto, Palmerston North, New Zealand

7-22 Recital, Auckland, New Zealand

7-25 Recital, Wellington, New Zealand

7-27 Recital, Blenheim, New Zealand

7-29 Recital, Nelson, New Zealand

8-1 Concerto, National Orchestra of the New Zealand

Broadcasting Service, John Hopkins, Town Hall, Wellington, New Zealand, Brahms 2

8-2 Recital, The Hutt, New Zealand

8-5 Concerto, National Orchestra of the New Zealand Broadcasting Service, John Hopkins, Town Hall, Auckland, New Zealand, Brahms 2

8-14 Concerto, Orquesta Sinfónica Nacional, Jaime Bodmer, Teatro Municipal, Lima, Peru, Beethoven 5

8-16 Recital, Teatro Municipal, Lima, Peru

8-28 Recital, Asociación Wagneriana, Buenos Aires, Argentina

8-31 Recital, Museo Nacional de Arte Decorativo, Buenos Aires, Argentina

9-2 Recital, Teatro Colón, Buenos Aires, Argentina

9-11 Concerto, Orquesta Sinfónica Nacional, Carlos F. Cillario, Teatro Colón, Buenos Aires, Argentina, Beethoven 5

9-13 Recital, Asociación Musical, Cine Argentino, Argentina

10-15 Concerto, Connecticut Symphony, Jonel Perlea, American Shakespeare Festival Theatre, Stratford, CT, Brahms 1

10-29, Recital, Dwight Morrow High School, Englewood, NJ

11-12,13,14 Concerto, Buffalo Philharmonic, Josef Krips, Kleinhans Music Hall, Buffalo, NY, Beethoven 1

11-24,26 Concerto, Pittsburgh Symphony, William Steinberg, Syria Mosque, Pittsburgh, PA, Mozart 20

12-8,9 Concerto, Cincinnati Symphony, Haig Yaghjian, Music Hall, Cincinnati, OH, Rachmaninoff 3

1962

2-2 Concerto, Filharmonisk Selskaps Orkester (Oslo Philharmonic), Sverre Bruland, Universitetets Aula, Oslo, Norway, Rachmaninoff 3

2-8,9,11 Concerto, New York Philharmonic, Thomas

Schippers, Carnegie Hall, New York, NY, Rachmaninoff 3

2-15 Concerto, London Philharmonic, Malcolm Sargent, Festival Hall, London, England, Beethoven 4

3-11 Concerto, Orchestra of the Royal Opera House, Joseph Horovitz, Albert Hall, London, England, Beethoven 5

4-3 Concerto, Radio Eireann Symphony Orchestra, Tibor Paul, Olympia Theatre, Dublin, Ireland, Tchaikovsky 1

4-4 Recital, Olympia Theatre, Dublin, Ireland

6-19 Concerto, "Evenings By the River" Festival, East River Park Amphitheatre, New York, NY, Richard Korn, Brahms 2

6-27 Concerto, Grant Park Symphony, Irwin Hoffman, Chicago, IL, Brahms 2

6-29 Concerto, Grant Park Symphony, Irwin Hoffman, Chicago, IL, Rachmaninoff 3

10-12 Concerto, London Philharmonic, Kenneth Alwyn, Festival Hall, London, England, Rachmaninoff 3

12-13 Recital, Indiana University Auditorium, Bloomington, IN

1963

3-10 Recital, Carnegie Hall, New York, NY

3-21 Recital, Cullen Auditorium, University of Houston, Houston, TX

5-19 Recital, Shared, onboard *SS France*

6-30 Recital, Kenwood House, London, England

8-6 Concerto, Philharmonia Orchestra, Norman Del Mar, Albert Hall, London, England, Beethoven 5

9-8 Recital onboard *SS Independence*

10-? Concerto, Scottish National Orchestra, Alexander Gibson, Glasgow, Scotland, Beethoven 4

11-1 Concerto, Scottish National Orchestra, Alexander Gibson, Usher Hall, Edinburgh, Scotland, Beethoven 4

11-3 Concerto, Scottish National Orchestra, Alexander Gibson, Festival Hall, London, England, Beethoven 4
11-6 Recital, Hochschule, ?
11-25 Recital, Indiana University Auditorium, Bloomington, IN
12-9 Recital, Festival Hall, London, England
12-15 Recital, Carnegie Hall, New York, NY

1964
2-1 Recital, Bilbao, Spain
2-2 Recital, Bilbao, Spain
2-4 Recital, Las Palmas de Gran Canaria, Spain
2-6 Concerto, Orquesta de Las Palmas de Gran Canaria, Enrique Garcia Asensio, Spain
2-10,17 Recitals, Teatro Marquina, Madrid, Spain
2-27 Concerto, Philharmonia Orchestra, Carlo Maria Giulini, Festival Hall, London, England, Rachmaninoff 2
4-4 Concerto, Philharmonia Orchestra, Stanley Pope, Festival Hall, London, England, Beethoven 5
4-25 Recital, University of Alabama, Tuscaloosa, AL
6-11 Recital, Teatro Colón, Bogotá, Colombia
6-18 Concertos, Orquesta Sinfónica de Colombia, Olav Roots, Teatro Colón, Bogotá, Colombia, Beethoven 4, Rachmaninoff 3
6-22 Recital, Teatro Colón, Bogotá, Colombia
6-25 Recital, Teatro Municipal, Lima, Peru
6-27 Recital, Teatro Colón, Buenos Aires, Argentina
6-28 Recital, Teatro San Martín, Buenos Aires, Argentina
7-7 Recital, Teatro Astral, Buenos Aires, Argentina
7-11 Recital, Teatro Colón, Buenos Aires, Argentina
7-13 Recital, Teatro Gran Odeón, Concordia, Uruguay
7-21 Recital, Teatro Acassuso, Buenos Aires, Argentina

8-13 Recital, Palazzo Pitti, Florence, Italy
8-23 Recital, Théâtre d'Hammamet, Tunis, Tunisia
10-3 Recital, Washington Irving High School, New York, NY
10-16 Recital, Penn State University, State College, PA
10-18 Recital, Guildhall, Plymouth, England
10-2 Concerto, Orchestre de la Suisse Romande, Gianfranco Rivoli, Victoria Hall, Geneva, Switzerland, Brahms 1
11-13 Recital, Millikin University, Decatur, IL
11-15 Recital, Tuskegee Institute, Tuskegee, AL
11-22 Recital, Tennessee Agricultural and Industrial State University, Nashville, TN
11-26 Recital, Sociedad Filarmónica, Bilbao, Spain
11-27 Recital, Teatro Carrión, Valladolid, Spain
11-28 Recital, Teatro Gayarre, Pamplona, Spain
11-30 Recital, Teatro Principal, Valencia, Spain
12-2 Recital, Bilbao, Spain
12-10 Recital, Teatro Victoria Eugenia, San Sebastián, Spain
12-13 Recital, Palacio de la Música, Barcelona, Spain
12-14 Recital, Teatro Marquina, Madrid, Spain
12-15 Recital, Conservatorio de Música, Málaga, Spain

1965
1-? Concerto, Nashville Symphony, Nashville, TN
1-7 Recital, Morehead State University, Morehead, KY
1-21 Recital, Victoria Hall, Geneva, Switzerland
1-24 Concertos, L'Orchestre Classique de Tunis, Anis Fuleihan, Théâtre Municipal, Tunis, Tunisia, Mozart 21, Beethoven 4
2-22 Recital, Indiana University Auditorium, Bloomington, IN
3-5 Recital, Metropolitan Museum, New York, NY
3-18,19,20,21 Concerto, New York Philharmonic, Seiji Ozawa, Philharmonic Hall, Lincoln Center, New York, NY, Mozart 21
3-21 Concerto, Orchestra of America, Richard Korn,

Carnegie Hall, New York, NY, Adaskin Capriccio

4-9 Concerto, Duluth Symphony, Hermann Herz, National Guard Armory, Duluth, MN, Beethoven 5

5-? Recitals and Concertos in Lima, Peru

5-30 Concerto, City of Birmingham Symphony, Harold Gray, Town Hall, Birmingham, England, Tchaikovsky 1

10-13 Recital, Johannesburg, South Africa

10-15 Recital, Feather Market Hall, Port Elizabeth, South Africa

10-16 Recital, Konservatoriumsaal, Stellenbosch, South Africa

10-19 Recital, Temple Hall, Cape Town, South Africa

10-21 Concertos, South Africa Municipal Orchestra, David Wooldridge, City Hall, Cape Town, South Africa, Mozart 21, Brahms 2

10-22 Recital, City Hall, Pietermaritzburg, South Africa

10-24 Concerto, Durban Municipal Orchestra, Frits Schuurman, City Hall, Durban, South Africa, Brahms 2

10-26 Concerto, South African Broadcasting Corporation Symphony Orchestra, Franco Mannino, City Hall, Johannesburg, South Africa, Mozart 21

10-29 Concerto, South African Broadcasting Corporation Symphony Orchestra, Franco Mannino, Pretoria, South Africa, Rachmaninoff 3

10-31 Recital, South African Broadcasting Corporation, South Africa,

11-2 Recital, Voortrekker Memorial Hall, Pretoria, South Africa

11-4 Recital, University Great Hall, Johannesburg, South Africa

11-9 Recital, Large City Hall, Bulawayo, Zimbabwe

11-11 Recital, Athenaeum Hall, Salisbury (now Harare), Zimbabwe

12-1 Recital, Marymount College, Salina, KS

12-2 Recital, State Teachers College, Pittsburg, KS

1966

1-15 Recital, Mission Playhouse, San Gabriel, CA

1-22,23 Recitals, Music Center, Los Angeles, CA

1-25 Concertos, Oklahoma City Symphony, Guy Fraser
Harrison, Oklahoma City, OK, Chopin 2, Ravel G

2-7 Recital, Rutgers University, New Brunswick, NJ

2-19 Recital, Washington Irving High School, New York, NY

3-4 Recital, Ohio University, Athens, OH

3-15 Recital, Hogg Auditorium, University of Texas, Austin,
TX

3-24 Concerto, Boston Symphony, Erich Leinsdorf, Symphony
Hall, Boston, MA, Brahms 2

3-25 Recital, Biltmore Ballroom, New York, NY

4-12 Concerto, Boston Symphony, Erich Leinsdorf, Jorgensen
Auditorium, University of Connecticut, Storrs, CT, Brahms 2

4-14 Concerto, Boston Symphony, Erich Leinsdorf, Academy
of Music, Brooklyn, NY, Brahms 2

4-16 Concerto, Boston Symphony, Erich Leinsdorf, Carnegie
Hall, New York, NY, Brahms 2

4-20 Recital, Capitol Theatre, Ottawa, Canada

5-1,2 Concerto, Des Moines Symphony, Frank Noyes, Des
Moines, IA, Beethoven 4

5-30,31 Recitals, Jai Hind Hall, Bombay, India

6-3 Recital, Hong Kong City Concert Hall, Hong Kong

5-30 Recital, Taj Crystal Room, Bombay

5-31 Recital, Patkar Hall, Bombay, India

6-3 Recital, Hong Kong

6-21 Concerto, Japan Philharmonic Symphony, Akeo
Watanabe, Bunka Kaikan Hall, Tokyo, Japan, Rachmaninoff 3

6-19 Recital, Tokyo

6-24 Concerto, Sapporo Symphony, Akeo Watanabe, Citizen's Hall, Sapporo, Japan, Beethoven 4

7-2,3,4 Concerto, Boston Symphony, Erich Leinsdorf, Tanglewood, MA, Brahms 2

7-19 Recital, Teatro Broadway, Buenos Aires, Argentina

7-23 Recital, Teatro Colón, Buenos Aires, Argentina

7-25 Recital, Salon Blanco Municipal, Buenos Aires, Argentina

7-28 Recital, Mozarteum Argentino, Buenos Aires, Argentina

8-2 Concertos, Orquesta Sinfónica Provincial de Santa Fe, Olgerts Bistevins, Teatro Municipal, Santa Fe, Argentina, Mozart 21, Beethoven 4

8-5 Concerto, Orquesta Sinfónica de Córdoba, Teatro Rivera Indarte, Córdoba, Argentina, Brahms 2

8-9 Recital, Teatro San Martín, Tucumán, Argentina

8-11 Recital, Teatro Municipal de Olavarría, Buenos Aires, Argentina

8-14 Concerto, Orquesta Sinfónica Nacional, Choo-Hoey, Teatro Colón, Buenos Aires, Argentina, Brahms 2

8-14 Recital, Teatro Argentino, Buenos Aires, Argentina

8-18? Concerto, Orquesta Filarmónica Municipal, Agustin Cullell, Teatro Municipal, Santiago, Chile, Brahms 2

8-20 Concerto, Orquesta Filarmónica Municipal, Agustin Cullell, Teatro Cariola, Santiago, Chile, Brahms 2

9-2,4 Concerto, Orquesta Sinfónica Nacional, Luis Herrera de la Fuente, Teatro Municipal, Lima, Peru, Brahms 2

9-9 Concertos, Orquesta Sinfónica de Colombia, Olav Roots, Teatro Colón, Bogotá, Colombia, Mozart 21, Brahms 2

9-12 Recital, Biblioteca Luis Ángel Arango, Bogotá, Colombia

9-29, 10-1,3 Concertos, Dallas Symphony, Donald Johanos, Memorial Auditorium, Dallas, TX, Chopin 2, Ravel G

10-10,11 Concerto, Kalamazoo Symphony, Gregory Millar,

Kalamazoo, MI, Chopin 2
10-16 Concerto, Radio-Orchester Beromünster, Erich Schmid, Studio Zürich, Switzerland, Brahms 2
10-26 Concerto, Orchestre de la Suisse Romande, Jean-Marie Auberson, Société Suisse de Radiodiffusion et Télévision, Geneva, Switzerland, Rachmaninoff 3
10-30,11-1 Concerto, Honolulu Symphony, George Barati, Honolulu, HI, Chopin 2
11-6 Recital, Chicago, IL
12-4 Recital, Indiana University Auditorium, Bloomington, IN
12-? to 1-5-67 Russia Tour

1967
1-9,10 Concerto, Omaha Symphony, Joseph Levine, Omaha, NE, Beethoven 5
1-16 Concerto, Evansville Philharmonic, Minas Christian, Coliseum, Evansville, IN, Beethoven 4
1-19 Recital, Carnegie Hall, New York, NY
1-28 Concerto, Colorado Springs Symphony, Walter Eisenberg, Palmer High School Auditorium, Colorado Springs, CO, Beethoven 4
2-1 Recital, Tufts University, Medford, MA
2-4 Recital, New Bedford, MA
3-2 Recital, Hertz Hall, San Francisco, CA
3-3 Recital, University of California, Berkeley, CA
3-4 Concerto, Melbourne Symphony, Malcolm Sargent, Town Hall, Melbourne, Australia, Beethoven 5
3-16,17,18 Concerto, West Australian Symphony, Thomas Mayer, Winthrop Hall, Perth, Australia, Ravel G
3-21 Concerto, West Australian Symphony, Thomas Mayer, Winthrop Hall, Perth, Australia, Beethoven 5

3-29 Recital, Town Hall, Wangaratta, Australia

3-31 Recital, Civic Centre, Shepparton, Australia

4-5 Concerto, New Zealand Broadcasting Corporation Symphony Orchestra, Alceo Galliera, Town Hall Wellington, New Zealand, Beethoven 4

4-8 Concerto, New Zealand Broadcasting Corporation Symphony Orchestra, Alceo Galliera, Civic Theatre, Christchurch, New Zealand, Beethoven 4

4-10 Concerto, New Zealand Broadcasting Corporation Symphony Orchestra, Alceo Galliera, Town Hall, Dunedin, New Zealand, Ravel G

4-13 Recital, Civic Theatre, Invercargill, New Zealand

4-15 Recital, Town Hall, Dunedin, New Zealand

4-17 Recital, Civic Theatre, Christchurch, New Zealand

4-19 Recital, School of Music, Nelson, New Zealand

4-22 Recital, North Opera House, Palmerston, New Zealand

4-24, Recital, Town Hall, Wellington, New Zealand

4-27 Concerto, New Zealand Broadcasting Corporation Symphony Orchestra, Alceo Galliera, Town Hall, Auckland, New Zealand, Ravel G

4-29 Concerto, New Zealand Broadcasting Corporation Symphony Orchestra, Alceo Galliera, New Zealand, Beethoven 2

5-3,4 Concertos, Melbourne Symphony, Malcolm Sargent, Town Hall, Melbourne, Australia, Beethoven 2 & 4

5-6,8 Concerto, Melbourne Symphony, Malcolm Sargent, Town Hall, Melbourne, Australia, Beethoven 5

5-11 Recital, Memorial Hall, Sale, Australia

5-13 Recital, Town Hall, Sydney, Australia

5-17 Recital, RSL Hall, Southport, Australia

5-19 Concerto, Queensland Symphony, Rudolf Pekarek, City Hall, Brisbane, Australia, Chopin 2

5-22 Recital, Tropical Theatre, Cairns, Australia

5-23 Recital, Theatre Royal, Townsville, Australia

5-25 Recital, Mackay, Australia

5-27 Recital, Municipal Theatre, Rockhampton, Australia

6-1,2,3 Concerto, Compton Symphony, Mackenzie, Compton, Australia, Beethoven 5

8-4 Concerto, New York Chamber Orchestra, Jorge Mester, Lincoln Center Philharmonic Hall, New York, NY, Mozart 21

9-25,26, 10-2 Concertos, Dallas Symphony, Donald Johanos, Dallas, TX, Beethoven 1,2,3,4,5 & Choral Fantasy

11-4 Recital, Metropolitan Museum, New York, NY

11-5 Recital, CBS Camera 3 TV

11-6 Concerto, Norwalk Symphony, Quinto Maganini, Norwalk, Connecticut, Beethoven 3

11-22 Concerto, Baltimore Symphony, Pierino Gamba, Baltimore, MD, Chopin 2

11-30, 12-1 Concerto, Indianapolis Symphony, Izler Solomon, Clowes Hall, Indianapolis, IN, Chopin 2

12-5 to 12-26 Russia Tour: approximately ten appearances, Chopin 2, Brahms 2, Beethoven 4, three different solo programs.

12-8 Recital, Baku, Azerbaijan

12-9 Concerto, Baku

12-11 Concerto, Yerevan, Armenia

12-13 Recital, Yerevan, Armenia

12-16 Concerto, Moscow State Philharmonic, Moscow, Russia

12-19 Concertos, Leningrad State Philharmonic, Edouard Grikurov, Leningrad, Russia, Chopin 2, Brahms 2

12-21 Recital, Leningrad State Philharmonic, Leningrad, Russia

1968

1-8 Recital, Queen Elizabeth Hall, London, England

1-27 Recital, Washington Irving High School, New York, NY

3-8 Recital, Lehigh University, Bethlehem, PA

3-12,15,18 Concertos, Venezuela Symphony, Gonzalo Castellanos, Caracas, Venezuela, Beethoven 1,2,3,4,5

4-8,9 Concerto, Albany Symphony, Julius Hegyi, Albany, NY, Rachmaninoff 2

4-18,19 Concerto, Florida Symphony, Hermann Herz, Peabody Auditorium, Orlando, FL, Brahms 2

4-24 Concerto, Orchestre Municipal de Strasbourg, Alceo Galliera, Strasbourg, Germany, Tchaikovsky 1

4-30 Concertos, New Orleans Philharmonic-Symphony, Werner Torkanowsky, Municipal Auditorium, New Orleans, LA, Ravel G, Chopin 2

5-2 Concerto, Pueblo Civic Symphony, Memorial Hall, Pueblo, CO, Rachmaninoff 2

6-3 Recital, Teatro Presidente, Panama City, Panama

6-8 Recital Teatro Colón, Buenos Aires, Argentina

6-10 Recital Asociación Wagneriana, Buenos Aires, Argentina

6-16 Recital, Teatro Argentino, Buenos Aires, Argentina

6-14 Concerto, Orquesta Sinfónica de la Universidad Nacional de Cuyo, Teatro Independencia, Mendoza, Argentina, Chopin 2

7-10 Recital, Northern Illinois University, DeKalb, IL

8-26 Concerto, International Juventus Orchestra, Nicolas Flagello, S. Maria a Gradillo, Positano, Italy, Rachmaninoff 2

8-30 Concerto, Oslo Philharmonic, Øivin Fjeldstad, Freia-salen, Oslo, Norway, Rachmaninoff 2

9-29 Recital, Nazareth College, Rochester, NY

10-6 Recital, Indiana University Auditorium, Bloomington, IN

10-11 Recital, Hertz Hall, University of California, Berkeley, CA

10-14,15 Concerto, Denver Symphony, Vladimir Golschmann, Auditorium Theatre, Denver, CO, Chopin 2

10-23 Ohio State

10-25 Recital, Women's Club Auditorium, Richmond, VA

10-28 Recital, Dade County Auditorium, Miami, FL

10-30 Recital, Biblioteca Luis-Ángel Arango Sala de Conciertos, Bogotá, Colombia

12-13,14 Concerto, Toledo Symphony, Serge Fournier, Peristyle Theatre, Toledo, OH, Beethoven 5

1969

1-25 Recital, Auditorium, Hunter College, New York, NY

1-25,26 Concerto, Edmonton Symphony, Lawrence Leonard, Edmonton, Canada, Brahms 2

2-1 Concerto, Philharmonic Symphony of Westchester, John Barnett, Westchester, NY, Chopin 2

2-7 Concerto, New Jersey Symphony, Henry Lewis, Montclair, NJ, Rachmaninoff 3

2-8 Concerto, New Jersey Symphony, Henry Lewis, Millburn, NJ, Rachmaninoff 3

2-12 Recital, Wheatley School, Old Westbury, NY

2-17 Concerto, New Jersey Symphony, Henry Lewis, Adelphi University, Garden City, NY, Rachmaninoff 3

3-4 Recital, Wisconsin State University, Stevens Point, WI

7-30 Concerto, Flagstaff Summer Festival Orchestra, Izler Solomon, Northern Arizona University Auditorium, Flagstaff, Arizona, Beethoven 4

8-2,3 Concerto, Flagstaff Summer Festival Orchestra, Izler Solomon, Northern Arizona University Auditorium, Flagstaff, Arizona, Tchaikovsky 1

8-25 Concerto, Salerno Festival Orchestra, Nicolas Flagello, Salerno, Italy, Tchaikovsky 1

10-1 Recital, Colby College, Waterville, ME
10-4 Recital, Washington Irving High School, New York, NY
10-12 Recital, Indiana University Auditorium, Bloomington, IN
10-19,20 Concerto, Calgary Philharmonic, Maurice Handford, Jubilee Auditorium, Calgary, Canada, Chopin 2
10-25,26 Concerto, Edmonton Symphony, Lawrence Leonard, Jubilee Auditorium, Edmonton, Canada, Brahms 2
12-13,14 Concerto, Toledo Orchestra, Toledo, OH

1970
1-27 Recital, SUNY Fredonia, Fredonia, NY
2-3 Recital, Musikhalle Kleiner Saal, Hamburg, Germany
2-5 Recital, Hochschule für Musik und Theater, Munich, Germany
2-7 Recital, Brahms-saal, Musikverein, Vienna, Austria
2-12 Recital, Hochschule, Berlin, Germany
2-22 Concerto, Wiener Symphoniker, Hans Swarowsky, Österreichischer Rundfunk, Vienna, Austria, Rachmaninoff 3
2-25 Recital Teatro Real, Madrid, Spain
2-26 Recital Conservatorio de Música, Málaga, Spain
2-27 Recital, Teatro Principal, Valencia, Spain
3-4 Recital, Teatro Pérez Galdós, Las Palmas de Gran Canaria, Spain
3-6 Concertos, Orquesta Filarmónica, Marçal Gols, Las Palmas de Gran Canaria, Spain, Chopin 2, Beethoven 4
3-10,11 Concerto, SABC Symphony, Francesco Mander, Civic Theatre, Johannesburg, South Africa, Rachmaninoff 3
3-12 Concerto, Cape Town Symphony Orchestra, Anton Hartman, City Hall, Cape Town, South Africa, Beethoven 4
3-13 Recital, Konservatorium vir Musiek, Stellenbosch, South Africa

3-14 Recital, Temple Hall, Cape Town, South Africa

3-20 Recital, University of Pretoria, Pretoria, South Africa

3-22 Recital, University Great Hall, Johannesburg, South Africa

3-24 Recital, Harry Margolis Hall, Harare, Zimbabwe

4-4 Recital, Washington Performing Arts Society, Washington, DC

4-12 Recital, Orchestra Hall, Chicago, IL

6-25 Recital, Peabody College, Nashville, TN

11-3 Recital, Cornell University, Ithaca, NY

11-8,10 Concerto, Honolulu Symphony, Robert LaMarchina, Honolulu, HI, Beethoven 5

11-11 Recital, Hilo High School Auditorium, Hilo, HI

11-12 Concerto, Maui Philharmonic, Baldwin Auditorium, Wailuku, HI, Beethoven 5

11-15 Recital, San Francisco, CA

11-19 Recital, Washington and Lee University, Lexington, VA

11-26 Recital, Dalhousie University, Halifax, Canada

12-6 Recital, Carnegie Hall, New York, NY

12-? Concerto

12-13 Recital, Queen Elizabeth Hall, London, England

12-20,22 Concerto, Oklahoma City Symphony, Oklahoma City, OK

1971

1-3 Concerto, Hallé Orchestra, Maurice Handford, Free Trade Hall, Manchester, England, Chopin 2

1-7,8 Concerto, Indianapolis Symphony, Izler Solomon, Clowes Memorial Hall, Indianapolis, IN, Brahms 2

2-25 Concerto, Indianapolis Symphony, Izler Solomon, Bloomington, IN, Brahms 2

4-6 Recital, Woolsey Hall, New Haven, CT

4-19 Concerto, Tulsa Philharmonic, Franco Autori, Tulsa Municipal Theater, Tulsa, OK, Brahms 2

4-29 Recital aboard *SS Nieuw Amsterdam*

6-9 Concerto, Orchestre de la Suisse Romande, Jean Meylan, Grand Studio Ernest Ansermet, Geneva, Switzerland, Rachmaninoff 2

10-27 Recital, Rutgers University, New Brunswick, NJ

11-13,14 Concerto, Edmonton Symphony, Ted Kardash, Edmonton, Canada, Schumann

11-15,16 Recital, University of Calgary, Calgary, Canada

12-6,7 Concerto, Shreveport Symphony, John Shenaut, Civic Theatre, Shreveport, LA, Beethoven 4

12-18 Recital, Washington Irving High School, New York, NY

1972

1-5 Recital, Norwegian Broadcasting Corporation, Norway

1-23 Recital, Shared, Carnegie Hall, New York, NY

1-25 Recital, Alice Tully Hall, New York, NY

7-26 Recital, Adirondack/Champlain Festival, Burlington, VT

7-30 Recital, Adirondack/Champlain Festival, Schroon Lake, NY

9-2 Chamber Recital, Brahms Quintet, Berkshire String Quartet, Music Mountain, Falls Village, CT

10-1 Recital, Diligentia Theatre, The Hague, Netherlands

10-2 Recital, Concertgebouw Small Hall, Amsterdam, Netherlands

10-? Concerto, Residentie-Orkest, Congresgebouw, The Hague, Netherlands, ?

10-19 Recital, University of Manitoba, Winnipeg, Canada

10-28,29 Concerto, Winnipeg Symphony, Winnipeg, Canada, Chopin 2

12-2 Concerto, Waterbury Symphony, Waterbury, CT,

Beethoven 4
12-25 Recital, Alice Tully Hall, New York, NY

1973
1-9 Concertos, Oklahoma City Symphony, Guy Fraser
Harrison, Civic Center Music Hall, Oklahoma City, OK,
Dohnányi Variations, Liszt Hungarian Fantasy
1-14 Recital, Queen Elizabeth Hall, London, England
3-6 Concertos, National Orchestral Association, Leon Barzin,
Carnegie Hall, New York, NY, Mozart 21, Beethoven 4,
Brahms 2
3-10, Concerto, Municipal Concerts Orchestra, Julius
Grossman, Alice Tully Hall, New York, NY, Chopin 2
4-4 Recital, Biblioteca Luis-Ángel Arango Sala de Conciertos,
Bogotá, Colombia
4-5 Recital, Cali, Colombia
4-6 Recital, Cúcuta, Colombia
5-8 Recital, Town Hall, New York, NY
6-28 Recital, Peabody College, Nashville, TN
10-16 Concerto, Harrisburg Symphony, Edwin McArthur,
Harrisburg, PA, Brahms 2
10-25 Recital, Jersey City State College, Jersey City, NJ
10-30 Recital, Musicians Club, Richmond, VA
11-6 Recital, Indiana University Auditorium, Bloomington, IN
12-14 Recital, Queen Elizabeth Hall, London, England
12-14 Concerto, Residentie-Orkest, Hiroyuki Iwaki,
Concertgebouw, Amsterdam, Netherlands, Tchaikovsky 1

1974
2-13 Recital, Hunter College, New York, NY
3-12 Concerto, Omaha Symphony, Yuri Krasnapolsky, Omaha,
NE, Chopin 2

10-17 Recital Indiana University Auditorium, Bloomington, IN
11-4 Recital, Queen Elizabeth Hall, London, England
11-20 Recital, Curtis Institute, Philadelphia, PA
12-2 Recital, Carnegie Hall, New York, NY

1975
1-18 Concertos, Evansville Philharmonic, Minas Christian, Evansville, IN, Gershwin F, Rhapsody in Blue
2-2,3 Concertos, Shreveport Symphony, John Shenaut, Shreveport, LA, Beethoven 3, Ravel G, Ravel LH
2-5 Recital, Robinson Auditorium, Little Rock, AR
2-13 Concerto, Durban Symphony Orchestra, Durban, South Africa, Chopin 2
2-14 Concerto, Pact Symphony Orchestra, Leo Quayle, Transvaal, South Africa, Ravel LH
2-16 Recital, University Great Hall, Johannesburg, South Africa
2-18 Recital, Large City Hall, South Africa
2-20 Recital, City Hall, South Africa
2-22 Recital, Queenstown, South Africa
2-25,26 Concerto, National Symphony Orchestra of the South African Broadcasting Corporation, Anton Hartman, City Hall, Johannesburg, South Africa, Brahms 2
3-3 Recital, Port Elizabeth, South Africa
3-20,21,22,25 Concerto, New York Philharmonic, Pierre Boulez, New York, NY, Ravel LH
5-20 Recital, Norwegian Broadcasting Corporation, Norway
7-8 Recital, Cheltenham International Festival, Cheltenham, England
10-24 Recital, Miami University, Oxford, OH
11-16 Concerto, St. Louis Symphony, Leonard Slatkin, Powell Hall, St. Louis, MO, Rachmaninoff 2

11-17 Recital, Edison Theatre at Washington University, St. Louis, MO

12-15 Concerto, Naumburg ad hoc ensemble, Carnegie Hall, New York, NY, Bach 3-keyboard

1976

1-14 Recital, Theatre Royal, St. Helens, England

1-21 Recital, Sioux Falls Coliseum, Sioux Falls, SD

2-24 Concerto, Fort Wayne Philharmonic, Thomas Briccetti, Fort Wayne, IN, Rachmaninoff Paganini

5-6 Concertos, Maracaibo, Venezuela, Beethoven 4, Rhapsody in Blue

5-11 Recital, Quito, Ecuador

5-13 Recital, Rio de Janeiro, Brazil

5-18 Recital, Sala Cecília Meireles, Rio de Janeiro, Brazil

5-? Concerto, SODRE Orchestra, Juan Protasi, Rio de Janeiro, Brazil, Beethoven 4

5-21 Recital, Ministerio de Educación y Cultura, Montevideo, Uruguay

5-22 Concerto, Montevideo, Uruguay, Beethoven 3

5-28 Concerto, Chile, Brahms 2

6-2 Concerto, Orquesta Sinfónica Nacional, Gerald Brown, Teatro San José, San José, Costa Rica, Tchaikovsky 1

7-23 Recital, Piper's Opera House, Virginia City, Nevada

8-12 Concertos, St. Louis Symphony, Leonard Slatkin, Southern Illinois University, Edwardsville, IL, Rachmaninoff Paganini, Rachmaninoff 3

10-8,9 Concerto, Edmonton Symphony, Pierre Hétu, Jubilee Auditorium, Edmonton, Canada, Dohnányi Variations

10-16,17 Concerto, Sacramento Symphony, Sacramento, CA

10-22,23,24 Concerto, Milwaukee Symphony, Kenneth

Schermerhorn, Milwaukee, WI, Chopin 2
12-2,4 Concerto, St. Louis Symphony, Powell Hall, St. Louis,
MO
12-7 Concerto, Lincoln Symphony, Robert Emile, O'Donnell
Auditorium, Lincoln, NE, Brahms 2
12-13 Recital, Carnegie Hall, New York, NY

1977
1-21,22 Concerto, Louisville Orchestra, Daniel Spurlock,
Louisville, KY, Ravel G
1-27 Concerto, Musikselskabet, Karsten Andersen,
Konsertpaleet, Bergen, Norway, Brahms 2
2-21 Recital, Place des Arts, Montreal, Canada
4-6 Recital, East Carolina University, Greenville, NC
4-17 Recital, Orchestra Hall, Chicago, IL
6-15 Recital, Peabody Conservatory, Baltimore, MD
7-17 Recital, McPherson Playhouse, Victoria, Canada
9-29, 10-1,2 Concertos, St. Louis Symphony, Powell Hall, St,
Louis, MO, Rachmaninoff 1 & 4
10-3 Recital, Grace United Methodist Church, St. Louis. MO
10-21 Recital, Allegheny College, Meadville, PA
10-28 Recital, aboard *SS Rotterdam*
12-5 Concerto and Recital, Sala Fénix, Barcelona, Spain,
Beethoven 5

1978
1-12 Recital, St. Andrew's Presbyterian Church, Toronto,
Canada
1-28,29 Concerto, Des Moines Symphony, Yuri Krasnapolsky,
Des Moines, IA, Brahms 2
2-4 Recital, Royce Hall, UCLA, Los Angeles, CA
2-16,17,18 Atlanta Symphony, Sung Kwak, Atlanta, GA,

Rachmaninoff 4

2-22 Recital, Millikin University, Decatur, IL

3-9 Recording for Norwegian Radio, Oslo, Norway

4-7 Recital, University of Houston, Houston, TX

4-10 Concertos, University of Houston Symphony, Igor Buketoff, Houston, TX, Mozart 21, Chopin 2, Rachmaninoff 3

4-14 Recital, St. Olaf College, Northfield, MN

4-29 Concerto, Philadelphia College of the Performing Arts Symphony Orchestra, Joseph Primavera, Shubert Theatre, Philadelphia, PA, Chopin 2

5-3 Recital, Carnegie Hall, New York, NY

6-17,18 Concerto, Orquesta Sinfónica de Minería, Jorge Velazco, Mexico City, Mexico, Rachmaninoff Paganini

7-5,7 Recitals, Beechwood and Seaview Ballrooms, Newport, RI

8-19 Recital, St. Michaels University School, Victoria, Canada

10-22 Concerto, Mount St. Joseph Performing Arts Orchestra, James Martin, Cincinnati, OH, Chopin 2

10-28 Concerto, Victoria Symphony, Harry Lyall, Victoria College Auditorium, Victoria, Canada, Chopin 2

11-4 Concerto, Philharmonic-Symphony Society of New York, Andre Kostelanetz, Avery Fisher Hall, New York, NY, Rachmaninoff 1

11-8 Recital, First Presbyterian Church, Stamford, CT

1979

1-30 Recital, Mississippi Valley State University, Itta Bena, MS

2-14,15 Concerto, Wheeling Symphony, Jeff Holland Cook, Wheeling, WV, Brahms 2

2-24,25 Concerto, Long Beach Symphony, James Paul, Terrace Theatre, Long Beach, CA, Beethoven 4

5-24 Concertos, Cultural Center of the Philippines Orchestra,

Luis C. Valencia, Manila, Philippines, Beethoven 5, Rachmaninoff 3

11-2 Recital, Hiram College, Hiram, OH

12-1 Concerto, Oshkosh Symphony, Henri Pensis, Civic Auditorium, Oshkosh, WI, Chopin 1

12-8,9 Concerto, Houston Symphony, Efrem Kurtz, Jones Hall, Houston, TX, Schumann

1980

2-7 Recital, Queen Elizabeth Hall, London, England

2-24 Recital, University of Houston, Houston, TX

3-3 Recital, Glassboro State College, Glassboro, NJ

3-20 Recital, The Bohemians Club, New York, NY

4-24 Recital, Butler University, Indianapolis, IN

4-25 Concerto, Butler University Symphony, Jason Wiley, Indianapolis, IN, Rachmaninoff 1

5-1 Recital, Place des Arts, Montreal, Canada

9-5 Recital, University of Houston, Houston, TX

9-13 Recital, Alice Tully Hall, New York, NY

10-4 Concerto, South Dakota Symphony, Emanuel Vardi, Sioux Falls, SD, Rachmaninoff 3

10-25 Concerto, Philharmonic Symphony of Westchester, Westchester, NY

11-? Concerto, American Philharmonic Orchestra, Carnegie Hall, New York, NY

11-? Recital, University of Toronto, Toronto, Canada

11-15,16 Concerto, Arkansas Symphony, Little Rock, AR, Chopin 1

12-10 Recital, University of Houston, Houston, TX

12-18 Recital, Alice Tully Hall, New York, NY

1981

2-19 Recital, Queen Elizabeth Hall, London, England

3-15 Concerto, Hastings Civic Symphony, Hastings, NE

4-21,22 Concerto, Fort Lauderdale Symphony, Emerson Buckley, War Memorial Auditorium, Fort Lauderdale, FL, Rachmaninoff 1

4-24 Recital, Butler University, Indianapolis, IN

4-? Recital, Civic Auditorium, Portland, OR

5-21 Recital, Homi Bhabha Auditorium, Bombay, India

5-24 Recital, City Hall Concert Hall, Hong Kong

6-4 Recital, Dr. Sun Yat-sen Hall, Taipei, Taiwan

6-6 Recital, Chung Hsing Hall, Taichung, Taiwan

6-13 Recital, University of Western Australia, Perth, Australia

7-7 Recital, New South Wales Conservatorium, Sydney, Australia

7-28 Recital, Trinity Church, New York, NY

10-4 Concerto, Reading Symphony, Rajah Theatre, Reading, PA, Beethoven 4

10-9? Concerto, Asheville Symphony, Asheville, NC, Brahms 1

10-17 Concertos, Oshkosh Symphony, Henri Pensis, Civic Auditorium, Oshkosh, WI, Gershwin F, Rhapsody in Blue

10-24 Concerto, Westchester Symphony, Harrison, NY

10-25 Concerto, Westchester Symphony, White Plains, NY

10-30 Recital, Civic Auditorium, Portland, OR

11-6 Recital, Carnegie Hall, New York, NY

11-29 Recital, Orchestra Hall, Chicago, IL

12-3 Recital, Dartmouth College, Hanover, NH

1982

1-26 Recital, Agnes Scott College, Atlanta, GA

2-? Recital, Gaines Auditorium of Presser Hall, Decatur, GA

2-26 Recital, University of Houston, Houston, TX

3-21 Recital, Queen Elizabeth Hall, London, England

4-28 Recital, Ambassador Auditorium, Pasadena, CA
10-2 Recital, Portland State University, Portland, OR
10-11 Recital, Jones Hall, Houston, TX
10-31 Recital, Carnegie Hall, New York, NY

1983
2-18 Chamber/Solo Recital, University of Houston, Houston, TX
2-28 Recital, L'Institut Canadien, Québec City, Canada
3-3 Recital, University of Houston, Houston, TX
3-23 Recital, MTNA Convention, Houston, TX
4-5 Recital, Bulgaria State Union of Theatre and Music, Sofia, Bulgaria
4-7 Concerto, Burgas State Philharmonic, Mihail Popov, Burgas, Bulgaria
4-12 Recital, Mississippi State University, Starkville, MS
5-11 Concerto, Symphonie Canadiana, Yondani Butt, Vancouver, Canada
5-15 Recital, Herbst Theater, San Francisco, CA
10-2 Recital, Queen Elizabeth Hall, London, England
11-11 Recital, Mercer University, Macon, GA
11-12 Concerto, Arkansas Symphony, Robert Henderson, Robinson Auditorium, Little Rock, AR, Chopin 1
11-18 Recital, Palisades Presbyterian Church, New York, NY
11-27 Recital, Orchestra Hall, Chicago, IL

1984
1-12,13 Concerto, Houston Symphony, Houston, TX, Rachmaninoff Paganini
1-14 Concerto, Rhode Island Philharmonic, Alvaro Cassuto, Performing Arts Center, Providence, RI, Brahms 1
1-22 Recital, University of Houston, Houston, TX

1-31 Concerto, Baton Rouge Symphony, James Paul, Centroplex Performing Arts Theatre, Baton Rouge, LA, Mozart 21

2-23,24 Concerto, Florida Chamber Orchestra, James Brooks, Bailey Hall, Ft. Lauderdale, FL, Beethoven 3

2-25 Concerto, Florida Chamber Orchestra, James Brooks, Florida Atlantic University, Boca Raton, FL, Beethoven 3

3-24 Recital, Brahms-Saal, Vienna, Austria

3-? Concerto, Vienna Radio Symphony, Vienna, Austria

4-15 Recital, Western Connecticut State University, Danbury, CT

4-24 Concerto, National Orchestra of New York, Harold Farberman, New York, NY, Liszt 1

4-28 Recital, Christopher Newport College, Newport News, VA

6-25 Recital, California Music Teachers Association Convention

10-7 Recital, 92nd St. Y, New York, NY

11-12 Recital, Salle Gaveau, Paris, France

12-9 Recital, Washington Heights YMHA, New York, NY

1985

1-12,13 Concerto, Houston Symphony, Raymond Leppard, Jones Hall, Houston, TX, Rachmaninoff Paganini

1-20 Recital, University of Houston, Houston, TX

2-9 Recital, Beethoven Society, Alice Tully Hall, New York, NY

3-6 Chamber Recital, Beethoven Wind Quintet, University of Houston, Houston, TX

3-15 Recital, St. Louis Conservatory, St. Louis, MO

3-24 Recital, Queen Elizabeth Hall, London, England

4-13,14 Concerto, Des Moines Symphony, Yuri Krasnapolsky, Des Moines, IA, Chopin 2

5-24,26 Concerto, Orquesta Filarmónica de la Universidad

Nacional Autónoma de México, Jorge Velazco, Nezahualcóyotl Centro Cultural Universitario, Mexico City, Mexico, Chopin 2

9-28 Recital, Hartwick College, Onconta, NY

10-1 Recital, Ithaca College, Ithaca, NY

10-2 Recital, Union College, Schenectady, NY

10-6 Recital, Carnegie Hall, New York, NY

10-24 Recital, US Merchant Marine Academy, Bowditch Auditorium, Kings Point, NY

1986

1-17 Recital, University of Houston, Houston, TX

3-14 Recital, Masonic Scottish Temple, Guthrie, OK

5-1 Recital, Terrace Theater, Kennedy Center, Washington, DC

6-13 Recital, Salle Gaveau, Paris, France

8-2, Recital, Buenos Aires, Argentina

8-7 Concerto, Buenos Aires Philharmonic, Adrian Pages, Teatro Colón, Buenos Aires, Argentina, Chopin 2

9-12,13 Concerto, Lehigh Valley Chamber Orchestra, Donald Spieth, Beethoven 3

10-11 Concerto, Sioux City Symphony, Thomas Lewis, Chopin 2

10-15 Recital, New York, NY

10-16 Recital, Philadelphia, PA

10-19 Concerto, Greater Trenton Symphony, Kurt Klippstatter, War Memorial Building, Trenton, Chopin 2

10-25 Concerto, Julius Grossman Orchestra, Julius Grossman, Alice Tully Hall, New York, NY

11-16 Concerto, Philadelphia Academy of Music, Joseph Silverstein, Beethoven 3

11-28,30 Concerto, Orquesta Filarmónica de la Universidad Nacional Autónoma de México, Jorge Velazco, Mexico City,

Mexico, Liszt 1
11-29 Concerto, Orquesta Filarmónica de la Universidad
Nacional Autónoma de México, Jorge Velazco, Pavillon
Chinois, Mexico City, Mexico, Beethoven 3
12-4 Recital, Centenary College, Shreveport, LA

1987
1-16 Recital, University of Houston, Houston, TX
1-21 Recital, St. Paul's Chapel, New York, NY
2-15,17 Concerto, Baton Rouge Symphony, James Paul, Baton
Rouge, LA, Brahms 2
3-22? Recital (shared), Butler University, Indianapolis, IN
3-23 Concerto, Hidetaro Suzuki Chamber Orchestra, Butler
University, Indianapolis, IN, Beethoven 3
4-11 Concerto, Des Moines Symphony, Yuri Krasnapolsky, Des
Moines Civic Center, Des Moines, IA, Chopin 2
5-5 Recital, Art Center of Northern New Jersey, New Milford,
NJ
5-7 Recital, Carnegie Hall, New York, NY
7-27 Recital, Damrosch Park, New York, NY
8-8 Concerto, Strawberry Creek Music Festival, Yehuda Gilad,
Pepperdine University, Malibu, CA, Chopin 2
10-9 Recital, Mercer University, Macon, GA
10-13 Recital, SUNY Buffalo, NY

1988
1-2 Recital, University of Houston, Houston, TX
1-12,14 Concerto, Orquesta Filarmónica de la Universidad
Nacional Autónoma de México, Jorge Velazco, Mexico City,
Mexico, Rachmaninoff 2
1-21 Recital, University of Houston, Houston, TX
2-22 Recital, Civic Theatre, Chicago, IL

2-28 Recital, Carnegie Hall, New York, NY
2-13 Concerto, Toronto Pops Orchestra, Massey Hall, Chopin 2
2-22 Recital, Civic Theatre, Chicago, IL
2-23 Recital, Jewish Community Center, Skokie, IL
2-26 Recital, Oshkosh Grand Opera House, Oshkosh, WI
2-28 Recital, Carnegie Hall, New York, NY
3-30 Recital, Pepperdine University, Malibu, CA
4-19 Recital, Chapman College, Orange, CA
4-20 Recital, California State University, Sacramento, CA
4-24,26 Concerto, Napa Valley Symphony, CA, Rachmaninoff 2
? Beethoven marathon, Obra Cultural de la Caja Ahorros Provincial San Fernando de Sevilla, Seville, Spain
7-24 Recital, Rutgers University, New Brunswick, NJ
9-23 Recital, Queen Elizabeth Hall, London, England
10-9 Recital, Muhlenberg College, Allentown, PA
10-12 Recital, Charlotte, NC
10-22 Concerto, Baton Rouge Symphony, James Paul, Carnegie Hall, New York, NY, Beethoven 4

1989
1-8 Recital, Iowa State University, Ames, IA
1-14,15 Concerto, Orquesta Filarmónica de la Universidad Nacional Autónoma de México, Jorge Velazco, Mexico City, Mexico, Beethoven 4
9-5 Recital, Damrosch Park, New York, NY
10-1 Recital, Glassboro Center for the Arts, Glassboro, NJ
10-5 Recital, The Morning Series, NY
10-10 Recital, Princeton University, Princeton, NJ
10-12 Recital, Spirit Square Center for the Arts, Charlotte, NC
10-15 Recital, Hackley Performing Arts Center, Tarrytown, NY

10-17 Recital, Carnegie Hall, New York, NY

1990
2-5 Recital, St. Louis Conservatory, St. Louis, MO
3-10 Recital, Celebrity Performances, Gloucester, MA
3-14 Recital, Potsdam College, New York, NY
3-20 Recital, Juilliard Theatre, New York, NY
3-25 Recital, Charleston Heights Arts Center, Las Vegas, NV
5-19 Concerto, Waukegan Symphony, Waukegan, IL,
Rachmaninoff 2
5-31 Concerto, Orquesta Santa Cecilia, Jacques Bodmer,
Pamplona, Spain, Chopin 2
6-10 Recital, University of Houston, Houston, TX
6-11 Recital, Texas A&M University, College Station, TX
8-25 Recital, Schloss vor Husum, Husum, Germany
9-19 Recital, Wigmore Hall, London, England
11-5 Chamber Recital, University of Calgary, Calgary, Canada
12-3 Recital, Davidson College, Davidson, NC
12-16 Recital, Alice Tully Hall, New York, NY

1991
2-14 Recital, Del Mar College, Corpus Christi, TX
5-4 Concerto, Las Cruces Symphony, Marianna Gabbi, Las
Cruces, NM, Mozart 21
6-4 Recital, Texas Christian University, Fort Worth, TX
8-19? Recital, Schloss vor Husum, Husum, Germany
10-27 Recital, University of Alabama at Birmingham,
Birmingham, AL
11-11 Recital, Texas A&M University, College Station, TX

1992
1-30 Concerto, Chamber Players of Toronto, Paavo Järvi,

Toronto, Canada, Mozart 12
2-2 Recital, University of Toronto, Toronto, Canada
3-17 Recital, University of Nevada, Las Vegas, NV
3-19 Recital, Northwest Church, Fresno, CA
3-26 Recital, Goldsmiths' Hall, London, England
7-18 Recital, Oregon Coast Music Festival, Coos Bay, OR
7-27? Concerto, Oregon Coast Music Festival Orchestra, James
Paul, Coos Bay, OR, Rachmaninoff Paganini
7-31 Recital, Bowdoin Festival, Brunswick, ME
9-14 Recital, Queen Elizabeth Hall, London, England
10-17 Concerto, Orquesta Sinfónica de Puerto Rico, Yuri
Krasnapolsky, San Juan, Puerto Rico, Chopin 2
10-31? Recital, Memphis State University, Memphis, TN
11-20 Concerto, University of Houston Symphony, Franz
Anton Krager, Houston, TX, Brahms 1

1993
1-24 Recital, University of Kansas, Lawrence, KS
1-31 Recital, California State University, Sacramento, CA
2-6 Recital, Harid Conservatory, Boca Raton, FL
3-3 Recital, Carnegie Hall, New York, NY
4-21 Recital, Universidad Nacional Autónoma de México,
Mexico City, Mexico
10-24 Recital, Bray Gallery, Flint, MI
10-29 Recital, New England Conservatory, Boston, MA

1994
1-14 Recital, University of Houston, Houston, TX
3-22 Recital, Hofstra University, Hempstead, NY
4-30 Recital, Folly Theater, Kansas City, MO
8-8 Recital, Manoir de Port-Breton, Dinard, France
8-23 Recital, Oregon Coast Music Festival, Coos Bay, OR

8-26 Concerto, Oregon Coast Music Festival Orchestra, James Paul, Coos Bay, OR, Schumann

8-30 Concerto, Oregon Coast Music Festival Orchestra, James Paul, Coos Bay, OR, Rachmaninoff 3

9-1 Recital, l'Ermitage Foundation, Los Angeles, CA

9-4 Recital, Los Angeles County Museum of Art, Los Angeles, CA

9-22,24 Concerto, Baton Rouge Symphony, Baton Rouge, LA, Chopin 2

12-2 Recital, Muhlenberg College, Allentown, PA

12-4 Recital, Longy School of Music, Boston, MA

1995

2-19 Recital, Consulate-General of Poland, New York, NY

2-22 Recital, University of Kansas, Lawrence, KS

3-22 Recital, Carnegie Hall, New York, NY

3-26 Recital, Wigmore Hall, London, England

5-15,16 Concerto, Orlando Symphony, Yuri Krasnapolsky, Orlando, FL, Chopin 2

7-10 Recital, University of Manitoba, Winnipeg, Canada

10-6 Recital, Terrace Theater, Kennedy Center, Washington, DC

10-7 Recital, Portland State University, Portland, OR

10-29 Recital, University of New Hampshire, Durham, NH

12-1 Recital, New England Conservatory, Boston, MA

1996

1-25 Concerto, Natal Philharmonic, Gérard Korsten, Durban, South Africa, Brahms 1

3-8 Recital, Southern Methodist University, Dallas, TX

3-25 Recital, Mayville State University, Mayville, ND

4-14 Recital, North Dakota Museum of Art, Grand Forks, ND

4-21 Recital, University of Kansas, Lawrence, KS
8-10,11 Concerto, Orquesta Sinfónica de Minería, Gregorio
Gutiérrez, Mexico City, Mexico, Liszt 1
10-4 Recital, University of Wisconsin-Whitewater, Whitewater,
WI

1997
1-30 Recital, Florida State University, Tallahassee, FL
2-23 Recital, California State University, Sacramento, CA
3-7 Recital, Friends of Music of Fairfield County, CT
3-16 Recital, Longy School of Music, Boston, MA
4-22 Recital, Sunset Center Theater, Carmel-by-the-Sea, CA
4-23 Recital, l'Ermitage Foundation, Los Angeles, CA
9-22 Recital, Carnegie Hall, New York, NY
11-24 Recital, Wigmore Hall, London, England

1998
1-9 Recital, Koninklijk Conservatorium, The Hague,
Netherlands
2-26 Recital, Grand Opera House, Oshkosh, WI
3-18 Concerto, Hunter College Symphony, Clayton
Westermann, New York, NY, Chopin 2
4-1 Recital, Fresno State Concert Hall, Fresno, CA
5-21 Concerto, London Soloists Chamber Orchestra, The
Barbican, London, England, Beethoven 5
7-25 Concerto, Oregon Coast Music Festival Orchestra, James
Paul, Coos Bay, OR, Beethoven 5

1999
1-20 Recital, Sociedad Filarmónica de Bilbao, Bilbao, Spain
1-30 Recital, BDP Music Society, Lancashire, England
2-24 Recital, Juilliard Theater, New York, NY

3-7 Recital, Westport Town Hall, Westport, CT

6-11 Recital, University of North Carolina at Greensboro, Greensboro, NC

7-6 Recital, University of Manitoba, Winnipeg, Canada

10-17 Recital, California State University, Sacramento, CA

11-5 Recital, Wheaton College, Wheaton, IL

2000

2-11 Recital, Southeastern Oklahoma State University, Durant, OK

4-6 Recital, Ford Center for the Performing Arts, North York, Canada

9-22,23 Concerto, Lubbock Symphony, Guillermo Figueroa, Lubbock, TX, Chopin 2

10-3 Concerto, Woodlands Symphony, Dagang Chen, The Woodlands, TX, Beethoven 5

10-15 Concerto, Brazos Valley Symphony, Marcelo Bussiki, College Station, TX, Chopin 2

11-5 Recital, Del Mar College, Corpus Christi, TX

2001

1-26 Concerto, Hungarian Symphony Orchestra, Pécs, Zsolt Hamar, Madison Civic Center, Madison, WI, Beethoven 5

1-30 Recital, University of Evansville, Evansville, IN

4-11 Recital, Carnegie Hall, New York, NY

11-9 Concerto, Orquesta Sinfónica de Puerto Rico, Luis A. Ferré, San Juan, Puerto Rico, Chopin 2

10-21 Recital, University of Toronto, Toronto, Canada

10-28 Recital, Los Angeles County Museum of Art, Los Angeles, CA

12-13 Shared Recital, Alice Tully Hall, New York, NY

2002

7-28 Concerto, Brevard Music Center Festival Orchestra, David Effron, Brevard, NC, Chopin 2

10-26 Concerto, New Philharmonic of New Jersey, Karen Pinoci, The Community Theatre, Morristown, NJ, Beethoven 4

2003

3-3 Concerto, Murfreesboro Philharmonic, Murfreesboro, TN, Beethoven 5

4-24 Recital, Conservatorio de Música, Jaén, Spain

7-27 Recital, International Keyboard Institute and Festival, Mannes School of Music, New York, NY

11-1 Recital, George Mason University, Washington, DC

2004

9-25 Recital, l'Hermitage Foundation, Los Angeles, CA

11-23 Recital, College of Charleston, Charleston, SC

1-31 Recital, Miami Civic Music Association, Miami, FL

3-19 Recital, Greenwich House Music School, New York, NY

2005

2-27 Recital, Los Angeles County Museum of Art, Los Angeles, CA

10-21 Recital, Kean University, Union, NJ

11-5 Recital, Chicago College of Performing Arts, Chicago, IL

2006

3-17 Concerto, New York Sinfonietta, Ki-Sun Sing, Good Shepherd Church, New York, NY, Mozart 21

10-27 Recital, Chapman University, Orange, CA

9-19 Recital, University of Houston, Houston, TX

2007

1-13 Recital, University of Pittsburgh-Bradford, Bradford, PA

7-26 Recital, Oxford University, Oxford, England

2008

10-26 Recital, Los Angeles County Museum of Art, Los Angeles, CA

2009

4-15 Recital, Newberry Opera House, Newberry, SC

4-19 Recital, Teatro Campoamor, Oviedo, Spain

4-21 Recital, Alice Tully Hall, New York, NY

2015

6-18 Recital, Orpheus and Bacchus Festival, Bordeaux, France

2017

2-9 Recital, University of Houston, Houston, TX

Appendix D
SELECTED RECITAL PROGRAMS

Curtis Institute, Philadelphia, PA (Graduation Recital)
March 14, 1940
Bach-Busoni: Toccata, Adagio and Fugue in C Major, BWV 564
Schumann: *Variations on the name "Abegg,"* op. 1
Beethoven: Sonata in E Major, op. 109
Chopin: Nocturne in F-sharp Minor, op. 48, no. 2
Chopin: Étude in D-flat Major, op. 25, no. 8
Chopin: Étude in F Major, op. 25, no. 3
Chopin: Étude in F Minor, op. post.
Chopin: Étude in C-sharp Minor, op. 10. no. 4
Rachmaninoff: Prelude in E-flat Major, op. 23, no. 6
Ravel: "Alborada del gracioso" from *Miroirs*
Godowsky: *Music Box*
Balakirev: *Islamey,* op. 18

Carnegie Hall, New York, NY
January 4, 1945
Bach-Busoni: Toccata, Adagio and Fugue in C Major, BWV 564
Mendelssohn: *Variations sérieuses*, op. 54
Chopin: Sonata in B Minor, op. 58
Liszt-Paganini: Three Études
Prokofiev: *Mephisto Waltz*, op. 96, no. 3
Haufrecht: *Sicilian Suite*

Teatro Colón, Bogotá, Colombia

June 2, 1954
Bach-Busoni: Toccata, Adagio and Fugue in C Major, BWV 564
Schumann: *Arabeske*, op. 18
Brahms: *Variations on a Theme of Paganini*, op. 35
Ravel: *Miroirs:* "Oiseaux tristes," "Alborada del gracioso"
Chopin: 2 Impromptus, 2 Études
Liszt: *Mephisto Waltz* no. 1, S. 514

Parkteatret, Oslo, Norway
February 28, 1955
Beethoven: Sonata in A-flat Major, op. 110
Liszt: Sonata in B Minor
Dello Joio: Sonata No. 1
Chopin: Nocturne in C-sharp Minor, op. 27, no. 1
Chopin: Scherzo in B Minor, op. 20
Chopin Waltz in E Minor, op. post.
Chopin: *Andante spianato* et Grande Polonaise brillante, op. 22

Four recitals in Derby, England, 1959
1) January 16
Beethoven: Sonata in E Major, op. 109
Chopin: Impromptus (complete)
Franck: Prélude, Chorale and Fugue
Prokofiev: Sonata No. 3 in A Minor, op. 28
Strauss-Godowsky: *Die Fledermaus*

2) January 23
Beethoven: Sonata in G Major, op. 14, no. 2
Liszt: Sonata in B Minor
Liszt: *Grandes études de Paganini* (complete)

3) January 30
Mozart: Sonata in F Major, K. 332
Brahms: *Variations and Fugue on a Theme by Handel*, op. 24
Chopin: Études, op. 10 (complete)

4) February 6
Bach-Busoni: Toccata, Adagio and Fugue in C Major, BWV 564
Schumann: *Variations on the name "Abegg,"* op. 1
Chopin: Sonata in B Minor, op. 58
Ravel: *Gaspard de la nuit*
Rachmaninoff: 2 Preludes
Prokofiev: Toccata, op. 11

Programs for Australian Tour, 1961
1) May 11
Bach-Busoni: Toccata, Adagio and Fugue in C Major, BWV 564
Beethoven: Sonata in C-sharp Minor, op. 27, no. 2 ("Moonlight")
Chopin: Impromptus (complete)
Ravel: *Miroirs:* "Oiseaux tristes"
Strauss-Godowsky: *Die Fledermaus*

2) May 16
Beethoven: Sonata in G Major, op. 14, no. 2
Chopin: Sonata in B Minor, op. 58
Brahms: *Variations and Fugue on a Theme by Handel*, op. 24
Ravel: *Miroirs:* "Alborada del gracioso"

3) May 18
Bach-Busoni: Toccata, Adagio and Fugue in C Major, BWV

564

Brahms: *Variations on a Theme of Paganini*, op. 35
Ravel: *Gaspard de la nuit*
Rachmaninoff: 2 Preludes
Prokofiev: Toccata, op. 11

4) May 26
Beethoven: Sonata in G Major, op. 14, no. 2
Franck: Prélude, Chorale and Fugue
Chopin: Impromptus (complete)
Ravel: *Miroirs:* "Oiseaux tristes"
Strauss-Godowsky: *Die Fledermaus*

Memorial Hall, Sale, Australia
May 11, 1967
Beethoven: Sonata in F Minor, op. 57 ("Appassionata")
Chopin: Sonata in B-flat Minor, op. 35
Rachmaninoff: Étude-Tableau in C Minor, op. 39, no. 1
Rachmaninoff: Étude-Tableau in F Minor, op. 33, no. 1
Rachmaninoff: Étude-Tableau in D Minor, op. 39, no. 8
Rachmaninoff: Étude-Tableau in E-flat Minor, op. 33, no. 3
Albéniz: *Evocación*
Albéniz-Godowsky: *Triana*

Carnegie Hall, New York, NY
December 6, 1970
Schumann: Fantasie in C Major, op. 17
Ravel: *Miroirs:* "Oiseaux tristes," "Noctuelles," "Alborada del gracioso"
Chopin Scherzos (complete)
Encores:
Scriabin: Poème, op. 32, no. 1

Kreisler-Rachmaninoff: *Liebesleid*

Hunter College, New York, NY
February 13, 1974
Schumann: *Kreisleriana*, op. 16
Beethoven: Sonata in F Minor, op. 57 ("Appassionata")
Chopin: Impromptus (complete)
Ravel: *La Valse*

Ministerio de Educación y Cultura, Montevideo, Uruguay
May 21, 1976
Schumann: Fantasie in C Major, op. 17
Brahms: *Variations on a Theme of Paganini*, op. 35
Chopin: Études, op. 25 (complete)

Alice Tully Hall, New York, NY
September 13, 1980
Beethoven: Sonata in D Major, op. 28
Beethoven: Sonata in E-flat Major, op. 81a ("Les Adieux")
Beethoven: Sonata in F Minor, op. 57
Beethoven: Sonata in A-flat Major, op. 110

City Hall Concert Hall, Hong Kong
May 24, 1981
Franck: Prélude, Chorale and Fugue
Schumann: *Arabeske*, op. 18
Schumann: *Variations on the name "Abegg,"* op. 1
Beethoven: Sonata in A flat Major, op. 110
Chopin: Ballades (complete)

Portland State University, Portland, OR
October 2, 1982

Schumann: Fantasie in C Major, op. 17
Brahms: *Variations on a Theme of Paganini*, op. 35
Ravel: *Valses nobles et sentimentales*
Kreisler-Rachmaninoff: *Liebesleid*
Kreisler-Rachmaninoff: *Liebesfreud*

University of Houston, Houston, TX
January 21, 1988
Rachmaninoff: *Variations on a Theme of Corelli*, op. 42
Ravel: *Miroirs:* "Oiseaux tristes," "Noctuelles," "Alborada del gracioso"
Scriabin: Poème, op. 32, no. 1
Beethoven: Sonata in G Major, op. 14, no. 2
Mendelssohn: Three *Songs without Words:* E Major, F-sharp Minor, C Major ("Spinning Song")
Chopin: Sonata in B Minor, op. 58
Encores: Scriabin, Rachmaninoff, Chopin, Kreisler

Schloss vor Husum, Germany
September 19, 1991
Bach-Liszt: Fantasy and Fugue in G Minor, BWV 542
Czerny: *Variations on a Theme of Rode, "La ricordanza,"* op. 33
Clementi: Sonata in F Minor, op. 14, no. 3
Delibes-Dohnányi: Waltz
Ravel: *Valses nobles et sentimentales*
Chopin: Sonata in B Minor, op. 58

University of Houston, Houston, TX
January 14, 1994
Franck: Prélude, Chorale and Fugue
Beethoven: Sonata in E Major, op. 109
Debussy: *Pour le piano*

Chopin: Barcarolle, op. 60
Chopin: Impromptu No. 1 in A-flat Major, op. 29
Chopin: Ballade No. 3 in A-flat Major, op. 47
Chopin: Ballade No. 4 in F Minor, op. 52

College of Charleston, Charleston, South Carolina
November 23, 2004
Beethoven: Sonata in D Major, op. 28 ("Pastorale")
Schumann: *Carnaval*, op. 9
Rachmaninoff: *Variations on a Theme of Corelli*, op. 42
Albéniz: Tango
Albéniz-Godowsky: *Triana*
Encores: Chopin, Rachmaninoff

BIBLIOGRAPHY

Bain, Wilfred Conwell. *Indiana University School of Music: The Bain Regime, 1947-1973.* Unknown, 1982.

Barenboim, Daniel. *A Life in Music.* New York: Arcade Publishing, 2002.

Bauer, Harold. *Harold Bauer: His Book.* New York, W.W. Norton & Company, 1948.

Beauclerk, Charles. *Piano Man: A Life of John Ogdon.* London: Simon & Schuster, 2014.

Bellamy, Olivier. *Martha Argerich, L'enfant et les sortilèges.* Paris: Buchet/Chastel, 2010.

-----. "Simon, Abbey (piano). Frédéric Chopin: Sonates Nos. 2 et 3; Impromptus et Fantasie-Impromptu – Barcarolle – Berceuse - Quatre Scherzos - Quatre Ballades. *Le Monde de la Musique* (July-August 2002).

Burton, Humphrey. *Leonard Bernstein.* New York: Doubleday, 1994.

Brown, William. *Menahem Pressler: Artistry in Piano Teaching.* Bloomington: Indiana University Press, 2009.

Carr, Elizabeth. *Shura Cherkassky: The Piano's Last Czar.* Lanham, Maryland: Scarecrow Press, 2006.

Chasins, Abram. *Speaking of Pianists.* New York: Knopf, 1967.

Delgado, Imelda. *An Intimate Portrait of Sidney Foster: Pianist... Mentor.* Hamilton Books, 2013.

Draheim, Joachim. "Für Kenner und Liebhaber: Raritäten der Klaviermusik im Schloß vor Husum." *Üben & Musizieren* (January 1991): 46-48.

Dubal, David. *The Art of the Piano: Its Performers, Literature, and Recordings.* New York: Summit Books, 1994.

-----. *Evenings with Horowitz: A Personal Portrait*. New York: Birch Lane, 1991.

-----. *Reflections from the Keyboard: The World of the Concert Pianist*. New York: Summit Books, 1993.

Dybowski, Stanislaw. "Weekly Music Events." *Slowo Powszechne* (September 23, 1976).

Ehrlich, Cyril. "London Events with Pianists." *Musical Times* (December 1990).

Evans, Allan. *Ignaz Friedman: Romantic Master Pianist*. Bloomington: Indiana University Press, 2009.

Feder, Edgard. "Abbey Simon à Guichets Fermés." *France-Amérique* (September 25-October 1, 1980).

Fleming, Shirley. "Abbey Simon." *Musical America* (June, 1967): 19.

Foster, Sidney. "David Saperton," liner notes for *David Saperton plays Godowsky, Chopin and Strauss/Godowsky*, International Piano Archives, IPA LP 118-119.

Gillespie, John, Anna Gillespie. *Notable Twentieth-Century Pianists: A Bio-Critical Sourcebook*. Santa Barbara: Greenwood Publishing Group, 1995.

Gollin, James. *Pianist: A Biography of Eugene Istomin*. Bloomington, IN: Xlibris, 1994.

Graffman, Gary. *I Really Should be Practicing*. New York: Avon, 1981.

Graydon, Nell S. and Margaret Sizemore. *The Amazing Marriage of Marie Eustis and Josef Hofmann*. Columbia: University of South Carolina Press, 1965.

Guerry, Jack. *Silvio Scionti: Remembering a Master Pianist and Teacher*. Denton: University of North Texas Press, 1991.

Harden, Ingo. "Schumann Carnaval op. 9; Fantasie C-dur op. 17--Abbey Simon Turnabout TV-S 34 432 (1 SM 30)" *Fono Forum* (May, 1972): 391.

Hart, Stanley F., Susan Kohl Katz, Frank Vos. *The Lotos Experience: The Tradition Continues.* New York: The Lotos Club, 1996.

Henken, Morris. "Abbey Simon." *WFLN Philadelphia Guide to Events and Places* (December 1978): 14-16.

Hofmann, Josef. *Piano Playing: A Little Book of Simple Suggestions.* New York: The McClure Company, 1908.

-----. *Piano Playing with Piano Questions Answered.* Reprint, New York: Dover, 1976.

Horowitz, Joseph. *Conversations with Arrau.* New York: Knopf, 1982.

Hurok, Sol, and Ruth Goode. *Impresario.* Westport, Conn.: Greenwood, 1975.

Irizarry, Carmen. "Madrid." *High Fidelity/Musical America* (April 1965): 142.

Johannesen, Grant. *Journey of an American Pianist.* Salt Lake City: University of Utah Press, 2007.

Kaiser, Joachim: *Great Pianists of Our Time.* New York: Herder and Herder, 1971.

Kornblum, Howard. "Chopin: Twenty-one Nocturnes. Abbey Simon, piano. VOXBOX CDX 5146 [ADD]; two discs: 56:48, 54:24. Produced by Marc Aubort and Joanna Nickrenz." *Fanfare* (May/June 1996): 132.

Kozinn, Allan. "Abbey Simon: Classical Virtuoso." *Contemporary Keyboard* (October 1979): 16-18.

Lassimonne, Denise, Howard Ferguson. *Myra Hess: By Her friends.* New York, The Vanguard Press, 1966.

Lehmann, Stephen, Marion Faber. *Rudolf Serkin: A Life.* New York: Oxford University Press, 2003.

Loesser, Arthur. *Men, Women, and Pianos: A Social History.* New York: Dover, 1972.

Logan, George M. *The Indiana University School of Music: A*

History. Bloomington: Indiana University Press, 2000.

Lyle, Wilson. *A Dictionary of Pianists.* London: Robert Hale, 1985.

Mach, Elyse. *Great Pianists Speak for Themselves,* Vol. 1. New York: Dodd Mead, 1980.

------. *Great Pianists Speak for Themselves,* Vol. 2. New York: Dodd Mead, 1988.

Marcus, Adele. *Great Pianists Speak with Adele Marcus.* Neptune, N.J.: Paganiniana, 1979.

McKenna, Marian C. *Myra Hess.* London: Hamish Hamilton, 1966.

Mitchell, Mark and Allan Evans. *Moriz Rosenthal in Word and Music: A Legacy of the Nineteenth Century.* Bloomington: Indiana University Press, 2009.

Monsaingeon, Bruno. *Sviatoslav Richter: Notebooks and Conversations.* Princeton, N.J.: Princeton University Press, 2001.

Montparker, Carol. "Abbey Simon." *Clavier* (July-August 1984): 12-15.

Neuhaus, Heinrich. *The Art of Piano Playing.* New York: Praeger, 1973.

Newcomb, Ethel. *Leschetizky, As I Knew Him.* New York: D. Appleton & Company, 1921.

Noyle, Linda. *Pianists on playing.* Metuchen, NJ: Scarecrow Press, 1987.

Nicholas, Jeremy. *Godowsky, the Pianists' Pianist: A Biography of Leopold Godowsky.* London: Travis & Emery Music Bookshop, 2013.

Thompson, Jennifer N. and Miranda Harrison, eds. *John Koch: Painting a New York Life.* Scala publishers, 2001.

Ogdon, Brenda Lucas, Michael Kerr. *Virtuoso.* Suffolk: Arima Publishing, 2008.

Plaskin, Glenn. *Horowitz: A Biography of Vladimir Horowitz.* New

York: W. Morrow, 1983.

Rasmussen, Karl Aage and Gyldendalske Boghandel. *Sviatoslav Richter: pianist*. Lebanon, NH: University Press of New England, 2010.

Roberson, Steven Henry. *Lili Kraus: Hungarian Pianist, Texas Teacher, and Personality Extraordinaire*. Fort Worth: Texas Christian University Press, 2000.

Ross, Beryl. "This Week in Music." *ABC Radio Guide* (May 9, 1967).

Rubinstein, Arthur. *My Many Years*. New York: Alfred A. Knopf, 1980.

-----. *My Young Years*. New York: Alfred A. Knopf, 1973.

S (last name), E. "Liszt: Grandes Études de Paganini. Brahms: Variations on a Theme of Paganini." *Stereo Review* (May 1991).

Sachs, Harvey. *Rubinstein: A Life*. New York: Grove Press, 1995.

Schafer, Milton. "Debuts and Reappearances." *High Fidelity/ Musical America* (May 1965): 118.

Schnabel, Artur. *My Life and Music*. New York: Dover, 1988.

Schonberg, Harold C. *The Great Pianists*. New York: Simon and Schuster, 1963.

-----. *Horowitz: His Life and Music*. New York: Simon and Schuster, 1992.

Simon, Abbey. "Masterclass: Josef Hofmann's Berceuse." *Keyboard Classics* (September-October 1983): 40-41.

-----. "Masterclass: Beethoven's Bagatelles, op. 33." *Keyboard Classics* (September-October 1985): 38-39.

-----. "Vladimir Horowitz." *Undated essay*.

Slenczynska, Ruth. *Forbidden Childhood*. New York: Doubleday, 1957.

Unknown. "A Recording Session with Abbey Simon." *American Record Guide* (November 1980).

White, Theodore H. *In Search of History: a Personal Adventure*. New

York: Harper and Row, 1978.

Young, William and Nancy K. Young. *Music of the Great Depression*. Westport, CT: Greenwood Press, 2005.

Online Materials:
Houston PBS UH Moment: Abbey Simon/Houston International Piano Fest. on YouTube.com
Musical Concepts. Abbey Simon. on YouTube.com
Curtis Institute of Music website. *curtis.edu*
Chang, Hsia-Jung. *Mandala Studio Interviews: on YouTube.com*

Newspapers consulted:
ARGENTINA Buenos Aires: *Argentinisches Tageblatt; Herald; Clarín; Crítica; Democracia; La Época; France Journal; Freie Presse; El Hogar; El Mundo; Mundo Radial; La Nación; Noticias Gráficas; La Prensa; El Pueblo; Le Quotidien; La Razón; Standard*. Rosario: *La Capital*. AUSTRALIA *Australian Women's Weekly*. Adelaide: *News*. Bathurst: *Advocate*. Brisbane: *Courier Mail; Sunday Mail*. Cairns: *Post*. Canberra: *Times*. Mackay: *Daily Mercury*. Melbourne: *Age; Herald; Jewish Herald; Jewish News. Sun; Wangaratta Chronicle*. Perth: *Sunday Times; West Australian*. Queensland: *Catholic Leader*. Rockhampton: *Bulletin*. Southport: *Gold Coast Bulletin*. Sydney: *Bulletin; Daily Telegraph; Catholic Weekly; Morning Herald; Sun*. Townsville: *Daily Bulletin*. AUSTRIA Vienna: *Express; Im Rampenlicht; Kurier; Neue Wiener Tages Zeitung; Weltpresse*. BRAZIL Rio de Janeiro: *Jornal do Brasil*. CANADA Calgary: *The Albertan; Herald*. Edmonton: *Journal*. Montreal: *Gazette; La Presse*. Ottawa: *Citizen; Journal*. Québec: *Le Soleil*. Shawinigan Falls: *Standard*. Toronto: *Star*. Victoria: *Times*. Winnipeg: *Free Press*. CHILE Santiago: *El Mercurio*. CHINA Hong Kong: *China Mail; Standard; Star; South China Morning Post*. COLOMBIA Bogotá: *El Espectador; La República; El Siglo; El Tiempo*. DENMARK Copenhagen: *Berlingske Tidende; Børsen;*

Dagens Nyheder; Ekstrabladet; Land Og Folk; Nationaltidende; Politiken; Socialdemokraten. ENGLAND London: *Daily Mail; Daily Telegraph; The Guardian; Jewish Chronicle; Telegram; Times.* FRANCE Paris: *Opéra; Le Quotidien.* GERMANY Berlin: *Der Abend; Berliner Anzeiger; Berliner Anzeiger am Morgen; Der Kurier; Berliner Montags-Echo; Morgenpost; Steglitzer Anzeiger am Morgen; Der Tag; Der Tagesspiegel; Telegraf; Die Welt.* Essen: *Essener Allgemeine Zeitung; Essener Tageblatt.* Frankfurt: *Frankfurter Neue Presse; Frankfurter Rundschau.* Hamburg: *Hamburger Abendblatt; Die Welt.* Husum: *Husumer Nachrichten; Kieler Nachrichten.* Kassel: *Hessische Nachrichten; Kasseler Post; Kasseler Zeitung.* Koblenz: *Rhein-Zeitung.* Mannheim: *Allgemeine Zeitung; Mannheimer Morgen; Rhein-Neckar Zeitung.* Munich: *Abendzeitung.* Nuremberg: *Nuernberger Nachrichten; Nuernberger Zeitung.* Tübingen: *Schwaebisches Tagblatt.* Ulm: *Schwaebische Donauzeitung.* IRELAND Dublin: *Evening Herald; Evening Press; Evening Mail; Irish Independent; Irish Press; Irish Times.* ISRAEL Jerusalem: *Al Hamishmar; Post.* ITALY Florence: *Giornale del Mattino; La Nazione;* Milan: *L'Italia; La Notte.* Rome: *Il Giornale d'Italia; Il tempo; La Voce Republicana.* Naples: *Il Mattino.* JAPAN Tokyo: *Japan Times.* MEXICO Mexico City: *Excelsior.* NETHERLANDS Amsterdam: *De Tijd; De Volkskrant; Het Parool; Het Vrije Volk; Trouw.* The Hague: *Haagsche Courant; Haagsch Dagblad; Het Binnenhof; Nieuwe Courant; De Nieuwe Haagsche Courant; De Telegraaf; Vaderland.* Rotterdam: *Algemeen Dagblad; Nieuwe Rotterdamsche Courant.* NORWAY Oslo: *Aftenposten; Dagbladet; Morgenbladet; Morgenposten; Verdens Gang.* PANAMA Panama City: *La Estrella de Panamá.* PERU Lima: *El Comercio; La Crónica; La Prensa.* SCOTLAND Edinburgh: *Evening Dispatch; The Scotsman.* SOUTH AFRICA Cape Town: *Die Burger; The Cape Times; The Cape Argus; Rand Daily Mail.* Durban: *Daily Durban; Natal Mercury.* Johannesburg: *Die Transvaler; The Star; Sunday Times.* Port Elizabeth: *Eastern Province Herald.* Pretoria: *Praetoria News.* SPAIN Barcelona; *Diario de Barcelona; La Vanguardia Española.*

Bilbao: La Gaceta del Norte; Madrid: *ABC; El Alcázar; Arríba; Informaciones.* Málanga: *Sur Málaga.* San Sebastián: *Tele express.* Seville: *ABC.* Valladolid: *Valladolid Ciudad.* SWEDEN Stockholm: *Aftonbladet; Aftontidn; Dagens Nyheter; Morgontidningen; Tidningen; Svenska Dagbladet.* SWITZERLAND Geneva: *Weekly Tribune; Journal de Genève; La Suisse; Tribune de Genève.* TUNISIA Tunis: *L'Action; Corriere di Tunisi; La Presse.* URUGUAY Montevideo: *Acción; El Bien Público; El Día; El Diario; La Mañana; La Tribuna Popular.* USA Atlanta: *Journal.* Austin: *Statesman.* Baltimore: *Sun.* Baton Rouge: *Morning Advocate; State Times.* Bloomington, IN: *Daily Herald-Tribune.* Boston: *Globe.* Buffalo: *Courier-Express; Evening News.* Colorado Springs: *Free Press.* Coos Bay: *World.* Charleston: *Post and Courier.* Charlotte: *Observer.* Chicago: *Daily News; Sun-Times; Tribune; Chicago's American.* Cincinnati: *Enquirer; Post.* Dallas: *Morning News.* Daytona Beach: *Morning Journal.* Decatur: *Daily Review; Herald.* Denver: *Post.* Duluth: *News-Tribune.* Evansville: *Courier.* Eugene: *Register-Guard.* Flagstaff: *Sun.* Flint: *Journal.* Fort Lauderdale: *News/Sun-Sentinel.* Fresno: *Bee.* Houston: *Chronicle; Post.* Indianapolis: *News; Star.* Kalamazoo: *Gazette.* Lawrence: *Journal-World.* Lehigh Valley: *The Morning Call.* Lincoln: *Star.* Los Angeles: *Herald-Examiner; Times.* Long Beach: *Independent.* Louisville: *Courier-Journal.* Ludington: *Daily News.* Macon: *Telegraph and News.* Meadville: *Tribune.* Miami: *Herald.* Milwaukee: *Journal; Sentinel.* Nashville: *Banner; Tennessean.* New Haven: *Journal-Courier; Register.* New Orleans: *Times-Picayune.* New York: *Musical America; Herald Tribune; Journal-American; Post; Times; New Yorske Listy; World Telegram and Sun.* Oklahoma City: *The Daily Oklahoman.* Omaha: *World Herald.* Oshkosh: *Northwestern.* Philadelphia: *The Evening Bulletin; Inquirer.* Phoenix: *Arizona Republic; Gazette.* Pittsburgh: *Post Gazette; Press.* Portland: *Oregonian; Journal.* Reading: *Eagle.* Richmond: *News Leader; Times-Dispatch.* Rochester: *Democrat and Chronicle.* Sacramento: *Bee.*

Salisbury, MD: *The Daily Times.* San Francisco: *Chronicle; Examiner.* Schenectady: *Gazette.* Shreveport: *Times; Journal.* Sioux Falls: *Argus-Leader.* St. Louis: *Post-Dispatch.* Stamford: *Advocate.* Stratford, CT: *Sunday Herald.* Toledo: *Blade.* Trenton: *The Trentonian.* Tulsa: *Daily World.* Tuscaloosa: *News.* Victoria: *Advocate.* Washington: *Times-Herald; Post.* Westport: *The Hour.* VENEZUELA Caracas: *El Mundo; El Nacional; El Universal.* RHODESIA (NOW ZIMBABWE) Salisbury (now Harare): *Rhodesian Herald.*

INDEX

A

"Chattering Monkeys at the Sacred Lake of Wendit", 33

"The Gardens of Buitenzorg", 33

Music Box, 36, 307

Studies on Chopin's Études, 33

Triakontameron, 33

Godowsky, Leopold Jr., 15

Godowsky, Vanita, 15

Gold, Shelly, 126

Goldberg, Albert, 245

Gols, Marçal, 285

Golschmann, Vladimir, 284

Goodman, Benny, 56

Goodman, Richard, 23, 204

Goodwin, Noël, 254

Goosen, J.F., 251

Goossens, Eugene, 90, 239

Gottlieb, Victor, 26

Gould, Glenn, 69, 101, 174

Graffman, Gary, 26, 185, 192 315

Gray, Harold, 84, 264, 265, 270, 277

Great Depression, 14, 319

Grieg, Edvard

  Piano Concerto in A Minor, op. 16, 17, 70, 72, 80, 88, 180, 199, 241, 263, 264, 265

Grikurov, Edouard, 123, 282

Grossman, Julius, 288, 297

Groves, Charles, 80, 263, 266, 268, 269

Grüner-Hegge, Odd, 263, 267, 270

Gulda, Friedrich, 67, 78, 79, 80, 205

Guller, Youra, 80

Gunn, Glenn Dillard, 246

Gutiérrez, Gregorio, 303

H

Haendel, Ida, 261

Hall, John Farnsworth, 271

Hamar, Zsolt, 304

Handford, Maurice, 285, 286

Hannikainen, Tauno, 267

Harrell, Lynn, 147

Harrison, Guy Fraser, 278, 288

Harshaw, Margaret, 102

Hartman, Anton, 285, 289

Haufrecht, Herbert

  Sicilian Suite, 55, 307

Hegyi, Julius, 283

Heifetz, Jascha, 12, 56

Helfgott, David, 99, 100, 162

Henahan, Donal, 250

Henderson, Robert, 217, 295

Henle, Fritz, 43

Herz, Hermann, 277, 283

Hess, Myra, 73, 205, 316, 317

Hétu, Pierre, 290

HMV Records, 90, 94, 239, 241, 242, 243

Hoffman, Irwin, 274

Hofmann, Josef, 6, 15, 16, 17, 18, 24, 26, 27, 28, 32, 35, 56, 60, 160, 166, 194, 196, 198, 199, 205, 206, 209, 217, 234

  bench, 166

  Chromaticon, 16

  Kaleidoskop, 16

  piano action, 166

  suspension system, 206

Hopkins, John, 272, 273

Horn and Hardart, 13, 20
Horovitz, Joseph, 274
Horowitz, Vladimir, 56, 60, 114, 115, 221, 130, 134, 156, 159, 167, 172, 183, 191, 198, 199, 205, 206, 207, 223, 248, 315, 316, 317, 318
Houseman, John, 139
Hurok, Sol, 61, 96, 110, 225, 120, 121, 124, 126, 316
Hutcheson, Ernest, 13
Hye-Knudsen, Johan, 268

I

Indiana University, 9, 10, 102, 105, 130, 134, 181, 223, 233, 274, 275, 276, 280, 283, 285, 288, 289, 314, 315, 316, 317
Irving, Robert, 93, 241, 276, 278, 283, 285, 287
Iturbi, José, 95, 132, 269
Iwaki, Hiroyuki, 288

J

Jacob, Bernard, 270
Janigro, Antonio, 269
Janis, Byron, 192
Järvi, Paavo, 300
Jaslowitz, Bernard, 156
Jazz, 12, 24, 100, 139, 205, 208
Johanos, Donald, 279, 282
Johnson, Christopher, 9, 223
Judson, Arthur, 30, 59
Juilliard, 4, 13, 27, 31, 103, 128, 139, 145, 148, 187, 191, 192, 195, 209, 228, 300, 303

K

Kapell, William, 70, 71
Karajan, Herbert von, 207
Kardash, Ted, 287
Kastendieck, Miles, 252
Katchen, Julius, 40, 62, 80, 81
Katims, Milton, 138, 148, 200
Keene, Constance, 40
Kisch, Royalton, 267, 270
Kissin, Evgeny, 207
Klein, Howard, 251
Klippstatter, Kurt, 297
Koch, John, 51, 52, 53, 59, 69, 317
Korevaar, David, 9, 222, 229
Korn, Richard, 274, 276
Korsten, Gérard, 302
Kostelanetz, André, 139, 292
Kozinn, Allan, 258
Krager, Franz Anton, 301
Krasnapolsky, Yuri, 140, 147, 288, 291, 296, 298, 301, 302
Kreisler-Rachmaninoff
  Liebesfreud, 232, 220
  Liebesleid, 32, 232, 220
Krips, Josef, 62, 261, 273
Kuerti, Anton, 195
Kurtz, Efrem, 57, 92, 139, 260, 293
Kushner, Leon, 47
Kwak, Sung, 139

L

LaMarchina, Robert, 286
Landowska, Wanda, 54
Leinsdorf, Erich, 116, 119, 278
Leonard, Lawrence, 284, 285
Leppard, Raymond, 296

Made in the USA
Middletown, DE
22 December 2018